LOVE SPEAKS™

21 WAYS TO RECOGNIZE
GOD'S MULTI-FACETED VOICE

BY

CARL WESLEY
ANDERSON

www.LoveSpeaks.Today

BORN TO BLAZE
MINISTRIES

PRAISE FOR *Love Speaks*

"The very heart of this book is an invitation to understand how much we are deeply loved, totally known, and seen by the Father. Carl does such a great job inviting us into a new journey of recognizing the voice of the Glorious Trinity, and how that is so different and how very personal it can be for each one of us. In this book, Carl, with such care and great detail, lays out before us the inexhaustible ways in which God has spoken, both past and present. This book will be a great resource in understanding your friendship with God!"

—**Rachel Carroll,** Co-Senior Leader, Building Contenders, San Diego

"For anyone who wants to grow in hearing God's voice, Love Speaks *is for you. In this book, Carl searches the Word of God for how He is speaking the message of love to people. This book would make a great devotional study for individuals or groups. I highly recommend* Love Speaks *to anyone wanting to expand their relational exchange with God! "*

—**Danny Silk,** President of Loving On Purpose
   Author of *Keep Your Love On, Loving Our Kids On Purpose & Culture of Honor*

"Carl Wesley Anderson is a dynamic and gifted storyteller, teacher, and communicator. He hits a home run with Love Speaks *in teaching us how to be more in tune with God—and understand how the Holy Spirit works to pursue an intimate relationship with each of us. The book compels one to recognize and respond to the 21 different ways that Love Speaks—opening up new, untapped avenues to deepen our relationship with the Father. Highly endorse, highly recommend!"*

—**Rodney and Angel Holscher Hatfield,** SERV OTHERS

"Anyone who has ever had any kind of a true encounter with the living Lord,

by default wants more! I've walked with God for a lot of years but probably like you, long to hear God speaking more often, directly to me, with the assurance that it really is His voice.

"In Love Speaks, Carl Anderson gives a biblically based, behind the scenes look, at how we can recognize God's voice. And the page turner for me, were all the true life stories that illustrate each of the various ways in which God speaks. Some of them, jaw-dropping examples of God's creative responses to our prayers.

"If you need to be convinced that God "enjoys" hearing from you and your eagerness to hear from Him, read this book! Guaranteed you will develop a new awareness of His voice with an anticipation that God wants to and WILL speak with you every day!"

—**Todd Isberner,** President of Share Media Services

"Rev. Carl Anderson has written a very timely teaching on how to understand God speaking to us. Even though we are born for such a time as this, these days often are marked by intense battle and demonic turbulence (in all forms and shapes). As confusion often abounds, we need to hear from God all the more (cf. Rom. 8:6). In a humble, gentle, and extensive way Brother Carl brings us to living with God... with His unconditional heart and with His living voice. Many examples make this vital instruction easier to read and understand. I gladly endorse this man of God and his very opportune book Love Speaks to you.

—**Father Marc van Rossem,** Priest, serving in The Netherlands & China

"Jesus promised His followers would know His voice (John 10). Sadly, many Christians have not mastered the art of hearing His voice. Carl Anderson, in this excellent book, Love Speaks, has given us a clear, fresh, unique and Biblically-based presentation, written for every day followers of Jesus. Carl shares illustrations and stories that give practical insight to enable people to better hear the voice of the Lord."

—**Rev. Alan & Dorothy Langstaff,** Kairos Ministries

"Love Speaks *by Carl Anderson is an amazing and unique gift to the Body of Christ in our time. It covers the bases as well as or better than any other book I am aware of, and maintains biblical balance with practical usability for real people looking for answers in how to discern God's voice and truth and guidance. I trust it will receive a broad readership and become the first of many more books from this anointed and committed brother in our Lord!"*

—**Dr. Lance Wonders,** Academic Dean, ACTS International Bible College, Twin Cities, Minnesota

"When we finished reading Brother Carl's manuscript, as past magazine publishers we immediately recognized a prominent theme running through and that is how "God speaks to mankind." Brother Carl outlines through scripture all the many ways from first person audible to third person words of knowledge and everything in between.

"Page after page, chapter after chapter, you will discover the many different ways that God gets and stays in contact with His people. And He does this through the varying ministries of the Holy Trinity: the Father, Son and Holy Spirit.

"Just as an angler carries a myriad selection of lures to fish, so too does God speak in a myriad of ways. As anglers, we learned years ago to keep changing our presentation methods to stay up with the changing nature of the fish. Carl's new book confirms that God acts in similar ways. God has a multi-faceted approach with constantly changing methods to "catch" our attention and minister His love to us, and through us, to others.

"We highly recommend Carl's book. It will inspire you to both grow in God's love, and share His love in becoming a better "fisher of men" as Jesus has called all of us to be."

—**Al and Ron Lindner,** Lindner Media

"I have known Carl Anderson for over 25 years. In a day where hearing God's Voice is paramount, Carl's newest book addresses and equips the reader in hearing the Voice that saves, guides, and strengthens those who heed it!"

—**Chuck Porta,** Founder, Ram's Horn Ministries

"Carl Anderson's book will inspire anyone wanting to know how to hear from God. It is well balanced with scripture and narratives to keep you engaged throughout. Carl is a master story teller, who's love for God comes through on every page, and his excitement for us as believers to hear from God is contagious! I would highly recommend this readable and thoughtful book to anyone who is on the journey of going deeper in their faith."

—**Donna E. Johnson,** M.S./M.A., Assistant Campus Pastor, Bethel University, St. Paul, Minnesota

"The title of this book whets our appetite for a feast. Indeed the title reminds us that our God is the God who speaks, in his Word and through his Son. And by speaking God reveals himself as the Lover. Rather than discerning God's character a priori, Anderson lets our Trinitarian God speak by his Word—and enriches our understanding of the Word from his own experience.

"Anderson offers us twenty-one ways to expect to hear from God. I am grateful to see that Anderson, from a Pentecostal perspective, confirmed that the Holy Spirit only works in agreement with God's Word, neither adding nor subtracting from that Word.

"Yet too many Evangelicals, while agreeing in principle, forget to expect the active leadership of the Spirit. His is also an important emphasis that should correct a dead and merely 'ethical' kind of Christianity (Do this! Don't do that!). If I have specific disagreements with the book, these can all be resolved by going to the Word of God who speaks—as Anderson would have us do.

"As a Reformed Evangelical, I am glad to call Anderson a friend and pleased to see this new book —a gift to God's church. May God use Anderson's book to draw us closer to the Lover who Speaks, expecting to hear Him."

—**Pastor Rick Shenk,** Senior Pastor, Village Evangelical Free Church

"A comprehensive and practical and personal approach to hearing the voice of God. Read it and listen for His love for you."

—**Jane Campbell,** Editorial Director, Chosen Books, a division of Baker Publishing Group

"Carl has provided a wonderful map and guidebook that I encourage you to read. He highlights many ways we can hear and discern the voice of God. This book has helped me hear God clearer, celebrate the diversity of how He speaks, and increased my desire to spend more time in His presence."

—**Mitch,** Evangelist, Author and Founder of Crown Jesus Ministries, Ireland

"Carl Anderson's book strikes me as a biblically sound, readable primer for hearing the voice of God, accessible to the average believer. The writing is simple, direct and full of gems designed to draw his audience into a more intimate life of communication with the Three."

—**R. Loren Sandford,** author, conference speaker, founding pastor, New Song Church and Ministries, Denver, Colorado

"I've worked with Brother Carl for well over two decades now, and I've always been amazed at how good a "hearer" of God's voice he is. So much of his ministry is based around being able to listen and obey, having an ability to track the Holy Spirit and move with Him. It's been an honour and a blessing to see the man in his ministry. In Love Speaks, Carl teaches us all what he demonstrates in ministry life: a keen ability to hear and obey the multi-faceted voice of the Lord."

—**Rónán Johnston,** Worship Leader, Song Writer & Author, Dublin, Ireland

To all my fellow travelers on this Kingdom journey of discovery,
longing to hear God's voice of love more clearly and more often,
with assurance that it really is HIM.
This book is for you.

LOVE

"The Lord appeared to me from afar, saying,

'I HAVE LOVED YOU with an everlasting love;

therefore I have drawn you with lovingkindness.

SPEAKS

'Call to Me, and I will answer you,

and I WILL TELL YOU

great and mighty things, which you do not know.'"

(Jeremiah 31:3, 33:3)

Edited by Sarah Elizabeth Anderson and Ron Olson.

Cover and Interior Design by Suzann Beck, BeckHaus Design, Inc.

Born to Blaze Ministries Publishing, Apple Valley, Minnesota, U.S.A.

Printed in the United States of America.

Email Contact: Carl@borntoblaze.com

http://www.BornToBlaze.com

Our Vision: "To Empower & Equip Believers as Witnesses for the Savior, to Call People to Repentance, & to Inspire Passionate Discipleship as We Prepare for Christ's Return"

SUBSCRIBE to Carl's YouTube Channel, www.youtube.com, Search "Carl Wesley Anderson"

SPEAKING: http://BornToBlaze.com/invite-carl

FACEBOOK: https://www.facebook.com/carlwesleyandersonjunior/

For instant access to all of our Love Speaks discipleship tools, including the Book, e-Book, Kindle Edition, Audio Book (read by the Author), the Love Speaks Masterclass (online training course for individuals & small group study), the Love Speaks Documentary Film Series "Video-On-Demand" Service (including Broadcast Versions and Special Director's Cuts), or to subscribe to our latest "Listener Updates e-Letter," please visit us at

http://www.LoveSpeaks.Today

ISBN 978-0-9762910-5-3

Library of Congress Control Number: 2018951840

TABLE OF CONTENTS

Section II: 7 Common Ways the Lord Speaks

Section III: 7 Uncommon Ways the Lord Speaks

LOVE SPEAKS

Testimonial from Carl

Why I wrote and created the world-wide "LOVE SPEAKS" PLATFORM including the book, Kindle Edition, Masterclass, and Documentary Film Series for Broadcast/Streaming...

In 2014 I was diagnosed with Stage 3b Melanoma. A very deadly form of cancer. The odds of my survival were low. I was devastated.

Yet, instead of blaming God or running away, I ran to the LORD!

He embraced me in His presence daily.

That first summer I was faced with 5 possible treatments, and He spoke to me in 8 different "contacts" in one weekend, to lead me into the hardest of all 5 with the most side-effects. It was actually an easy decision to take the toughest path, because I felt His love so strongly in confirmation, and I knew I was battling the Enemy who was causing this cancer to attack me. I suffered through 4+ continuous years of treatments, including 69 weeks of enduring a high fever through them to battle the cancer.

I suddenly realized the Trinity was reaching out to me almost continuously in Their LOVE. And it was EASY to hear Their voice and recognize the "contacts" They were making in answer to my intimate lifestyle of prayer as a dialogue with God.

I say, "They" because of a mystery: the Father, His Son, Jesus Christ our LORD, & the Holy Spirit are One God in Three Persons!

And They love us and believe in us!

So I began to write, "Love Speaks" and I discovered through Scripture, Salvation-History, and personal experience 21 different "ways" that They are making contact with all of Their children.

As I write this, the world is in crises, with "wars and rumors of wars" and many other Global threats. You may be facing isolation, anxiety, fear, sadness, grief, or other trials of faith, wondering where the voice of God is?

I too felt these same emotions at times during my treatments. Yet... I have come out the other side of cancer and am a SURVIVOR today.

His voice is continuously speaking to lead you deeper in relationship with Him and to help you learn to become a stronger witness of His love to those around you.

Through my entire battle with cancer, I discovered a great reality: the last recorded words of Jesus Christ, before His ascension, are absolutely true:

> *"And Lo, I am WITH YOU ALWAYS, even to the end of the age"*
> *(Matthew 28:20).*

> *And His presence truly goes before you, beside you, and His glory*
> *is your rear guard (Isaiah 58:8).*

So no matter what wilderness you may be wandering in or trials of fire you may be facing, HIS LOVE IS SPEAKING.

So, keep listening!

Soli Deo Gloria (to God Alone the Glory), Amen.

—*Rev. Carl Wesley Anderson, Jr. 1st February, 2024.*

P.S. *The book you are reading now is the 2nd Edition, a special expanded version with Study Guide questions at the end of each Chapter to help you grow deeper and interact with the Holy Spirit in that new "WAY" you have just learned.*

And we've now added the special Resources at the end of this book to help you grow even more!

Each Chapter of this book has a corresponding Documentary Film Episode highlighting God's faithfulness in Salvation-History (21 Chapters, 21 Episodes) and also its own Masterclass Equipping Session, and each of these Resources are complimentary in wisdom and insight to each other (Chapters of the book, Episodes in the Series, and Equipping Sessions in the Masterclass).

FOREWORD BY J. LEE GRADY

The Bible promises that God will guide us. But many Christians find it difficult to hear God's voice. And in some charismatic churches we complicate things when we try to make guidance mystical or weird—as if you have to hear an audible voice from Heaven about what color shirt to wear *(see Chapter 21 on 'The Audible Voice of the Father': it is the final Chapter because it is the rarest form of Guidance)*!

That is why I am so glad my friend Carl Wesley Anderson has written this insightful book, Love Speaks. It is a book filled with Scripture, teaching, exhortation, Salvation-History, personal examples, modern examples, and applications to build your faith.

God's guidance should not be difficult for us if we truly know that our heavenly Father loves us and wants to direct our lives. Years ago I learned several particular (of the 21 Ways in this book) that began to really help me connect deeper with God.

Here are a few with Carl's corresponding Chapters (WAYS) to recognize God's multi-faceted voice.

Firstly, you can hear God's voice by reading and studying the Bible *(see Chapter 1, "The Established Word")*. Friends have sometimes complained to me: "I just never hear God speaking." Yet when I ask if they read the Bible regularly, they say they are too busy.

God supernaturally inspired 40 authors over a period of 1,600 years to compile His love letter to us. After the Bible was written in Hebrew and Greek, many people were martyred because they translated it in a modern language.

And related to the Established Word; you can hear God's voice when you read Scripture with a prayerful heart and it is illuminated directly to you *(see Chapter 2, "The Living Word")*. British preacher Charles Spurgeon recognized this years ago when he wrote, "When I have been in trouble, I have read the Bible until a text has seemed to stand out of the Book, and salute me, saying, 'I was written specially for you.'"

Next, you can hear the voice of the Holy Spirit *(see Chapters 3-5, 10-12, and 15-18 for many WAYS to interact with the Holy Spirit)*. He speaks through His supernatural inspiration. He comforts us and actively speaks to us through our redeemed human spirit. Many times it is simply a deep sense of inward knowing. This ability to hear the Spirit's voice inside us is developed over the years as we grow in Christ. As you allow more of the Spirit's presence and power in your life, you will set aside your selfish agendas and sinful habits so God can communicate without any hindrance.

Finally, you can hear the Father's unique voice through circumstances *(see especially Chapter 7, "Providence" and Chapter 13, "Holy Coincidences" to learn more)*. Not everything that happens to you is God's will. But God is sovereign, and He has power over nature, over government leaders and over all the details of your life. He opens doors that no man can shut. As Carl so aptly puts it, "Believe that the Father's love for you is so real, He has already visited your tomorrow, so He can speak into your life today."

In this book, Carl Wesley Anderson offers 21 unique WAYS that God lovingly speaks and directs us. I pray you will open your heart, tune your ears and listen for one of my favorite ways to hear: that still, small voice of God in your life *(see Chapter 4)*.

Put on your seatbelts—because listening to God and following His direction is truly the adventure of a lifetime.

J. Lee Grady
Former Editor, *Charisma* magazine
Director, The Mordecai Project
Author, *Set My Heart on Fire* and other books

Introduction

"Can You Hear Him—NOW?"

God is an ever-present God who is speaking in every generation. The question is, how clearly can you recognize His creative, multi-faceted voice?

He revealed Himself to Moses as the "I AM." A person's name reveals something of their identity—of who they are. God wanted us to know this aspect of His name, for His name reveals His nature. He is the "I AM." He is ever-present. For you, today.

He was, He is, and He is to come.

He revealed Himself to Jeremiah as the God who is love, as He takes initiative to love you first. He said, *"I HAVE LOVED YOU with an everlasting love; therefore I have drawn you with lovingkindness"* (Jeremiah 31:3).

And out of His divine love nature, He speaks personally, *"Call to Me, and I will answer you, and I WILL TELL YOU..."* (Jeremiah 33:3).

Thus, His love, and His voice, are forever intertwined.

Down through the centuries, many Christians have testified of experiencing God's love through hearing His voice by personal contact with Him.

He revealed Himself to Martin Luther in His established Word. Luther came to such a strong conviction of the importance of the Word that he was able to stand strong in the face of adversity. When put on trial for his convictions of the truth of grace through faith alone, he remarked in simple conviction, "My conscience is captive to the Word of God."[1]

It was said of Luther that he read his Bible with more zeal than anyone had read it for a thousand years. Thus, I begin this book with this absolute

---

1 Quoted from Heiko Oberman, *Luther: Man Between God and the Devil* (English edition, Yale Publishing, 1989).

foundation of God's voice speaking to you: His holy Bible, the Word. In fact, this is the number one way to hear from God, and the tried-and-true test of all the other ways to hear. (You can read more of this way in Chapter 1.)

Can you really hear His voice?... The answer is an emphatic, "Yes!"

Another Christian who made a profound impact for many believers is Roman Catholic leader St. Francis of Assisi. His practical ministry of love to the poor, for animals, and for all creation has inspired people in every generation since the 12th Century.

And St. Francis felt the love of God through hearing the voice of God. The *actual* voice.

Yes, he did. In fact, it happens to be the rarest aspect of God speaking: The Father's Audible Voice. (You can read more of this way, and the story, in Chapter 21.)

The Bible is the most common way God speaks to us. The audible voice of the Father is the least common way. And in between these two bookends of ways, there is an adventure of listening and receiving confirmation that will surprise you far beyond any experience you've had with God thus far.

I chose Moses, Jeremiah, and these stories to open this introduction as they represent the shared experience of millions of Christians down through the centuries. We all need to hear from God better, and re-center our lives around daily commitment to our Lord Jesus Christ.

Both Scripture and salvation-history teach us that He has spoken, is speaking today, and will continue to speak.

By "salvation-history" I mean that connected stream of history in which God keeps appearing, revealing Himself, relating to a people through covenant, and unfolding His pre-creational plan of salvation centered in Christ, the God-man. Thus, God might just choose to speak to you today in creative ways, just as He has always spoken, through the many facets of His voice.

Why Did I Write This Book?

I wrote this book to help everyday followers of Christ like me develop a new awareness of the voice of God calling out in His love. And I want to open up non-Christians to the idea that a personal relationship with the Father, through commitment to following His Son Jesus Christ, is the best choice you can ever make. His Holy Spirit becomes alive inside of you, and through Him, you can communicate in an ongoing dialogue with God the Father and God the Son.

The Lord is breaking into the chaos all around us and being a good, good Father to us all. His love is eternal.

He has already visited tomorrow, so He can speak and bring hope to your heart, today.

When I check the breaking news stories every morning, I find that the world has gone mad. Nations are being shaken. Societies are crumbling. Politics are spinning out of control. Even the earth itself seems to be affected and is being shaken with global epidemics and natural disasters. People are afraid. The times are uncertain.

Perhaps you are attending church on Sunday and just living out the mundane of the daily grind of life, not feeling a personal contact with God in those common moments. Is His love real, and for you, today?

Or, perhaps you are in the midst of some kind of trial of faith, and wondering if God can really be "ever-present" for you, personally. Is His love real, and for you, today?

What if He is actually taking initiative to speak to you every week, in His love, in the midst of your circumstances, be they *mundane* or *extraordinary*?

Can you really hear His voice and thus experience His love no matter what is happening today, or what may happen tomorrow? The answer is an emphatic, "Yes!"

In over three decades of reaching out in faith to hear the voice of God, I have realized that every time I recognize a *contact* from the Lord to me personally, I feel the love of the Father. His personal, eternal love is reaching out to me in the midst of uncertain times.

And the more contacts you have with God on a regular basis, the more you experience His leadings and His love.

And what about hearing from God when you don't have all the answers? What if I told you that many followers of Jesus have had deep, meaningful contact with God, and felt His love through hearing His voice, in the midst of their trials? It's true.

During the years of writing of this book, I myself have been in a particular trial of faith. I have been in a real difficult battle in fact. Some days I succumbed to unbelief, doubt, and even fear. At times I even cried out, "Why me, God?" "Why am I battling cancer?"

To which there seemed to be no immediate answer.

Yet during those very times, His voice continually called out to me and I experienced His presence and His love, in spite of not understanding the "why."

"Agape is a love for the unworthy..."

I never felt alone. I always felt loved. And I kept hearing His voice speaking to me.

My days of knowing His love and hearing His voice far outweighed the days of doubt.

His love has spoken to me over and over again, even though I didn't, and still don't, have all the answers to my "why?" questions.

Defining the Title: LOVE. How do we spell the word, "LOVE?"

For a Christian only, we don't spell LOVE, L-O-V-E. Instead, we spell it like this: A-G-A-P-E. That's right.

Agape.

This word is unique to the Christian's understanding of God. For the ancient Greeks (and the modern world) the words that describe love include a variety of ways like friendship, or love for a *worthy* object, like a sports team, or a *worthy* person, like a spouse or a child. The revolutionary event of the cross of Jesus Christ reveals a revolutionary love that is as impactful in modern times as it was then.

"*Agape* is a love for the *unworthy*, for one who has forfeited all right to the lover's devotion," writes Bruce Milne. "The Old Testament has witness for this in God's love for Israel, and in Hosea's love for his faithless wife.

"Holiness and love conjoin perfectly in the person and work of Jesus Christ. As God, He embodies divine holiness that is separate from and resistant to all sin and evil, yet His very coming is God's loving, gracious response to human guilt and helplessness.

"They unite also in the ministry of God the Holy Spirit whose essential ministry is the renewal and sanctification of God's people in fulfillment of God's purpose of love (*agape*)."[2]

Revolutionary, yes? So Paul writes, *"But God demonstrates His own love (agape) toward us, in that while we were yet sinners, Christ died for us"* (Romans 5:8).

So LOVE is GOD's LOVE, as GOD IS LOVE (*also see* 1 John 4:7-19).

Agape love.

But in our culture of misunderstanding of certain words, it is helpful to define just who GOD is to a Christian.

How do we spell the word, "GOD?"

For a Christian only, we don't spell GOD, G-O-D. Instead, we spell Him like this: Father-Son-Holy Spirit. This is called by many, the Trinity or Triune God.

---

2 Bruce Milne, *Know the Truth: A Handbook of Christian Belief* (InterVarsity Press, 1982, 1998), p. 88.

This revelation, relationship, and intimate voice is only accessible to a Christian. Many millions of people outside of true faith in Christ are praying to God from a distance. They still spell GOD, G-O-D.

And people outside true faith in Christ are kept from an intimate relationship with their Heavenly Father through their sinful nature. It still separates them from Him. Thus, without Jesus you cannot really know God as Father.

Enter: *agape*.

As soon as a person opens their heart in repentance to Christ, His love and His voice are poured out.

And even many people inside a true relationship with Christ have been raised in religious backgrounds that simply did not emphasize intimacy with God in hearing His voice. But change can happen, starting today! We get the exclusive opportunity to worship Him up close. In fact, we worship Him from within, for His Kingdom has come within our hearts. It's a choice every person has to make to say, "Yes!" Almighty God can become Intimate Abba to a follower of Christ.

The Trinity Speaks

As Jonathan Edwards once noted after studying the topic of the Triune God extensively, "I think [the doctrine of the Trinity] to be the highest and deepest of all Divine mysteries."[3]

As a diamond or special gemstone reflects the light shone upon it in many facets, so God's glory upon you continually reflects many aspects of His voice to discern and His love to experience, and all 3 Persons of the Trinity are actively involved.

To put it very simply, as you study each way God speaks, think of His contact with you in these terms (while remembering that this is all a mystery):

1) The Father speaks primarily externally, through His Providence, circumstances, nature and creation, and other ways.

---

3 Jonathan Edwards, *Works* (England: Banner of Truth Trust, From an unpublished treatise on the Trinity).

These signs of His love are quite literally everywhere. And each sign then bears witness within your spirit, through the Holy Spirit's confirmation.

"For God (the Father) so loved (agape) the world that He gave His one and only son" (John 3:16).

2) The Son, Jesus Christ

speaks primarily through both His Word (the Bible) and through His Body (other believers). We are all part of the one Body of Christ no matter what our church background. His Word (the Bible) is the foundation of all revelation and the trusted source of confirmation for everything we hear from God.

"The Son of God (Jesus) who loved (agape) me, and gave Himself for me" (Galatians 2:20).

3) The Holy Spirit

speaks primarily internally, from within your human spirit, as He now inhabits your heart with the divine Kingdom of God. His voice flows out of your mind and can be discerned by your spirit. And He confirms all direction at least two or three times through both internal and external means.

"I urge you by the love (agape) of the (Holy) Spirit" (Romans 15:30).

Note: The Holy Spirit as a Person comes to abide inside every believer in Jesus Christ. His workings require the believer to actively participate in a sanctifying, holy lifestyle that involves a dying to self and old, selfish priorities.

So throughout this book, perhaps consider a fresh surrender to Jesus Christ, and a fresh commitment to participation with the Holy Spirit, as He leads you to die to yourself and your old ways, and learn new ways to communicate with Him.

Thus, with the Holy Spirit's help, you can learn to truly listen to God's multi-faceted voice and follow Christ who said, *"If anyone wishes to come after Me, let him deny himself, and take up his cross, and follow Me"* (Matthew 16:24).

Defining the Title: SPEAKS. 21 Distinct Ways

Now the second word to define is, SPEAKS.

The promise from Jeremiah is, *"Call to Me, and I will answer you, and I will TELL YOU..."* (Jeremiah 33:3). The premise of this book is that there 21 ways that God's answer, His *telling*, might be coming. His voice is multi-faceted, and so amazing that sometimes He sends His answer in multiple ways through creative means and circumstances.

There are three main sections with seven ways in each, categorized from "very common" to "common" to "uncommon" for a total of 21 ways. So there are 21 chapters to read. Each one contains a possible new way that God might be contacting you this very week. As mentioned, all of them require an ongoing prayer dialogue between the Holy Spirit and you.

Your faith will grow the more ways you recognize His voice. And the more ways you recognize, the closer you will draw near to God, even as He draws near to you in His *agape*.

As you approach each way God speaks, remember two opposite truths, held in tension and part of the mystery of the Trinity:

1) Each Person of the Trinity is part of the One God, so each Person is involved in unity in every contact in this book, though one of them might be primary.

2) Sometimes it is the Father Himself taking initiative, sometimes it's Jesus, and sometimes it is the Holy Spirit taking initiative to speak.

Note: At all times, Father's love is the ultimate source and, Love Speaks!

And His love brings His security to His sons and daughters, pouring through Jesus and the Holy Spirit. You are a child of God. You can hear from your Father directly. And you can call Him, "Abba" (*see* Romans 8:15).

Practical Application, and the "Counterfeit Voices"

The fourth section is a very practical section with applications and challenges. It isn't enough to just hear the voice and experience the love of God for yourself. The world around you is waiting to receive what you've been given. This section will help you form new interactions with God through His Holy Spirit, and new ways to share Father's love with people.

The Appendix adds another dimension to this teaching. It is called, "Counterfeit Voices." There are many "counterfeit voices" to be aware of through the influence of New Age and other false religions.

For example, New Age teachings promote a loss of God as the glorious, infinite, personal Trinity. "Humans are simply congealed energy, the All in self-reflective mode. You create your own reality. Both death and morality are an illusion, and hence 'we are God.' These teachings not only misunderstand the fallen nature of man and our human condition, but the seriousness of our sin before God. There is no Savior to cleanse our guilty hearts, no personal, loving God to share our tears."[4]

This Appendix will help you discern the original from the counterfeit in your everyday life.

My Prayer For You

I am praying for you, the reader of this book. *"May the Father give you a spirit of wisdom & revelation of the knowledge of Him"* (Ephesians 1:17-18).

I am praying you will recognize the multi-faceted aspects of God's wonderful voice, and increase your weekly contacts with Him in an ongoing dialogue.

I am praying that every time you recognize a contact from the Lord to you personally, you will know that it is your Heavenly Father reaching out to you

---

4 Bruce Milne, *Know the Truth: A Handbook of Christian Belief* (InterVarsity Press, 1982, 1988), p. 139.

in His unshakable, eternal love in the midst of uncertain times.

I am praying that as you read this book, you will establish a strong communication signal from God, and you will never again experience a dropped call or weak signal in prayer, like people do with their mobile phones.

God will never again have to say to you, "Can you hear Me—NOW?"

God is still *ever-present*. He is the *I AM*. And, His everlasting love speaks.

Can you hear Him, NOW?

SECTION 1

7

VERY COMMON

WAYS THE LORD SPEAKS

LOVE SPEAKS

WAY #1: THE ESTABLISHED WORD

Give Me the Book!

    "In the beginning was the Word (Logos, Greek), and the Word was with God, and the Word was God. He was in the beginning with God" (John 1:1-2).

On a visit to southwest England a few years ago, I decided to visit the town of Bristol, where John and Charles Wesley had their key base of ministry. They helped lead the Methodist movement, and since I was named after them with my middle name (my middle name is Wesley), I thought the least I could do was search out where they used to live, pray, study the Bible, and preach.

They saw revival spread from there outward and all over England and the world. I had heard that their original ministry base was there and still preserved. I walked to the place where I thought it was, but all around me instead was a very modern shopping mall. I kept walking, and suddenly the walls of a huge store seemed to give way to a small stone walkway with a statue of Wesley on his horse in the front. The walkway led back to an old building, the oldest surviving Methodist church and building in the world.

Modern developers had literally built this huge, modern shopping mall all around it!

The inside was an amazing gathering room with a wrap-around balcony and a stunning wooden pulpit two stories high with impressive stairs leading up to it. From there some 250 years ago, the focal point was the preaching of the Word, and the preacher could be seen plainly, both by those standing on the floor and those gathered round on the upper level.

I knew that the Word of God was important to the Wesley brothers, and the revival power of God that accompanied the Word preached had brought thousands of people to Christ in the decades of the mid-1700s and beyond.

I mounted the stairs and stood prayerfully in their pulpit. As I did so, I began to pray and even sense the presence of God. An old King James Edition of the Bible was open in front of me and I prayed for a deeper impartation of the understanding of the Word of God. The walls around me themselves seemed to speak. People had stood all around that pulpit and literally trembled as they heard the power of the Word preached by the revivalists of that day.

> Always let the Bible lead the way.

I love John Wesley's passion for the study of the Word. The centrality of Scripture and its function as the core of belief for every Christian caused him to call himself, "a man of one book."

This chapter will now highlight how emphasizing the study of the Word of God is the most common way in all of Christendom that God is speaking. It is the beginning, middle, and end of every understanding we have of God communicating to us.

In fact, the Bible is the foremost authority in our lives, and though this book lists 21 different ways that God can potentially be speaking to you today, this first one is the anchor of all the rest. Without it, you would be a ship caught adrift in the waves of experience without an anchor of truth.

In fact, the many experiences you'll read about in this book that have happened to me, as the author, and to countless other Christians down through the centuries, are not the basis of teaching or truth.

From the outset, I want you, as the reader, to be encouraged to always keep Scripture as the source of all teaching in this book and the practical applications of each Section. Study the Word for yourself and develop your own firm convictions. Do not fall for the trap of forming your beliefs merely on the basis of your own spiritual experiences or the experiences of other people.

Always let the Bible lead the way.

Let's define this first way of hearing from God in the Word.

The Established Word of Jesus, a simple definition. *Logos,* Greek. This word can be best defined as, "the established body of Truth" in the whole of Scripture. Expect that Jesus will guide you every time you study the Word in its original context.

The *Logos* is important for doctrine, correction, training in righteousness, and truly understanding how the God of both Testaments has chosen to lead, train, and speak to His people in all generations. Whenever you sit down to a Bible study and learn about the time the original passage was written, and try to understand the exact context of what the writer was trying to communicate, you are studying the Logos.

> *"For you have been born again, not of seed which is perishable but imperishable, that is, through the living and abiding Word (Logos) of God."* (1 Peter 1:23).

Theologians build their lives upon careful study of the historical contexts, the nuances of original languages like Hebrew, Latin, and Greek, and understanding the audience and the author. Sometimes it is helpful to read their thoughts on a particular passage, though you do not need to be a theologian to understand it.

You always ask yourself the famous six questions as you study the context of the Bible: Who, What, Why, Where, When, and How?

The Father Reveals His Son Through His Word

So how does God speak today through His Word? Let's turn to a few scriptures that best answer that question in light of its importance for balance in the beginning of this journey of seeking to hear all the ways that God is speaking in the midst of these uncertain times.

In John chapter 1, John writes,

> *"In the beginning was the Word, and the Word was with God, and the Word was God. He was in the beginning with God"* (John 1:1-2).

In Hebrews chapter 1 we read,

> *"God, after he spoke long ago to the fathers by the prophets in many portions and in many ways, in these last days has spoken to us by His Son, whom He appointed heir of all things, through whom also He made the world. And He is the radiance of His glory and the exact representation of His nature, and upholds all things by the word of His power"* (Hebrews 1:1-2a).

Oh wondrous thought! The Father spoke through many various ways down through the centuries, and now He speaks through His Son, and His Son is the exact representation of His glory and majesty.

> *"God has spoken!" wrote Andrew Murray. "When man speaks it is the revelation of himself. When God, who dwells in light that is inaccessible, speaks out of the heights of His glory, it is that He may reveal Himself. The Son Himself had to come as the Word of God to us, the bearer of the life and love of the Father. The Son Himself had to come to bring us into living contact with the Divine Being, to dwell in our heart, as He dwells in God's heart, and so to give us the living experience of what it means that God speaks to us."* [5]

---

5   Andrew Murray, *The Holiest of All: an Exposition of the Epistle to the Hebrews* (Retypset edition, 1993, Baker Book House Company).

And Paul gives us this:

"Every scripture is God-breathed (given by His inspiration) and profitable for instruction, for reproof and conviction of sin, for correction of error and discipline in obedience, and for training in righteousness (in holy living, in conformity to God's will in thought, purpose, and action)" (2 Timothy 3:16, The Amplified Translation).

And then let's turn back to John 1 for a moment.

"And the Word became flesh, and dwelt among us, and we beheld His glory, glory as of the only begotten from the Father, full of grace and truth" (John 1:14).

How's that for a firm foundation? The first place to start in your journey of daring to listen and begin a dialogue with God is right there in front of you, in your Bible.

The Word is the Living Jesus!

He is alive on every page.

Scripture is teeming with life, and all the Father's life is found in His Son. "It is not flesh and blood that reveals Christ," wrote Bonhoeffer, quoting from Matthew 16:17 and Peter's revelation of who Christ was, "but the Father in heaven, where and when He will."[6]

> Do not fall for the trap of forming your beliefs merely on the basis of your own spiritual experiences or the experiences of other people.

I remember hearing a preacher many years ago, and He was revealing how Jesus was present, in some way, in every single book of the 66 books of the Bible. If you search for Jesus, you can find Him somewhere in every book. Allow the Father to guide you to the true revelation of the Son throughout the Word.

---

6 Dietrich Bonhoeffer, *Christ the Center, A New Translation* (Harper & Row Publishers, 1978), p. 51.

What My Scripture Says, I Say

"For many Christians the supreme reason for according the Bible the status of God's Word written is simply the fact that GOD HIMSELF addresses us in it," writes Bruce Milne. "God speaks in the words in the Bible in such a manner as to remove all doubt as to its divine origin, character and authority. In the final analysis only God can be an adequate witness to himself. All other testimony such as historical evidence or philosophical deduction can at best possess only secondary value.

"Multitudes of Christians in every generation have testified that, as they read the Bible and hear it expounded, they are moved to recognize its inherent authority. This was focused by Augustine when he put into God's mouth the words, 'Indeed, O man, what my Scripture says, I say.'"[7]

And for Martin Luther, his firm convictions of the truths of Ephesians 2 led him to absolutely stand upon the importance of the Bible as the source of revelation of God's truth.

Give Me The Book!

Let us pause here and return for a moment to John Wesley, and how he considered the study of the Logos, the established Word, the foundation for all of our seeking and discovering God's will and the answers to our most basic questions.

"I am a creature of a day, passing through life as an arrow through the air. I am a spirit come from God, and returning to God: just hovering over the great gulf; till, a few moments hence, I am no more seen; I drop into an unchangeable eternity!

"I want to know one thing,—the way to heaven; how to land safe on that happy shore.

"God himself has condescended to teach me the way. For this very end He came from heaven.

"He has written it down in a book.

---

7 Bruce Milne, *Know the Truth: A Handbook of Christian Belief* (InterVarsity Press, 1982, 1988), p. 45.

"O give me that book! At any price, give me the book of God!

"I have it: here is knowledge enough for me. Let me be *homo unius libri: a man of One Book!*

"Here then I am, far from the busy ways of men. I sit down alone; only God is here. In His presence I open, I read His book; for this end, to find the way to heaven. Is there a doubt concerning the meaning of what I read? Does anything appear dark or intricate?

"I lift up my heart to the Father of Lights: 'Lord, is it not said in Your Word, 'if any man lack wisdom, let him ask of God?' You give liberally.

"You have said, 'if any be willing to do Your will, he shall know.' I am willing to do, let me know Your will.

"I then search after and consider parallel passages of Scripture, 'comparing spiritual things with spiritual.'

"I meditate therein with all the attention and earnestness of which my mind is capable. If any doubt still remains, I consult those who are experienced in the things of God: and then the writings whereby, being dead, they yet speak."[8]

So if you follow in Wesley's footsteps you will find the will of God and His understandings speaking to you in many ways.

I love Wesley's technique of comparing parallel passages, meditating on the Word, and consulting others to help confirm truth. I love his passion for Scripture.

I, too, want to be a "man of one book."

Another "man of one book" was a short and stout plumber in the northwest of England, a few centuries after Wesley. He became one of the Pentecostal movement's most widely-known evangelists. His name was Smith Wigglesworth. He never learned how to read up until the time of his conversion. After his conversion, he asked his wife to help him learn how to

---

8 John Wesley, Preface to his published *53 Sermons* (Nashville: Abingdon Press, 1983), p. 13.

read so that he could read the New Testament on his own.

He shared, "Fill your head and your heart with the Scriptures. Memorize passages from the Word so you can learn to quote it. You must be so soaked with the Word of God, so filled with it, that you yourself are a living epistle, known and read of all men. I have a love for the Word, and an absolute confidence in the God of the Word."[9]

Wigglesworth only read the New Testament the rest of his life.

Tips for Sword Sharpening

Think of the Word as a sword, always by your side. Paul talks about comparing the Word to a sword in Ephesians. A sword needs sharpening to be an effective weapon; a blunt blade will do no harm to your enemy.

Sharpening your sword of established truth is akin to careful study, meditation, and application of the Word in obedience of faith.

It also requires practice.

Picture yourself out for a walk down the path in medieval times. You round the bend in the road and suddenly are faced with the edge of a battlefield. You were not aware that a battle was taking place. As you enter the edge of the field, your enemy notices you and begins to advance in your direction. The honest truth is, you will not live very long unless you know how to draw your sharpened sword out of its sheath and begin to use it.

When you objectively study and meditate on the Logos, you need to ask yourself this question:

What DID it mean?

In other words, learn who the original author was, who the original intended audience was, and the historical backdrop to the situation. All Scripture is God-breathed, so in its original context it contains power.

---

9 Stanley Howard Frodsham, *Smith Wigglesworth: Apostle of Faith* (Radiant Books, 1948), p. 111.

Another element in studying the Logos can be summarized in three simple steps:

1. Observation (What does it say?)

2. Interpretation (What does it mean?)

3. Application (What does it mean to me personally?)

Conformity to the Word of God always brings holiness and leads to obedience and action. Being able to answer number 3 in all honesty can bring a wonderful sense of the presence of God to you.

Practical Application:
By Study & Strong Belief You Swim Against the Stream

Understand that by taking a position of objective study you are swimming against the rising tide of an all-inclusive, one-world religion that is sweeping the West (and many mainline churches, too) in post-modernism. For example,

1. Biblical beliefs are out. They are "so last century" in people's minds. They are now irrelevant—to be discarded and not held.

2. Being "fully alive" is in—no matter what religion inspires passion.

3. There's no room for objective reality or absolute truth.

4. The "higher form of knowing" would be based on mystical experiences and self-knowledge. The latter supposedly leads to "knowing a universal god—or the spirit of love in everyone."[10]

That is where society in the West is currently heading. There is also a stream of mystical delusion in the Church; whole groups base their Sunday morning services on "experience in the Holy Spirit" without a balanced emphasis on the study of the Word. Many people today have come to

10 Adapted partially from a blog entitled, *"From Gnostic Roots to Occult Revival"* by The Lighthouse Trails Research Group.

value emotions and feelings in place of truth. It's time to develop both a balanced view of "experiences with God's Spirit" and learning the "truth of God's word."

As you learn to emphasize study of the Word, you will grow daily and find any experiences deeper as you anchor them in the truth. Learn the context of it, learn to formulate strong understandings by comparing scripture with scripture, and staying true to its original meaning and intent.

And when you study it and memorize it, you can stand on it and hold firm, and thus develop strong convictions about it.

Practical Application: Stand on the Rock of the Word

You can also imagine the Logos as the bed-rock of established truth that you can stand upon to be elevated above your circumstances and share in God's vision for them.

Here is a sample of five general situations where you can achieve victory by meditating and standing upon the established Word of God. On the left is the *need* and on the right is the *answer*.

Memorize the scriptures on the right and no matter what your own circumstance, believe them to be true. Meditate and stand upon the Word in faith.

It is like you are truly "in Christ" as you stand upon His Word; it is the Old Testament word picture of Christ as our "high tower" of strong defense against our enemy.

I encourage you to study the Word of God and learn to discipline yourself daily in consecration to the truth in any area of need that may not be on this list.

Whatever the need, there are answers in the Word!

THE NEED	THE ANSWER
Healing	Isaiah 53:4-5, 1 Peter 2:24
Encouragement	Psalm 27, 2 Corinthians 4
Repentance	Psalm 51, 1 John 1:9
Peace	Psalm 23, Philippians 4:6-7
National Crisis	2 Kings 19:14-19, Revelation 12:11

Practical Application: Develop Your Own Non-negotiables

When I use the term *non-negotiable*, I am reminding you that your faith, and mine, is rooted in firm commitment.

Jesus is called, among other titles, "the faithful witness" ("witness" means martyr) in the Book of Revelation.

He is called that for a reason.

His blood was shed as He remained true to the Father against all the human and Satanic opposition of His life. He was uncompromising against sin and embodied the fullness of the truth.

He is still the truth and is calling people to "witness" to that truth today.

When you take a stand for Jesus, and you truly study His word, it speaks to you. HE speaks to you. And you then develop your own firm convictions.

No matter what pressures come your way, with governmental authorities or other people asking you to conform, to abandon "absolute truth" and submit to their religious openness, you must be able to stand firm.

Unique in this world-gone-mad of earthly religions and global terrorism is the concept of who GOD is to a believer when it comes to listening prayers.

I find great comfort, in the midst of worldwide terrorism and religious upheavals, that there is a distinct difference between myself, a follower of Christ and, say, a Muslim person or a Hindu person or a Buddhist person.

Jesus Christ stands alone as God's challenger of every other earthly, man-made religion. He alone brings us revelation that God is a Father and longs to speak, in His love, to His people. He gives me "ears to hear" Him, up close and personal. Muslims, Hindus, Buddhists and others simply never experience God on a personal level of a love relationship. Jesus brought us access to our Father, through the Holy Spirit. Both His Father and our Father. That is life-changing.

Christians are the only people on earth that share this love relationship, with open lines of communication between our Father and ourselves. He comes through the Person of Jesus and the power of the Holy Spirit.

Martin Luther declared boldly, in his famous speech when he was summoned before the religious leaders to give an account of his writings, "My conscience is captive to the word of God."[11]

Perhaps some of you will become "faithful martyrs" as you testify in the coming years of your relationship with Jesus, and what it really means to you.

Here are three of my "non-negotiables" (my "hills to die on") if I am ever called to publicly testify of my relationship with Jesus Christ in opposition to some kind of governmental regulation:

1) **Jesus is the only way, and the best way, to develop relationship with God the Father.** There are not many paths to God. There is only one God, and one path, and Jesus is that path.

2) **Jesus is Lord.** I submit to His Lordship first and foremost and will not allow any government to control my spiritual life. I only worship Jesus as Lord.

3) **God's Word is filled with absolute truth and faithful promises,** and I will absolutely follow it and trust in it.

"And they (followers of Jesus) overcame him (Satan) because of the blood of the Lamb and the word of their testimony, and they

---

11 Quoted from Heiko Oberman, *Luther: Man Between God and the Devil* (English edition, Yale Publishing, 1989).

did not love their life even unto death" (Revelation 12:11).

Dietrich Bonhoeffer once said, "To endure the cross is not tragedy; it is the suffering which is the fruit of an exclusive allegiance to Jesus Christ."

Begin today in emphasizing study of the Word of God, learning sound doctrine, and developing new disciplines (like the discipline of memorizing the Word) and it will light the way in the darkness in front of you.

Become a "man of one book" or "a woman of one book."

So here is our very first way of God's leading and speaking. It is the eternal and established Word, speaking. It is the most common, and the bedrock foundation, for all the other 20 in this book.

———

If you don't understand the various applications and importance of the Established Word of God for your life, please pause here and re-read tomorrow certain paragraphs until you really grasp the revelations and applications of becoming a "man or woman of one book."

And—most importantly—if for some reason you are reading this and haven't yet made a personal commitment to Jesus Christ as LORD, through repentance of your sins and a fresh consecration to Him for the onward journey of your life, please turn to page 333 of this book and pray the prayer that is printed for you.

It is called simply, *"A Prayer of Repentance From Sin."*

Why?

The simple answer: as you move ahead to the next 20 WAYS (Chapters), each of them requires the presence of the Holy Spirit inside of you to truly grasp with your mind, feel with your heart, and personally motivate you to learn new ways to interact with Him.

He is only accessible to those who have made a personal commitment to Jesus Christ and have received forgiveness of sins, the love of the Father and the presence of the Spirit within.

So if this applies to you, pause now, go pray that prayer, begin to sense His presence, and return to begin the next and following Chapters in this adventure of hearing God's voice.

And if you already love the LORD, please continue now.

Very Common Ways	
WAY	SCRIPTURE
1 The Established Word of Jesus	*John 1:1*

Questions for Deeper Study:

1. What is the difference between observing text and interpreting text?

2. Why does asking "What Does it Mean? (to you personally) require personal integrity?

3. Why does the Word (Scripture) supersede all other ways to hear God's voice?

4. Write out one of your very own non-negotiable Doctrines (your own "hill to die on") from the Established Word.

Keep listening!

CHAPTER

Way #2: The Living Word of Jesus

Baked Fresh Daily

"So *faith comes by hearing, and hearing by the word (Rhema, Greek) of Christ"* (Romans 10:17).

On a sunny morning in the summer of 1939, Dietrich Bonhoeffer set out on a prayer walk through the streets of New York to seek a personal answer to a dilemma. Adolf Hitler had risen to power and the evil Nazi regime was growing in strength in Germany. Europe loomed on the knife's edge of war.

Bonhoeffer had retreated for a short time in America, and while he felt secure, he also felt a responsibility to potentially return and be with his own people. What did God want for him?

Only a few years before, he had taken a group of his Bible School students for a special weekend retreat together in Northern Germany, before the Nazis had closed it and scattered his students in hiding. There, nestled in on the shores of the sea, he had taught them that Love Speaks.

"When you read the Bible," he told his students, "you must think that here and now, God is speaking with you. You can't be a Christian unless you hear from God. He wants to speak to you personally, not just in principles, and beliefs, and orthodox theology. But God wants to speak to you personally."[12]

As he meandered the streets of New York City that morning, he realized he needed to practice what he preached. He needed to hear for himself a word from God.

I can imagine him, walking and praying saying something like, "What should I do? Father, speak to me."

As he walked, he paused on a bench and opened his Bible. He stumbled upon a scripture from Isaiah that seemed to be illuminated in his spirit.

"He who believes will not flee" (Isaiah 28:16).

It was as if Jesus Himself was shouting an answer from heaven for his particular situation at that moment. Bonhoeffer knew that God was speaking to him directly to return to Germany and help his people in the midst of great spiritual darkness.

He departed the harbor on the very last ship that was allowed to leave as the war began.

He would never return to America.

As he arrived in the overspreading evil of Europe, he brought the light of Jesus Christ directly into the darkness. Sometimes, the voice of the Word will call you into the darkest places to shine the brightest for Him.

This chapter will focus our attention on the second of the two Greek words that are used in the New Testament for the term *word*. If you put into practice, on a daily basis, the truths found in this chapter, you too will develop an "absolute confidence in the God of the Word" like Wigglesworth did.

---

12 Quote from Dietrich Bonhoeffer in *Bonhoeffer: Pastor, Martyr, Prophet, Spy* by Eric Metaxas (Thomas Nelson, 2010).

In Scripture, there are two separate Greek words, with two completely complementary meanings, for understanding Jesus as the "Word." In essence, there are two different words for the word *word*. The previous chapter talked about the first of these: Logos. As a refresher, it means, "The established body of Truth" in the whole of Scripture. When you study it, you are asking yourself, "What DID IT MEAN?"

> **The Living Word of Jesus, a simple definition.** *Rhema*, Greek. This is the other word in the Greek that is translated "word of God." This word can best be defined as the living, breathing, personal and fully applicable Word of God. It's whenever you personally recognize that God may be speaking a "word from the Word" to you. It breathes new life into your spirit, opens your spiritual eyes, and adds fresh illumination from the Word into your spirit.

When Paul writes to the church at Rome he shares this revelation, *"So faith comes by hearing, and hearing by the word (rhema) of Christ"* (Romans 10:17).

He specifically uses the word *rhema*, and so he's talking about the power of the "Living Word" to bring growth in faith. I think in the past two thousand years of strong historical church doctrines and traditions we have lost something of the power of these words. As I read them, Paul is simply sharing that our faith is grown by hearing (listening to what God is saying in the Word) and applying the fresh Living Word of Christ into our personal situation.

Ask yourself this question: have you ever sat down to study the Word of God, and as you are reading along, suddenly a particular passage of the Scripture literally seems to shine like a brilliant light into your heart and you feel the nearness of God?

Do you believe that He is speaking that Scripture directly to you for your particular situation?

If your answer is "yes" to this question, you can rejoice that by the Holy Spirit, Jesus Himself, the Living Word, has utilized the Word itself to shout an answer from Heaven to your particular situation.

YOUR
WORD

is a lamp unto my feet

and a light to my path.

(Psalm 119:105)

That is the power of *rhema* for you, and the *rhema* of the Word is the other edge of the Sword of the Spirit; it penetrates the darkness and illuminates your heart with light. So you have "established truth" on one side and "living truth" on the other. The two sides of your sword, sharpened in balance, can bring daily answers to your questions.

> "Your Word is a lamp unto my feet and a light to my path"
> (Psalm 119:105).

The poetic psalmist understood a thousand years before the appearance of Jesus the Messiah how important it is that we allow the Word of God to speak personally to us and lighten the darkness around us, like a flickering candle light on the path ahead.

When you study and meditate on the *rhema*, you are asking yourself this question:

What DOES it mean <u>TO ME</u>?

What does it mean to me, personally? In other words, apply faith and your current situation to the text. Could it be that Jesus Himself is initiating contact with you through His Word, and shouting an answer to your prayers before you call out?

All Scripture is God-breathed, so in its fresh and relevant context it contains power.

It takes integrity to make sure you receive confirmation from another scripture, or another source from the Holy Spirit, before making any key decisions after receiving the *rhema* Word.

Ask yourself, "Is Jesus really saying this to me?"

There could be multiple interpretations and guidance for you in every *rhema*, so get ready for an adventure, and remember to apply obedience and action by faith in the text to your situation.

Here are a few examples from church history where common people received guidance and comfort from the Living Word for their lives.

The Word Alive in 17th Century Scotland

During a time of intense persecution of the church in Scotland, a group of courageous men and women arose. It was the 17th century, and political and religious upheaval caused the people of God, known then as the Covenanters, to have to take a stand to not abandon the orthodox faith of their fathers.

Many were driven from their homes, some were imprisoned, and some became martyrs for their faith (and convictions of the importance of obedience to the Word of God).

One of the inspiring stories I uncovered comes from the life of Alexander Peden. Peden was a powerful preacher and was driven by the authorities to live a life on the run. He traveled through the countryside, sleeping in barns and haystacks, and secretly meeting with small groups of believers and encouraging them to remain true to the faith.

Early one morning he walked up the side of a mountain and spent many hours in prayer and in his Scriptures. An eyewitness account records what happened next.

"He returned singing the 32nd Psalm, from the 7th verse to the end, then repeated that verse,

> 'Thou art my hiding place, thou shalt
>
> From trouble keep me free:
>
> Thou with songs of deliverance
>
> About shalt compass me.'

"These and the following," he said, "are sweet lines, which I got at the mountain-side this morning, and I will get more tomorrow; and so will get daily provision. He is never behind with any who put their trust in Him, and we will go on in His strength, making mention of His righteousness, and His only."[13]

---

13 John Howie, quoting from the life of Alexander Peden, *The Scots Worthies* (Banner of Truth Trust, Edinburgh, Scotland, 1870), pp. 515-516.

The Living Word fed His servant, and the encouragement kept Peden on the move, in the midst of persecution, strengthened by God's presence in His Word.

Isn't that beautiful? You will notice that Peden exercised the spiritual discipline of waiting on God to receive from Him. The key here is EXPECTATION. After you have spoken in prayer to God and await His presence, believe and expect that God will respond to you and share, in His love, a fresh Word just for you.

A "Talent" of Gold

Another wonderful example of Jesus personally speaking to us in situations through His Word is from the life of an intercessor, Rees Howells, in Wales in the first half of the 20th Century.

After an incredible revival in Africa in 1922, Rees and his wife returned to Wales and during a time of prayer with some friends, they began to pray for a Bible college to be formed in Wales, as there were so many young people responding to God's call but they had nowhere to be trained.

Here's how the narrative went.

"It never dawned on Mr. Howells that he was to have a part in it. But as they got down to pray, the Lord said to him, 'Be careful how you pray. I am going to build a college, and build it through you!'

"It came as such a shock to him that the only thing he could say was, 'If You are really speaking to me, confirm it through the Word,' and that night the confirmation came to him through I Chronicles 28, where these three promises stood out before him:

'Be strong...and do it...for the Lord God will be with you; He will not fail you, nor forsake you, until you have finished all the work...of the house of the Lord.'

'There shall be with you...every willing, skillful man, for any manner of service' (verses 20, 21); and the third from the next chapter (29:4), that the Lord would give him a "talent" of gold, which from the margin of his Scofield Bible he learned was worth 6,150 pounds Sterling exactly.

"A short while later, as Mr. and Mrs. Howells were walking along the Mumbles Road, which skirts Swansea Bay, they passed a large estate on the rising ground overlooking the bay, and noticed that the house was vacant.

"They went up to the gate, and found the name of the place to be Glynderwen, and as they stood there, the Lord's word came, 'This is the College!'"[14]

During one period, the disappointed Howells cried out in prayer, "But you haven't given me the money!"

God replied, "Didn't I promise you a talent of gold? If you believe, go on your knees right here and claim that place."

So he knelt down there on the lawn by a little bridge and claimed it by faith, with no money at the time.

The story continues that although that estate was at the time worth more than 10,000 pounds Sterling, after much prayer and fasting, the owner agreed to sell it to Howells for 6,300 pounds. But Howells had to refuse that generous offer, as the Lord had very specifically given the figure of 6,150, and not a penny more!

The man agreed and they signed an agreement. At the time of the signing, Rees had to pay the deposit within 10 days, and on the 10th day, he was still 140 pounds Sterling short. But he was a man of true faith!

"In faith he set out to the office without it. He hadn't been there long when Mrs. Howells arrived. She had followed him down with the post, and in it were three checks, which made up the 140 pounds Sterling to the very penny!"[15]

Here's the amazing end of the story. Just as the original Word had spoken to the situation, and so it came to pass, the presence of the Lord was hovering over the land, and skillful men of various backgrounds came and helped build the property into something beautiful.

---

14 Norman Grubb, *Rees Howells: Intercessor* (Christian Literature Crusade, 1952), pp. 174, 176.
15 Ibid., p. 181.

As for the finances, over a three month period, as the word spread that Howells was buying this estate in faith to begin a new work of a Bible college, multitudes of gifts from all kinds of people were sent, from the sum of 5 cents up to 300 pounds Sterling; and on the very day that they needed to pay the money in full, they added it all up.

It was indeed "a talent of gold": 6,150 pounds (with a few coins extra to buy some food)!

How's that for a LIVING word?

The Living Word Speaks Your Name

Anne Graham Lotz, daughter of Billy Graham, shares a story about the simplicity of receiving the Living Word at a special retreat where she was teaching. She had felt stretched and weak at this particular retreat. She shares,

"The morning of the first day, I opened the Daily Light, a volume of selected Scriptures I have read every day of my life. Here is the way I "heard" those Scriptures that morning,

"'Be strong...and work, for I am with you, Anne,' says the Lord of Hosts.

"Lord, You mean I can do all things through Christ who strengthens me?"

"'Yes, Anne, (Be) strong in the Lord and in the power of His might...the joy of the Lord is your strength.' The Lord turned to Anne and said, 'Go in this might of yours. If God is for you, Anne, who can be against you? Therefore, Anne, you have received mercy, so do not lose heart.'

"As I read those verses, I clearly and distinctly heard my Shepherd speaking to me with a heart filled with compassion, sensitive to the challenge that was facing me and with genuine understanding of my weakness. I was so encouraged and strengthened by His words that I was enabled to carry out my assignment triumphantly."[16]

---

16 Anne Graham Lotz, *Expecting to See Jesus* (Zondervan Publishing, 2011), pp. 170-171.

An Application to Receive the Living Word

Place yourself in the presence and glory of God through praise and worship and create an atmosphere of expectation.

Sometimes you can expect that the Holy Spirit will actually lead you as you open up your Bible and begin to ask Jesus for a "word from His Word." This can happen in many places in your Bible, like starting to read a particular story for example, or Bible character, or passage of wisdom, or prophetic utterance, or the words of Jesus in His teachings, or the apostle's words of doctrine.

As you read, if something bears witness with your spirit and encourages you, that is probably God breathing a word from His Word to you.

Expect that as you read, there will come a specific passage that will apply to you. And as you re-read it, you will "know-that-you-know-that-you-know" that Jesus Himself, the author and finisher of your faith, has taken a Scripture and made it personal and real for you.

One of my mentors, Dr. Lance Wonders, once described to me *rhema* words as God Himself "taking the initiative and shouting an answer of prayer from heaven, but through the pages of Scripture."

So, let's say for example that you have been in prayer for a particular personal situation. Sometimes the prayer has just been spoken, other times it may be something you are simply thinking about but haven't even prayed yet. (Yes, God knows your thoughts afar off.) Still other times it may be a prayer you have prayed and you have been persistent in your prayers and continually sought God until He answers.

True growth in faith would constitute two key actions. The first half is the study of the Word to receive general guidance and to understand better what it meant.

The other half is listening to the Living Word for specific guidance and daring to ask the question, "What does this mean to me, personally?"

So, 50% study and 50% listening equals 100% success in hearing God through His Word.

And dare to allow Jesus to personalize a passage and direct it to you with your first name. This is a powerful exercise and you can trust Him to do this for you.

The Holy Spirit is unlimited in His capacity and can utilize the same passage of Scripture to apply to thousands of hearts in thousands of places, all at the same time!

Just a final thought. Remember back to one of the ways God's provision came to the children of Israel as they endured their wilderness wanderings. The story of the manna falling from Heaven is recorded in both Exodus 16 and Numbers 11.

God actually fed the children of Israel with one loaf of bread at a time. It was a substance that fell from the sky and a unique blend of ingredients that both tasted good and sustained them for one full day of travel. They were not allowed to store the bread.

The provision of the Heavenly bread was only good for one day; it could not be eaten the next day. So faith had to be applied to each and every day in order for fresh provision to be enjoyed.

In John's gospel, Jesus was teaching us that He is "the Bread of life." We need to feed upon Him daily. The application of this wonderful truth, symbolized by the manna in the wilderness and of Jesus Himself being the Living Word, is that you need a fresh meal every day.

You, too, cannot live solely on the revelations He has given yesterday. You need to seek Him afresh every day to receive fresh bread as spiritual nourishment from His Word.

When was the last time you opened your Bible and felt God supply a fresh Word directly to you, perhaps with your own first name upon it, for your situation? If you have been praying for guidance, or in need of a touch of His love, then the answer should always be, "Today!"

Yes, today.

Stretch your faith and open your Bible and prepare your heart to receive. You can receive fresh bread, Living Bread, "baked fresh daily" and let it nourish your spirit and fill your heart with hope.

To summarize, here is our next way of God's leading and speaking. It is JESUS speaking IN HIS LIVING WORD. It is one of the most common of all the ways that Jesus, in His presence in the Trinity, speaks.

Very Common Ways

WAY		SCRIPTURE
1	The Established Word of Jesus	John 1:1
2	The Living Word of Jesus	Romans 10:17

Questions for Deeper Study:

1. What is the difference between studying the scriptures and devotional moments?

_____

_____

_____

2. Why is it important to balance both study and devotional inquiry?

_____

_____

_____

3. What does it mean to "go to man"? And what are the potential pitfalls?

_____

_____

_____

4. Based on what you have learned so far, what will you do differently when you need to hear from the LORD?

_____

_____

_____

Keep listening!

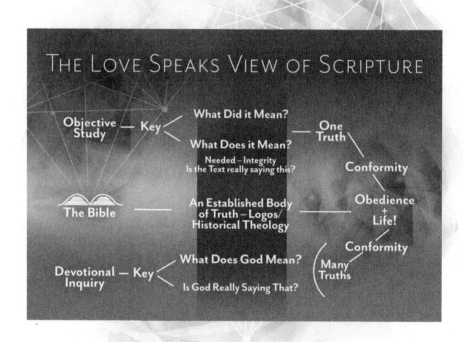

WAY #3: THE INNER WITNESS OF THE HOLY SPIRIT

Red Light, Yellow Light, Green Light

"So the church enjoyed peace, being built up; and going on in the fear of the Lord and in the comfort of the Holy Spirit, it continued to increase" (Acts 9:31).

Early in this journey of revisiting some of the more common ways and learning new ways to recognize the voice of God, we come to the subject of confirmation.

As you walk forward, and you are desiring to follow God's will, it is helpful to have some internal confirmation of the direction you sense you are to be traveling.

You might currently be praying over a situation and even have a scripture or two from the Word to stand upon.

What if you can have the direction of the Word AND have another confirmation from God Himself that the direction you are praying about is a good one? Or a bad one? Or perhaps you should be cautious and keep on praying?

You can!

The "inner witness" serves as a unique, instantly accessible, instantly available 24/7, divine and supernaturally natural means of confirming true direction from God.

It is one of the most common ways of God speaking, yet perhaps one of the least taught in most churches. And when you learn to access God's Spirit on an ongoing basis as a means for confirmation, you'll find that this one works alongside and in tandem with many of the other 20 ways taught in this book.

> **The Inner Witness of the Spirit, a simple definition.** A spiritual "sense" of PEACE and JOY in your inner spirit (like a green light or YES! in particular guidance, and originating from your inner spirit) OR a spiritual sense of "tightness" inside (a "yellow" light or a "red" light) witnessing, "CAUTION" or "NO!" to particular guidance.

So this form of listening is more of a *sense* from God's Spirit. I will explain more below that it is like an impulse of Holy Spirit to human spirit!

A Divine Glow to Light the Way in the Darkness

The Inner Witness is rooted in a very unique way that God used to lead His people in the Old Testament, through the high priest, in a method of discernment called the Urim and Thummim.

Here is the Scripture to study along with this.

> *"And you shall put in the breastplate of judgment the Urim and the Thummim, and they shall be over Aaron's heart when he goes in before the Lord"* (Exodus 28:30a).

Let me quote from Steve Sampson here, author and itinerant speaker. "This was a way for the priest to receive a "yes" or "no" witness from God. The word Urim means lights and perfections, while the word Thummim means truths and completeness. It is interesting how the wisdom of God put the two together—the Urim (light) for divine guidance, and the Thummim (truth) for integrity of heart.

"The Holy Spirit will only bear witness to truth. Whenever there was a need for divine guidance regarding a decision, the priest could peek into the pouch behind the breastplate to see if the Urim glowed. If the glow was present, he knew the Lord was speaking a yes. If there was no glow (inner burning), then he knew God was speaking a no, meaning not to take the action they were inquiring about.

"This is exactly what we do as believers. We become conscious of the inner glow, or that witness of the Spirit inside. We can be aware of the Spirit glowing with a resounding yes, or when there is a lack of glowing or burning, a resounding no. This is trusting the inner witness of the Holy Spirit within."[17]

I like to think of the inner witness kind of like the special gift of the elves to Frodo Baggins in the great "Lord of the Rings" trilogy. The elf queen, Galadriel, gave him the light of Earendil, their most beloved star. She said, "May it be a light to you in dark places when all other lights go out."[18]

In the power of the Holy Spirit, you always have an inner light to light the way in any spiritual darkness you encounter.

One of the key ways to always know in your heart that God speaks is through confirmation. In other words, He says something one way and then confirms it by a totally different way. And you and He alone know that He is speaking! He shares this principle in various scriptures, including Paul visiting Corinth and sharing,

> "This is the third time I am coming to you. In the mouth of two or
> three witnesses, every word shall be established" (2 Corinthians 13:1).

Paul's "third time" equaled "three witnesses" of confirmation of truth to the church there. God uses this same principal in guidance. Always look for confirmation in a variety of ways that He is speaking! This is why the inner

---

17 Steve Sampson, *You Can Hear The Voice of God: How God Speaks in Listening Prayer* (Chosen Books, a division of Baker Publishing Group, 2015), pp. 94-95.

18 Quote from, *The Lord of the Rings: The Return of the King,* film by director Peter Jackson & based upon the writings of J.R.R. Tolkien.

witness is powerful.

Let's turn to Scripture for a New Testament explanation of this amazing witness.

Red Light, Yellow Light, Green Light

Here is a simple way to work with the Holy Spirit whenever you are seeking fresh direction, or seeking to confirm a direction or a path and you already have at least the Word of God to light the way. Think for a moment of the three lights at a traffic intersection. You know what those lights signal.

Here are three scriptures from the Book of Acts that share some insights about this unique voice of the Holy Spirit. I'll start with the red light and move to the yellow light and finally, to the green light.

RED LIGHT: *"And having been forbidden by the Holy Spirit to speak the word in Asia"* (Acts 16:6).

Here the disciples most likely felt a tightness in their inner spirits when considering the path to Asia. It was the method the Spirit utilized to say "No!"

YELLOW LIGHT: *"Now while Paul was waiting for them at Athens, his spirit was being provoked within him as he was beholding the city full of idols"* (Acts 17:16).

Here we imagine Paul, interceding moment by moment, questioning his own involvement in deciding whether to confront the idolatry of Athens.

This "yellow light" or semi-tightness in his spirit is described as a kind of "provoking" as the Holy Spirit Himself was probably deeply grieved and attempting to lead Paul in helping him fulfill his ministry there.

GREEN LIGHT: *"And the disciples were continually FILLED WITH JOY with the Holy Spirit"* (Acts 13:52).

> *"So the church enjoyed peace, being built up, and going on in the fear of the LORD and in the comfort of the Holy Spirit"* (Acts 9:31).

Here we have two instances where the Holy Spirit was communicating a "green light" to all these disciples of Jesus. They felt the very joy, peace, and comfort of the Holy Spirit deep inside their own human spirits as they followed His leadings.

I have utilized this very simple application in prayer hundreds of times. As you get better at working along with the Holy Spirit at this, it will become quite natural. You will want to actively ask the Holy Spirit, in relation to a particular situation you are facing, "Lord, red, yellow, or green?" And then wait upon the Lord and see what you can sense in your inner spirit.

I think this approach is a little bit radical. I know that many of you are wondering by now how this and other approaches affect your mind. I mean, God gave you a mind and reason to be used, didn't He?

Yes! So this approach is radical because it tends to bypass the faculties of the natural mind.

> "Lord, is it red, yellow, or green?"

Spiritual Intuition

In the West, we have been taught that the pursuit of knowledge and the faculty of reason reign supreme. We live in a rational world with scientific proof explaining nearly everything around us, from the smallest micro-organisms to the largest black holes and new cosmoses being discovered yearly.

This is only half of the way God has fashioned us in His wisdom.

The other half is what I term the intuitive, the part of us that just "knows-that-we-know-that-we-know" without it being a rational discussion of physical proof.

The God of the Bible is the God who created man and woman uniquely in His own image, and breathed into them the Spirit of life, and created both the rational and intuitive inside each of us.

Genesis teaches clearly that the rational part of us and the intuitive part of us have been affected by the Fall. In a very real sense, the spirit of man became inactive after the Fall.

You will note in Genesis 3 that God forbade Adam and Eve from re-entering the intimate place of fellowship with Him, communicating Spirit-to-spirit. He did not allow them to eat or partake of the Tree of Life.

Jesus Christ Himself poured out the life-giving, life-filled Holy Spirit at His ascension, as a gift from the Father. We are reborn and our inner spirit becomes active once again and receives communication daily from Heaven.

"There is a faculty we may term 'spiritual intuition.' It is the most difficult to speak of because it is by far the deepest aspect of our beings and often defies neat and tidy categories," writes Andy and Jane Fitz-Gibbon. "In seeking the mind of God we need the humility to move beyond our own powers of reason and to seek an intuition given Spirit to spirit.

"It will often be in the form of an inner check or confirmation.

"That's it. Do That."

"No, don't do that."

"The inner "yes" and "amen" of God is often a fleeting impression like the gentle breeze felt but difficult to grasp hold of."[19]

So, to sum up the understanding of the inner witness, the Holy Spirit, as a Person of the Trinity, knows and understands you and lives in your human spirit.

As you pray and ask Him to speak, you can expect something like a set of traffic lights to be there; a kind of YES in your heart when the light is GREEN, meaning, "Go, and I am with you."

Or a kind of CAUTION light sometimes is the sign within if the situation needs you to step back and perhaps wait for further guidance, or to proceed with caution.

Or a "NO, don't do that" will be heard in your spirit, followed by almost a check or tightness inside.

Like a RED light.

---

19 Andy and Jane Fitz-Gibbon, *Prophetic Lifestyle and the Celtic Way,* p. 157.

Billy Graham Called to Preach by the Witness

On a beautiful evening in 1938, on the edge of a golf course, young Billy Graham was in prayer. He was asking God if he was being called to preach. God answered him through the inner witness of the Holy Spirit. He shares the experience in his own words.

"I walked through the late-night hours, struggling with the Holy Spirit over the call of God to be a minister. That was the last thing I wanted to be, and I had used all kinds of rationalizations to convince God to let me do something else.

"Many people responded to my preaching by confessing faith in Christ and being converted. My teachers and classmates seemed to affirm that this ministry was good and right for me. But did I want to preach for a lifetime?

"The inner, irresistible urge would not subside.

"Finally, I got down on my knees at the edge of one of the greens. Then I prostrated myself on the dewy turf. 'O God,' I sobbed, 'if you want me to serve you, I will.'

"The moonlight, the moss, the breeze, the green, the golf course—all the surroundings stayed the same. No voice from above. But in my spirit I knew I had been called to the ministry.

"And I knew my answer was yes.

"From that night in 1938 on, my purpose and objectives in life were set. I knew I would be a preacher of the gospel."[20]

For Billy Graham, the inner witness of the Holy Spirit green-lighted an international preaching ministry that literally has affected millions of souls for the Kingdom.

---

20 Billy Graham, *Just As I Am* (Harper Paperbacks, a division of HarperCollins Publishers, 1997), p. 63.

God Loves the Sound of Music

So how does the gentle witness square with your mind and its workings?

Let's call it a perfect balance of feeling and logic. Call it logic on fire.

The Holy Spirit's habitation and leading by intuition will become primary at times, while emotions, reason, logic, and even other people's emotions will become secondary as you seek His inner witness of confirmation.

Think of it like living between two opposites. Love can exist in the middle, as we see in the story of one of the most beloved movie musicals of all time, *The Sound of Music*.

Wild, spontaneous, passionate Maria begins her first day of work as a new nanny to the sound of a whistle. Captain Von Trapp is militarily trained, exact, rule-following, and major-general in the way he approaches fatherhood to his seven children.

He blows his whistle to assemble the children like a military battalion going off to war, while new recruit Maria, in all her free-spiritedness, dances around the bedroom in a rain storm. She and all the children dance and sing with the curtains as the rain pours in and they sing to "My Favorite Things."

There could not be a more unique example of reason vs. intuition between two characters in all of musical film history! Yet a story of love begins to blossom, and in the end, Love Speaks. There is a balance to be enjoyed between the two. The sound of the army whistle became the sound of music. God turned logic on fire through Captain Von Trapp and Maria's love story!

The Witness of the Spirit Brings the Experience of God's Love

The inner guidance of the Holy Spirit will deepen your intensity of love for personal relationship with Him.

You'll remember my opening story of John Wesley as we looked at the foundational way of God speaking through His Word. Wesley was indeed, "the man of one book," yet he also relates a very interesting story that happened shortly after he gave his heart to Christ and was converted.

Wesley and some others were in prayer together and seeking the presence of God's Spirit as they sought His direction in moving forward in evangelism. Here is what Wesley wrote of that all-night prayer meeting with a divine surprise, on December 31, 1738.

"About 3 o'clock in the morning, as we were continuing instant in prayer, the power of God came mightily upon us inasmuch that many cried out for exceeding joy, and many fell to the ground. As soon as we were recovered a little from the awe and the amazement at the Presence of His majesty, we broke out with one voice, 'We praise thee, O God, we acknowledge thee to be the Lord.'"[21]

Can you see the amazing moment of the Spirit's presence here, and how on the inside of each man present there came a witness of peace and joy? That was the inner YES of God's Spirit, a green light if you will, for all of them in their journey. Of course, this particular instance shows the power of gathering together for times of praise and worship and a beautiful expression of God's power sent to give them all a witness of peace and joy.

Note: learning to listen to the inner witness, is an ACTIVE stance in prayer, not a PASSIVE one. Wesley and the others here were actively seeking the presence of God and expecting that He would share His confirmation with them.

Satan loves to use passiveness as a lure to the harmful and mixture-filled direction of his demonic forces. The Spirit is the opposite; He works with those who are moving forward and seeking Him in active ways, as He Himself is always in motion.

It has always been this way. As you re-read the Book of Acts with this in mind, you will find the inner witness leading His people as they are actively pursuing the Kingdom and advancing the Kingdom.

You'll note that in Billy Graham's story, he was in the motion of prayer and actively seeking God's will and direction when the inner witness gave him a "Yes!"

---

21 E.M. Bounds, *The Classic Collection on Prayer* (Bridge-Logos Publishers, 2001).

Go To the Toilet NOW

Let me close this portion with a very practical example from my earlier life of itinerant ministry, and share a very real experience when the inner witness in another brother brought amazing results.

In February of 1995 I was invited to the United Kingdom to preach and encourage leaders in various places. Having flown all night with very little sleep from Minneapolis to London, I hurriedly collected my luggage at Gatwick Airport and hopped on the first available train to connect to another station which would lead me to Edinburgh, Scotland, for the first leg of my journey.

I was scheduled to stay at the home of a very good friend of mine, Iain. Iain was a leader of various ministries, including churches and parachurch ministries, and had invited me to preach on the Sunday at a new church-plant that was forming just south of Edinburgh.

I did not realize it at the time, but the Holy Spirit was upon me at Gatwick and I was being watched and followed!

So, off I go on a train, heading due north through the English countryside on my way up to Iain and a warm meal and bed in Edinburgh. About half-way through the train ride, I was so hungry for the presence of God that I could not watch a movie on my laptop.

I felt the inner witness of the Spirit encourage me to get up from my seat and move to the area in-between the train cars, where the toilets are located, to go and worship Jesus in song. I was hungry for the presence of God.

Usually nobody sits in the fold-out seats near the toilet, so this opportunity would afford me some privacy to worship God in secret (except for those who were using the toilets).

I had just settled into about 15 minutes of singing songs of worship when a man appeared from the train car opposite me.

He sat down near me and began to stare at me. I felt a little uncomfortable with this; after all, this was not a concert performance! I could notice out of the corner of my eye that he had a thick beard.

Then he spoke to me. "Hi. My name is John." (He did not give his last name, and to this day I have no idea what it was.)

I noticed he had an American accent like mine, and I began to look closer at his appearance. He was wearing a long, brown cloak with a hood, a brown belt covering his large waist, and had a thick white beard and wild hair. He looked like Gandalf from the Lord of the Rings movies, or perhaps John the Baptist himself. He continued speaking.

"I am a graduate of the Brownsville School of Revival. The Lord told me to take along with me a big jar of anointing oil and bring it to Edinburgh. It has been prayed over by the group of intercessors and the prayer teams in the Revival, and the oil is to go to a group of prayer warriors in Scotland for them to use to pray over their soil and anoint it for coming revivals.

"Today is my first day; I flew all night from New York and when I landed in Gatwick this morning, I saw you from across the luggage collection area and the Spirit prompted me inside and said, 'Follow him. Go wherever he goes.'

"I felt a green light in my spirit to follow you onto this particular train, though I did not know where you were sitting."

By this point I sat amazed. Deep inside, I knew that God was in this.

I asked him now how he happened to find me on this particular train.

"Oh, well, I was sitting in my seat when the Spirit spoke to me by His inner witness, and I felt Him prompt me to go to the toilet.

"I sat there and argued with God. 'But God, I really don't have to go to the toilet just now!'

'YES, YOU DO.'

"The Spirit kept giving me a green light in my spirit to go NOW.

"So I got up from my seat, and I came to the toilet closest to me, and here you are, singing praises to God. I knew you were somewhere on this train but now I see why the Spirit prompted me to go to the toilet!"

Iain met us at Edinburgh train station, and after a brief introduction, immediately offered John a bed for the night at his home. John then handed Iain this enormous jar of anointing oil and explained it was for intercessors in Edinburgh. Iain's face suddenly lit up, and a huge grin came over him. "Ah, well," he shared in his lovely accent, "I know where to bring this!"

He then shared that the Holy Spirit had recently led him to begin a city-wide prayer service, gathering over 150 intercessors and prayer warriors from all over Scotland, to begin to pray for revival to break out in Scotland.

So the next time God tells you to go to the toilet, you'd better obey the witness!

Very Common Ways

WAY		SCRIPTURE
1	The Established Word of Jesus	John 1:1
2	The Living Word of Jesus	Romans 10:17
3	The Inner Witness of the Holy Spirit	Acts 9:31

Questions for Deeper Study:

1. How can you increase the power of the Inner Witness (confirmation either way) to give you direction regarding your decisions?

2. How can reason alone prevent you from hearing the Holy Spirit?

3. How comfortable are you with following your intuition?

Keep listening!

NOTES:

_____

_____

_____

_____

Way #4: The Inner Voice of the Holy Spirit

Sensing the Divine Within

"And behold, the Lord was passing by! A great and strong wind blew, but the Lord was not in the wind. And after the wind an earthquake, but the Lord was not in the earthquake. And after the earthquake a fire, but the Lord was not in the fire; and after the fire, a still, small voice" (1 Kings 19:11a, 12b).

Some years ago when our first-born son was very small, we had just unpacked the car to enjoy a weekend at a friend's lake cabin. It was a hot summer day and I was planning to leave the back car windows open to air things out after a long journey.

As I was unloading the car, quite suddenly and quite naturally, I heard a still, small voice speak to me inside my heart.

He said simply, "Carl, you may want to shut that window."

He was referring to the rear window next to the baby car seat for my son. I quickly shrugged off that "voice" and dismissed the gentle Holy Spirit, leaving the car window open. Why would God, who rules the universe, be speaking to me about a rear car window anyway?

Well, to my surprise, when I came back out to the car the next morning, the back seat was full of water. I had to set my baby boy into a wet car seat, which in turn meant I had to change his diaper as soon as we got to the restaurant where we were going for breakfast. A huge thunderstorm had rolled in quite unexpectedly overnight, drenching the land and his car seat with bountiful rain, all because of the open window.

"Carl, are you trying to tell me that God actually foresaw the rain and was intimately speaking to you ahead of time out of personal concern for your son's diaper condition the next morning, and asked you gently to shut that window?"

Yes. Yes I am.

Many, many people describe the voice of the Lord like Elijah, who heard the "still, small voice" of the Spirit in that cave so many years ago.

They are right.

This is one of the more common ways of God speaking to you. You, too, can tune into that "still, small voice" or the almost whisper-like, gentle-sounding quality of the Lord's voice. Elijah heard it outwardly, but you will hear it inwardly, as a member of the New Covenant that brings the realized promise of an inward, directing voice right in your spirit.

> **The Inner Voice of the Spirit, a simple definition:** An inaudible voice, originating in your sanctified inner spirit. It flows out through your mind simultaneously as a "thought" or even a flood of thoughts.
>
> **Note:** It is usually short, to the point, powerful, and sometimes comes as a question, to which God expects you to ponder and answer Him.

You will note in this definition, this is not an audible voice. You'll have to wait until way number 21 to read of that particular contact from the Lord. The inaudible voice is way more common and way more consistent with the leadings of the Holy Spirit within.

Simple, and not too spooky, right?

Remember how simple Jesus tried to make this for all of us who would follow Him personally when He shared,

> *"My sheep hear my voice, and I know them, and they follow Me"*
> (John 10:27).

His voice is His voice, but given to us here on earth in the Person of the Holy Spirit.

A great scriptural example of a very practical outworking of this definition happened to Philip, the servant-turned-evangelist in the Book of Acts who found himself being directed to a particular road for a particular encounter with an Ethiopian.

The Scripture simply says, *"And the Spirit said to Philip, "Go up and join this chariot"* (Acts 8:29).

The Spirit Himself spoke to Philip as a voice in his mind, originating from his inner spirit, where the Spirit Himself dwells. It can't get too much simpler than that.

"The Spirit said."

And examples of this kind of inner guidance happened throughout the Book of Acts and down through the centuries of history.

Let's turn to one unique example from church history of a common, everyday man who learned to hear the inner voice for himself.

Quaking For God

Let me illustrate the inner voice through a unique man that literally "quaked" when the Spirit came upon him. Others "quaked" too, and people began to call his followers *Quakers*. His name was George Fox. Fox once told a magistrate to "tremble at the word of the Lord" and the name *Quaker* stuck. These men and women also sometimes "trembled" when moved by the Spirit in their meetings.

"My sheep

HEAR

MY

VOICE

and I know them,

and they follow Me."

(John 10:27)

When you read his lively journal, written during the 1600s in England, you find countless references with phrases like, "the power of the Lord was over all," or "the Word of the Lord came to me," or "the Word of the Lord was like a fire in me."

He pursued the Lord in the 17th century which had sprung Protestant churches all over the land. Many were emphasizing what Luther had called "Sola Scriptura" (Latin, "by the Word alone").

This taught that everything to maintain life and holiness and salvation is contained in the Logos of the Word.

The Puritans had also sprung up around this time, beginning to emphasize more of a balance of both the Word and the experience of the Holy Spirit. The Puritans, though, limited their "experience" to certain degrees and weren't known for much emphasis on personal guidance from the Spirit.

Then along came this young man who pursued the Spirit and received daily guidance as a result. He was like a pendulum swinging in the other direction from the "Word alone" that Luther had so strongly held.

"Fox realized, as few men have ever realized, that we are placed under the dispensation of the Spirit: that the power from on high with which the risen Christ promised to endue His People was no exceptional or transitory gift, but an Eternal Presence, an unfailing spring of energy, answering to new wants and new labors.

"He felt that the Spirit which had guided the fathers was waiting still to lead forward their children.

"That He who spoke through men of old was not withdrawn from the world like the gods of the Ancients, but ready in all ages to enter into holy souls and make them friends of God."[22]

In reading his journals, here is just one of many examples I found of how Fox heard the inner voice on almost a daily basis.

---

22 Bishop Brooke Foss Westcott, Bishop of Durham.

"On July 1, 1652, Fox reached the town of Ulverston, and paused outside St. Mary's Church. SENSING A DIVINE COMMAND TO GO INSIDE, Fox entered the church, jumped up on a seat, and lashed out at both minister and congregation.

"He claimed they should come out of their outward ordinances and traditions of men to the light of Jesus and the life of the Spirit. His preaching was so mesmerizing that it seemed that Fox had literally grabbed the congregation."[23]

To translate that phrase from 17th century English to modern day understanding, Fox "heard the inner voice" flowing from his inner spirit and into his mind saying, "Go in, George!"

Thus, as Fox preached in the fields, churchyards, town squares, and even taverns, the "divine command or inner voice" led him.

This is how it has always been! When you dare to begin to start each week with this simple way of trusting the inner voice, true adventures in the Holy Spirit will unfold before you.

The Voice Brings Peace, Assurance & Rest

Recently my oldest son Ethan embarked on a missions trip to Uganda with the youth group from our local church.

Both my wife and I had been praying for him before his journey, and this was the first time he was heading out into the world in missions for two whole weeks apart from us. As you can imagine, a mother has concern for her children. My beautiful Sarah, herself very practical and not much of a worrier, had been praying for him and asking the Father to watch over him. But even in her, sometimes anxious thoughts can arise.

A few weeks ago she was in the car on her way to bring Ethan in for his required shots before his trip, and the Holy Spirit spoke to her in His inner voice,

"He's gonna be okay."

---

23 H. Larry Ingle, *First Among Friends: George Fox & the Creation of Quakerism* (Oxford University Press, 1994).

That brought instant comfort to Sarah! The Lord was going to watch over our son.

And he was okay, and the Lord watched over him. He returned from Uganda all enthusiastic for Africa and world missions, and the fire that was lit within him by the Holy Spirit continues to burn strong.

Do you see the power in tuning in to the still, small voice, and have the Holy Spirit Himself speak a word of *trust* that is personal to her prayers and situation? Think of this in light of the difference of this very personal moment vs. just flipping open your Bible and reading some objective truth such as, *"trust in the Lord with all your heart"* or standing on a scripture about *"being secure in the Lord."* The Word, of course, is powerful, but when you combine the power of the Word with the personal voice of the Spirit, there is even more assurance.

There's power in the inner voice!

There's peace, assurance, and rest in the inner voice!

And the inner voice is one of the most common of all the ways the Spirit communicates. You just need to be sensitive and learn to actively listen.

What Does That Voice Sound Like?

The answer is, that voice sounds like you. What do I mean? I mean, it sounds like your voice, talking to yourself in a way.

To illustrate, I once heard a story of a pastor's wife who felt like God might be leading her and her husband to move. The move involved selling their house and packing up and moving to a whole different state.

This woman was a sweet "Southern gal" (meaning she was originally from the Deep South of the United States), with a Southern drawl for an accent. She ate grits for breakfast and talked like you would normally think a true Southern woman would talk. So God often just spoke to her in an accent!

For example, if you are an Irish male, you'll hear His voice like an Irishman talking to you in Irish lingo! And so on, and so on.

One day in prayer, the Lord spoke to the pastor himself that it was time to move. But he didn't want to make such a bold decision without his wife also hearing the same thing as confirmation. So he told her one day,

"Honey, I am going out to mow the lawn. While I am mowing, I want you to pray and ask the Lord if we are supposed to move away from here or not. I believe He has already spoken to me on this matter, but I need you to hear yourself so we have confirmation either way."

So she began to pray inside the house as he set about mowing their lawn. About half-way through the mowing, the Holy Spirit spoke to her, clear as day, with His inner voice.

The pastor came in from mowing and asked her what God had said.

She replied, "He said, 'Honey, the cloud is movin' and you best be movin' with it.'"

And the "cloud was moving" and they moved with it!

The Inner Voice is More Powerful than Fear and Doubt

Champion fisherman, author, and television host Al Lindner shares a very personal story in his book, *Reflections At First Light: A Fisherman's Devotional*. One day his wife Mary was diagnosed with breast cancer. The shock of the news hit him hard one night before she had to go in for an operation. The doctors had caught the cancer early and were confident they would be successful in the operation. However, the night before she went in, the Enemy was active in trying to bring fear, confusion and doubt to Al's mind.

"For the first time, doubt and fear came over me like a heavy blanket. I had the craziest, most insane thoughts I could ever imagine—thoughts only the author of insanity himself, the devil, could send my way. The fiery darts of the master deceiver battered me with dread and mistrust through the night as I stood on these words from God:

> 'For God has not given us the spirit of fear, but of power and of love and of a sound mind' (2 Timothy 1:7).

"I rose early the next morning and walked downstairs to check on Mary. She was sleeping like a baby with a smile on her face. Nevertheless, another wave of fear rushed over me, defying the peace I saw so evidently on Mary's face. I went outside where I could quote scriptures out loud and come boldly before the throne of God. I cried, 'Lord, you say in your Word'—when suddenly it felt as though my arm was grabbed and shaken.

I heard the Lord speak to my heart, 'Stop! I said she will be okay!'"[24]

And it was! The surgery was fully successful and Mary is a cancer survivor now of many years since this incident, whole and healed.

Does God Know the Outcome of Football Games?

I have personally heard the inner voice hundreds of times. I just naturally ask the Spirit all kinds of things, and though sometimes He is silent on an answer, or sometimes I do not hear clearly enough, often times He speaks and He answers me quite clearly. Usually in very short and direct sentences.

A few months ago, our own Minnesota Vikings finally made the playoffs. It had been several years of disappointing seasons and finally we had a shot.

I was quite busy in writing some material for the DVD/Online video course we have produced to be released with this book. On the Saturday I just plain asked the Holy Spirit a question, "Will the Vikings win tomorrow?"

The inner voice answered in my spirit, "No."

Talk about short and direct for an answer.

I asked for further details.

Nothing else came from the Spirit.

So on Sunday, already knowing in my spirit the outcome of the game, I did not even watch the first half, but worked diligently on my writing.

---

24 Al & Ron Lindner, *Reflections at First Light: A Fisherman's Devotional* (Eugene, Oregon: Harvest House Publishers, 2015).

Then I tuned in, just for fun, as I do love to watch the Vikings play. At the very end of the 4th quarter, just as there was enough time for the Vikings to kick a simple, 20-yard field goal to win an upset victory, I asked the Holy Spirit again, "Will the Vikings win?"

Again the voice spoke. "No."

And about 2 minutes later, our kicker missed a 20-yard field goal. The entire Vikings team and many thousands of fans were shocked. The other team won.

I turned off the television. And smiled. The Spirit had been right all along. And He did not even add, "I told you so."

What I really wanted to ask Him at this point was, how did He know that the kicker was going to miss?

Well, this is not a book about God's sovereignty, so I will not answer that question directly!

Yet for 2,000 years now, in every generation and within every single follower of Jesus, the Holy Spirit has a distinct, unique voice in your inner spiritual man and speaks to you through that voice. Sometimes, even you, might experience "a divine command" to do something like Fox did. Sometimes He will speak to confirm the Word. Sometimes the still, small voice will speak a "yes" or a "no."

Follow that voice and follow the Lord by faith.

Very Common Ways

WAY		SCRIPTURE
1	The Established Word of Jesus	John 1:1
2	The Living Word of Jesus	Romans 10:17
3	The Inner Witness of the Holy Spirit	Acts 9:31
4	The Inner Voice of the Holy Spirit	Acts 8:29

Questions for Deeper Study:

1. Why is it easy to NOT recognize the LORD's voice speaking to you?

_____

_____

_____

2. How can the Inner Voice speaking to you be challenging or something you may WANT to dismiss as not Him?

_____

_____

_____

3. How does one-way conversation inhibit true relationship and fellowship?

_____

_____

_____

4. What does it mean to pray and live in expectation?

_____

_____

_____

Keep listening!

NOTES:

_____

_____

_____

_____

WAY #5: THE DESIRES OF YOUR HEART

Holy Spirit Inception

"**A**nd Nathan said to the king, 'Go, do all that is in your heart, for the Lord is with you'" (2 Samuel 7:3).

Could it be that sometimes the Holy Spirit reaches out to you, deep inside, and leads you through your own desires, especially towards your calling in God?

It sure could, especially when He performs *Inception*!

And this is a very common, though rarely taught, way of the Lord reaching out to multitudes of people.

One of my son's favorite movies is the thriller, *Inception*, starring Leonardo DiCaprio. What is it about? "A thief, who steals corporate secrets through use of dream-sharing technology, is given the inverse task of planting an idea into the mind of a CEO."[25]

Holy Spirit Inception is the same idea, except it's not "a thief" like Satan who only comes to steal, kill and destroy, but it's the Father Himself,

---

25 Description from the IMDB website, http://www.imdb.com/title/tt1375666/

through the agency of Jesus and the Spirit. He not only creates you with a certain personality and talents and abilities, but He watches over you and is active to lead you. He guides you towards the best choices of utilizing those abilities.

> **Holy Spirit Inception, the Desires of Your Heart, a simple definition:** It is the activity of the Holy Spirit inside your heart, first planting seeds of destiny in you, then watering those same seeds and helping you fulfill the plans and purposes He has first placed there. He brings those seeds to full-grown maturity as you joyfully walk out your paths and follow your desires.

In other words, often times the Spirit guides by your own desires. Sometimes He put those desires there in the first place. And sometimes, almost spontaneously, you make decisions to move forward by faith toward your dreams. And He moves with you.

"For I am confident of this very thing, that He who began a good work in you will perfect it until the day of Christ Jesus" (Philippians 1:6).

Paul knew firsthand this idea and the very faithfulness of the Holy Spirit in both originating the good works in him, and bringing them continually forward as He sought to fulfill his own calling.

The Psalmist wrote, *"Delight yourself in the Lord; and He will give you the desires of your heart"* (Psalm 37:4).

Or as the Passion Translation puts it, "Make God the utmost delight and pleasure of your life; and He will provide for you what you desire the most."

The key here is maintaining a close relationship with the Holy Spirit, delighting always in the Presence of the Trinity, and trusting that as you have certain desires towards your own calling and gifting, those will fully align themselves with His purpose.

The process of maintaining your walk is fully up to you.

From Fireworks to Simple Desires

Let's look at two very different Scripture verses to help begin understanding this unique process of Holy Spirit Inception. It's God's guidance in a very supernaturally natural kind of way.

First, here's the original "first missionary journey" and how it all began with Paul.

> *"And at Antioch while they were ministering to the Lord and fasting, the Holy Spirit said, "Set apart for Me Barnabas and Saul for the work to which I have called them. Then, when they had fasted and prayed and laid their hands on them, they sent them away. So, being sent out by the Holy Spirit, they went"* (Acts 13:2-4).

Powerful, right? We have some very specific information about this prayer meeting. I call this "God's direction through fireworks," because it was kind of a spectacular supernatural event.

The Holy Spirit spoke (probably through the word of prophecy, though we are not told exactly how He spoke; that's pretty much like Jesus Himself showing up and directing them). They were also "sent out by the Holy Spirit" so His power and manifest presence were felt and displayed. And off they go!

Was it God's will that they go on their first missionary journey?

"Sure," you might say.

Well, how do you know?

Because the Holy Spirit spoke and directed the whole scene, didn't He? The first missionary journey included preaching and accompanying signs and wonders, acceptance of the gospel and new churches planted, opposition to the gospel and pain and suffering for the ambassadors. It's all there in chapters 13 and 14.

Acts chapter 15 speaks of a special gathering of leaders in Jerusalem. Paul gave a full report of his ministry. Both Jews, who were circumcised and grew up under the Law, and Gentiles, who were uncircumcised and knew nothing of the Law, were coming into the church in droves.

The council determined that the new converts, the Gentiles, were not under obligation to be circumcised, as their faith in Jesus set them free from such obligations, by grace. Verse 28 gives us a beautiful understanding of the Spirit's working:

"For it seemed good to the Holy Spirit and to us" (Acts 15:28).

In other words, the Holy Spirit was operating within the human conscience and heart of those gathered, and working together with them personally. God works within the most awesome gift He has created within mankind: the gift of man and woman's free-will.

Let's look now a little later in Acts 15. We find an interesting part of the story after the Council at Jerusalem.

"And after some days Paul said to Barnabas, "Let us return and visit the brethren in every city in which we proclaimed the word of the Lord, and see how they are" (Acts 15:36).

Paul and Barnabas then had an argument, and in their disagreement, each took a different companion and went forth.

"Paul chose Silas and departed, being committed by the brethren to the grace of the Lord" (Acts 15:40).

Was it God's will that they go on their second missionary journey?

"Sure," you might say.

Well, how do you know?

It's all there in the next few chapters of Acts. Look at all the places Paul visited. The Holy Spirit was working through the desires in the heart of Paul. His desire was to go forth and strengthen the brethren.

Think about the differences in this moment vs. the "fireworks" of Acts 13!

There was no prophetic voice saying, "Go forth!" There was no fasting, no prayer, no laying on of hands.

In fact, quite the opposite. There was a fight between the two apostles. Paul and Barnabas had a serious argument and emotions were stirred up and involved.

Yet, in all of this, I beg to ask the question, "Was it God's will for them to go?"

And the answer seems to be, "Yes!"

Off they go. We have no record of what Barnabas did as he brought John Mark and sailed off to Cyprus (verses 37-39). Yet we do have a very remarkable record, written by Luke, of the journey of Paul and Silas. It is called the "second missionary journey" and brought encouragement to young believers, the preaching of the Kingdom, miracles and new converts, persecutions and amazing deliverances, and more.

My point? Sometimes the Holy Spirit works WITH you. He is called, in the Greek, the "*Paracletos*" or "*One called alongside to help.*"

So just what is in your own heart to do for God? What are you good at? What are your gifts? There could be many different paths in front of you. Sometimes you have to pick one and start walking.

Trust in Him to be with you.

> "He who began a good work in you will perfect it ..."

Trust in Him, that just maybe, He planted that idea in your mind or in your heart in the first place without you realizing it. Perhaps you are actually following exactly the path you are called to follow. In other words, it was Holy Spirit Inception.

The Princess Bride

When I first got married and started out in itinerant evangelism, the Lord called me to a unique season of both owning my own video business and ministering at the same time. Somewhat like the Apostle Paul himself. Paul manufactured tents as a business to help support his own missionary endeavors during different seasons of his ministry.

How in the world did we follow this calling?

It all began for me at the age of 13. I had been filming family memories for a couple of years, and suddenly one night I got this "idea" in my head: maybe I could actually own my own business someday, and make money with my video camera! I remember staying up nearly all night with a true excitement inside of me. I did not yet know the Lord, but I did pray to Him that He would bless this path.

I loved the idea of making documentary films that would tell an emotional story and bless others.

Did God secretly plant this "idea" and "desire" in my mind?

I think so.

A door was opened towards my future at the age of 15, when a senior girl in my High School came up to me in the hallway.

"I see you filming all the events here. Can I hire you to film my wedding?" (She was 17, and turning 18 and getting married that summer.)

"Sure!" I excitedly replied.

"Well, how much do you charge?" she asked.

I had to think a minute. How much should I charge?

"How does $25 sound?" said I.

"Perfect. You're hired!"

And that was my first wedding booked for my new business. I shot it at age 15 and absolutely loved it.

I continued filming through my high school and college years, then stopped and gave up this business idea so I could get trained for ministry. During my training, I was living on the financial support of family and friends.

The brother I lived with left me a note one day in my room. "Have you considered having a business and being self-supportive for a season? The Apostle Paul did that, and the scriptures say he supported himself and his staff (Priscilla and Aquila at Corinth). He was a "tentmaker" and an "Apostle" at the same time, every once in awhile."

Hmmm, I thought. *I wonder? Should I consider this?*

A month later I was down in Florida at a ministry training camp, learning all about how to prophesy.

A woman led a session one afternoon, and she was calling people out of the audience and prophesying to them. She asked me to stand up. The Lord spoke through her and she "read my mail" so to speak.

He said, "Son, I am going to give you calluses upon your hands. I've called you to a season of working and ministering at the same time. You are going be a tentmaker like Paul, and you are going be able to say to people, 'I've not taken from you, but I've given to you.'"

Wow! I prayed about this, and felt the start of it would come in its own time.

My story continued with about three years of itinerant travel. I launched Born to Blaze Ministries by faith, and the Lord supported me financially through the gifts of others. I went on about 12 different missions to Europe and the U.K. in those years, as well as to a number of other nations, even as far as Kazakhstan.

Then in the summer of 1996, at the age of 26, the inner voice of the Holy Spirit spoke to me.

"Son, you travel all over the world telling people about Me, but you don't really know Me. I'm asking you to lay down your ministry for a while, and get to know Me better. I am your Father and I want you to get to know Me as your Father. I want you to find a wife and get married, start having children, and start your own wedding video business. I will help you get started."

The inner voice of the Holy Spirit spoke these things to me, and it was all confirmed in the Word. I studied the Apostle Paul and his work in making tents as a business venture in Corinth.

Every time I prayed about this, I felt the peace and joy of the inner witness about it. Also, I received some counsel from a friend of mine, and he confirmed this new direction.

As I prayed more, I received a Living Word one day as well. It was from I Thessalonians for this new season of life, *"and to make it your ambition to lead a quiet life and attend to your own business and work with your hands, just as we commanded you"* (I Thessalonians 4:11).

In the same week that summer, the Holy Spirit gave me the name of my new company, Princess Bride Video.

The movie, *The Princess Bride* was popular at that time. It was a great name for a wedding video company, as every bride is also a princess.

So I named the company Princess Bride Video on a Tuesday. On that very Friday, I was invited to preach at Cities Vineyard, a Vineyard church that had a lot of young people in their late teens and twenties.

On the way in I prayed, "Lord, you told me to get married, and I need a wife. This is the kind of place where you could answer my prayers for a wife and send one to me tonight. How about it, Lord?"

I opened the door of the church, and there, greeting me, was a beautiful young strawberry blonde missionary named Sarah. She was assigned as the greeter for that evening, and we shook hands.

To make a long story short, I married that strawberry blonde missionary exactly seven months to the day, later. To put the icing on the cake, her name, Sarah, means, "God's Princess." So God gave me my very own Princess Bride Video Company, and my very own Princess Bride in the same season!

For over 20 years, both Sarah and I served faithfully in following the Holy Spirit in this vision. I traveled throughout the world once in a while, visiting some 20 nations, and paid for all of my journeys myself through our video work. At the same time, we also started a family and raised three strawberry blonde children. I was a true tentmaker like the Apostle Paul was for this long season.

We even became known as one of the most successful wedding video companies in our whole region during those years. To God be the glory!

To sum up all the ways of the Lord speaking to me that you have learned thus far (they are all contained in the story):

— His established word.

— His living word.

— His inner witness.

— His inner voice.

— And, Holy Spirit Inception (my own desires in documentary filmmaking).

> The voice of the Lord is multi-faceted— He speaks in many ways.

That's at least five different ways the Lord was speaking to lead me down this path.

Can you begin to see how the voice of the Lord is truly "multi-faceted" and there are links running to and from the various facets of His voice at times?

The truth is, at certain times the Lord layers multiple ways among the 21 to direct you. How exciting! Sometimes, while in prayer over several days when I really need to hear from Father, He speaks like this and I have had up to eight or more unique contacts with Him to help me to make the wisest decisions!

And it all started with Holy Spirit Inception.

Some People Make Their Living Fishing

In the previous chapter I mentioned a story from the life of Al Lindner, and in the next chapter I share another one from his brother Ron. Al and

Ron were very special mentors early in my development as a Christian, and they also hired me for my very first job in media: I was a teenage intern at their television studio. They built their lives around one thing: Fishing.

Yes, I said *fishing*. You might not have heard their names, but if you are a fisherman or know someone who loves fishing, chances are their magazines, books, seminars, or 45+ years of a television show aired to millions of viewers would be familiar to you.

And they were led by the Holy Spirit into this lifetime of fishing success.

Al comments about his life directly after becoming a Christian, "To tell you the truth, I was relieved after receiving Jesus as Lord of my life that He did not ask me to go into some other endeavor. Here I was in my late thirties, and fishing was the only thing I knew how to do. He graciously allowed me to continue to fish."

His brother Ron also commented as he was beginning his journey with God leading the way, "If I could make $10,000 a year and work in the sport-fishing industry, I would be the happiest man in the world."[26]

Well, these two brothers are among the happiest men in the world. And they made their livings by fishing. And it seems it was "Holy Spirit Inception: the Desires of Their Hearts."

Former President Harry S. Truman, once said, "I have found the best way to give advice to your children is to find out what they want, and then advise them to do it."

Sounds a bit like Holy Spirit Inception. Follow your desires. Quite often, through confirmation and the right timing, you'll be following the Holy Spirit and be flowing right in the middle of the river of God's will for your life.

Remember the words of the prophet Nathan to young king David, *"And Nathan said to the king, 'Go, do all that is in your heart, for the Lord is with you.'"* (2 Samuel 7:3).

---

26 Al & Ron Lindner, *Reflections at First Light: A Fisherman's Devotional* (Eugene, Oregon: Harvest House Publishers, 2015).

Very Common Ways

WAY		SCRIPTURE
1	The Established Word of Jesus	*John 1:1*
2	The Living Word of Jesus	*Romans 10:17*
3	The Inner Witness of the Holy Spirit	*Acts 9:31*
4	The Inner Voice of the Holy Spirit	*Acts 8:29*
5	The Desires of Your Heart	*Psalm 37:4*

Questions for Deeper Study:

1. List desires/passions/dreams from your youth or young adulthood:

_____

_____

_____

_____

2. What were YOU born to do? What are the things that God placed in you that He wants you to bring forth?

_____

_____

_____

_____

3. How could you do those things for His glory?

_____

_____

_____

_____

Keep listening!

6

WAY #6: FATHER SPEAKS THROUGH ALL OF CREATION & NATURE

The Ocean of God's Love

"**A**nd God called to him from the midst of the burning bush, and said, "Moses, Moses!" And he said, "Here I am" (Exodus 3:4).

Most theologians would agree that when we speak of the Trinity, we most often associate the Father as the Father of creation (even though Paul reveals in Colossians that Jesus and the Holy Spirit were present in all of creation).

So you cannot always put the One God into neat-and-tidy scriptural containers.

Again, please note, I am distinguishing in this book the three voices of the Trinity, without in any way separating them from each other; they are truly One and inseparable! And they are always in unity together with every contact made.

Father Speaks through All of Creation and Nature, a simple definition: God our Father speaks in many outward ways every day, in-directly, through all of His creation and nature. These "outward signs" are confirmed inwardly by both the Word and the Spirit.

How do I define *creation or outward ways?*

Very simply: everything around you in your environment.

This includes, but is not limited to, your landscape, animals (like the birds of the sky and the fish in the sea), the seasons, weather-related events (like tidal waves, earthquakes, tsunamis, hurricanes, famines and so forth), sounds, shapes, clouds, sun and moon, stars and planets, and even the wind, rain, thunder, lightning and fire.

He is ever-present and possibly reaching out to communicate to you in all of these facets of His creation at all times!

You'll notice that other people are not in this list. That's because they belong in several other unique ways and we will study more about how God uses people, both Christians and non-Christians, in other chapters of this book.

Is "Mother Nature" Really Your Mama?

You'll need to refocus and possibly rethink all you've ever heard about "mother nature" in light of the broader understanding of the Father reaching out through nature. She is no Big Mama! Just the opposite is actually true: creation is an extension of the awesome majesty of the Father. It should be called "Father Nature" and not "Mother Nature."

Paul, when writing to the Romans, made it very clear that all people have an internal conscience and that the outward creation itself witnesses of the truth and reality of the nature of God Himself. You'll note the connection between the "outward creation" bearing witness to people's conscience internally.

"That which is known about God is evident to them, for since the creation of the world His invisible attributes, His eternal power and divine nature, have been clearly seen, being understood through what has been made, so that they are without excuse" (Romans 1:19).

Paul's whole point in this passage is that all people of all nations are under God's wrath because of their sinful choices to ignore the God who made them, and live contrary lives of corruption.

This is strong language.

Atheists have no excuse on the Judgment Day. God is present and His personal nature is revealed in all of His created nature, so to speak. And Paul goes on,

"For they exchanged the truth of God for a lie, and worshiped and served the creature rather than the Creator, who is blessed forever. Amen" (Romans 1:25).

There has been a rise in the political realm for decades now of topics like global warming, and nations are still convening and trying to figure out what to do about it.

There has also been a rise in what can be called *pantheism*, which is defined as the belief that the universe (or nature as the totality of everything) is identical with divinity, or that everything is composed of an all-encompassing, immanent god. Pantheists thus do not believe in a distinct personal God.

This whole misunderstanding of "mother nature" as "divine in itself" through pantheism is quite the opposite of the teaching of this book and this chapter.

The truth: God is your Father, and He is the Creator, and He is blessed forever. He deserves your personal worship, and all of His creation shouts praise and glory to Him, every day, everywhere.

Through sin and the curses upon the earth, mankind still denies the existence of God, but God still loves His creation and His people, and is continually reaching His arms of love THROUGH creation and nature to speak and communicate.

Let's turn now to the Old Testament, and open our eyes to many times in history that God the Father has utilized His creation to communicate directly.

He has always been a very personal God in an impersonal world.

Lightening, Smoke, Earthquakes & a Burning Bush

Throughout the Psalms and Prophets, we catch a sense of the wonderful, artistic, wild-at-heart Hebrew (or Far Eastern) way of looking at creation. It involved all the outward senses and they lived in a world that was full of nature, creation, and His presence in everything—*the trees of the field clap their hands, and the mountains and hills rejoice and sing (see Isaiah 55).*

It's a wonderful way to consider that God our Father is present in all of His creation every day. In fact, every day all of creation is both dying slowly and being renewed slowly. Change is everywhere. Life is exploding everywhere. He wants you to tune in to the explosion!

It was the Father who sent a dove with an olive branch to Noah after the flood, utilizing outward creation (both a bird of the sky and the branch of a tree) to speak to him *(Genesis 8:11)*.

It was the Father who gave Moses the outward sign of His presence and authority by a staff that was in his hand *(Exodus chapters 2 and 4)*.

It was the Father who spoke through thunder, lightning, smoke, a trumpet, and an earthquake on Mt. Sinai *(Exodus 19:16)*.

It was the Father who told the children of Israel to follow the cloud in the wilderness *(Numbers chapter 11)*.

And pausing again at Moses for a moment, what about that burning bush?

"And the angel of the Lord appeared to him in a blazing fire from the midst of a bush; and he looked, and behold, the bush was burning with fire, yet the bush was not consumed. God called to him from the bush, and said, "Moses, Moses!" And he said, "Here I am" (Exodus 2).

So here you have a combination of at least three of the Father's ways of communication: a burning bush (His creation/nature), an angel, and His voice itself. (We will look at both angels and His audible voice toward the end of this book in their own chapters.) For now, think of that burning bush as the Father reaching out in a personal contact with Moses.

"And God said to Moses, "I AM WHO I AM." In the original, it's the name *"YHWH."* In English, we make that name of the Lord "Yahweh."[27]

"Another, more literal translation of the original is, "I WILL BE THERE WITH YOU."

"This is Fox's translation, which emphasizes God's continuing presence in His creation, His "being there with us."

"And the symbolic nature of this epiphany suggests that this God, as dangerous, tempering, and purifying as fire, can burn in us without consuming."[28]

So, the Father is speaking through FIRE! And much later, John the Baptist would agree with Father's voice and purpose in the sending of the Holy Spirit through His Son. *"HE will baptize you with the Holy Spirit and FIRE"* (Luke 3:16b).

So to all followers of Jesus down to this very day, you have this wonderful promise from the midst of the fire of the Father: He will be there with you. That is His name, and His revelation to you, personally!

---

27 A more literal translation of Yahweh would be, "I be who I be" or, "I am and will be who I have always been, I will be who in the future I Myself choose to be, based on who I have always been." –Dr. Lance Wonders.

28 Thomas Cahill, *The Gifts of The Jews,* Ibid., (Fox's translation by Martin Buber and Franz Rosenzweig), pp. 109-110.

Down through the Gospels, we find Jesus spending time listening to His Father, and Father teaching Him what He was to share with us through many outward signs and simple illustrations.

For example, Father revealed Jesus as the Bread of life through a loaf of bread.

Father revealed Jesus as the Water of life through a conversation next to a well.

Father revealed Jesus was filled with the Holy Spirit through the appearing of something like a dove.

> He is ever-present and may be reaching out to you in all facets of His creation at all times!

Father revealed Jesus as perfect provision by causing a fish to be caught that contained the exact coin needed to pay tax to Caesar.

Father even provided the exact donkey for His Son to enter Jerusalem in triumph the week before His crucifixion. And on goes the list!

In these short examples we have a loaf of bread, a well with water, a bird (dove), a fish, and a donkey. All of them outward signs in creation and nature.

Signs of Father's Love

The Father has always poured His love into his children very experientially, through creation. There have been moments throughout salvation-history where multitudes of people have felt the love and power of God in creation.

I have studied for years many revivals, and I'm always drawn to the Great Awakening that happened in Britain and America in the 18th century with men like John and Charles Wesley, George Whitefield and Jonathan Edwards.

One of the more obscure revivalists of that generation was a young Welshman named Howell Harris. His ministry actually pre-dated Whitefield's and the Wesley's by a few years, and he was the first to take the gospel out of the churches and into the streets, the marketplaces, and the fields. He truly was the pioneer of Methodist field preaching, and both Wesley and Whitefield patterned their work after his.

He wrote in the year 1739 of his experience after conversion, where he felt the Father's love reaching out to him personally through His creation, like in times of meditation and also preaching in the fields of Wales.

"I was carried," he exclaimed, "as on wings through all my trials. I feared nothing, though my life was in danger from the threats of such as loved darkness rather than light; the fire of God did so burn in my soul that I could not rest day or night without doing something for my God and Savior. I WAS DRAWN ONWARDS BY THE LOVE I HAD EXPERIENCED, as a blind man is led, and therefore I could not take notice of anything in my way.

"My food and my drink was praising my God.

"A fire was kindled in my soul and I was clothed with power, and made altogether dead to earthly things."

It was said of him, "the words flowed scorching hot from the preacher's heart, and he would go on thus, pouring out old things and new for two, three, or even four hours. Indeed, we have instances of his services continuing without a break for six hours."[29]

I don't think that Harris would "fit" very well in most of our modern churches, with their service times planned to the minute and the allotted slots for preaching the word of 22 minutes and not a minute more!

In terms of guidance, he prayed daily for it, and felt the love of the Father and the influence of the Spirit guiding him in his itinerant evangelism.

---

29 Arnold Dallimore, *George Whitefield: the Life and Times of the Great Evangelist of the 18th Century Revival* (England: Banner of Truth Trust, 1970), pp. 240-241, the chapter about Howell Harris.

He wrote, "Oh! Send me where You will; I obey. I am Yours. Let me have the guidance of Your Holy Spirit; let me not go till You command; but when I am called, make me to go; rule me, guide me, assist me; Whatever You do, take not these signs of Your love away."[30]

Harris "saw and felt the signs" of Father's love as he walked in the fields and meditated, and as he beheld the sunrise and the sunset, and in so many other outward ways in Creation.

How wonderful to read of a man of God like this praying in such a way for the Father to guide Him, and to let the "signs" of His love lead him in his evangelism!

A Kiss from Your Heavenly Father

Father is speaking His personal love and care through all of creation and nature.

My family and I are part of a wonderful local church community, and our pastor's wife Jacque shared with us how she was going through a very difficult day.

Her emotions were heavy and she was experiencing rejection and hurt. She was deep in prayer, asking the Father to show her an outward sign of the reality of His love.

As she was spending time that afternoon quietly singing praises, she looked up into the sky.

Two airplanes, many miles up in the sky, had recently flown opposite patterns. They cast their long-line straight trails of vapor in a crisscross pattern, forming a giant "X" in the sky.

Suddenly it dawned upon the heart and mind of Jacque that this was the sign from the Father for His personal touch of love for her. She often signed her cards and love notes to her husband and her children and parents with an "x" to indicate a "kiss." Here she felt the Father was giving HER a kiss "in the sky." It was His special way of signing a love note to His daughter.

---

30 Ibid., p. 245.

She felt validated as a daughter of God, realizing that Father really did love her and was personally present in the midst of this difficult day. The witness of the Spirit within her brought a sense of joy and peace, too.

As for me, after I heard that story I have always become keenly aware of the letter "X" as sometimes it might just mean the Father is sending me a kiss from Heaven. A few months ago, on the very morning I was preparing this same material to teach to a Bible school, I asked the Holy Spirit for a recent example to share.

After I did so, I happened to look out of the window of my study where I do all of my writing and praying. Just outside my window, there were two sets of tracks from animals in the freshly fallen snow. They each went in different directions, and as they crisscrossed, together they formed a huge "X" right in front to me! A few days later that "X" was gone following a fresh snowstorm.

This "X" was a kiss from Father, just for me, just for that morning. I felt His love in reaching out to me.

So even down through history and into modern times, you and I can expect Father to speak in such mysterious ways like this.

The Ocean of God's Love

And what about animals, like the simplicity of the birds of the sky for example? When you learn to listen to God in nature, and worship and serve Him and thank Him for all of His Creation, you will find Him reaching out. Usually it's in the seemingly insignificant, most fleeting moments.

Out of the horrors of the Nazi concentration camps comes an illustration from Corrie Ten Boom. She was an amazing witness for Christ.

She lived through World War 2 and became an outspoken evangelist, sharing her message of Christ's power of forgiveness with countless people in the years following the war. She relates a story of Father's love in His Creation in her own words.

"When I was in a concentration camp during the last war, we had to stand every day for two or three hours for roll call, often in the icy-cold wind. That was something terrible.

"Once a woman guard used these hours to demonstrate her cruelty. I could hardly bear to see and hear what happened in front of me.

"Suddenly a skylark started to sing high in the sky. We all looked up, and when I looked to the sky and listened to its song, I looked still higher and thought of Psalm 103:11: 'For as the heavens are high above the earth, so great is His steadfast love toward those who fear Him.'

"Suddenly I saw that this love of God was a greater reality than the cruelty that I experienced myself and saw around me.

"Oh the love of God, how deep and great, far deeper than man's deepest hate.

"God sent that skylark every day for three weeks, just at the time of roll call, to give us an opportunity to turn away our eyes from the cruelty of men to THE OCEAN OF GOD'S LOVE."[31]

A Celestial Celebration

Earlier in the book I referenced a few stories from professional fisherman Al and Ron Lindner. Both are strong Christians with a deep faith and countless stories of how the Lord has spoken to them in guidance. God has used their love of fishing as a witness, and they have shared Christ's love with many people.

A favorite moment in Ron's testimony happened the night he surrendered his life to Jesus Christ in a special meeting with an evangelist. After that meeting, he went home and was reading and re-reading a small booklet that he had received that explained the gospel. He shares what happened next:

---

31 Corrie Ten Boom, *Marching Orders for the End Battle* (Fort Washington, P.A.: CLC Publications, 1969, 2012), pp. 53-54.

"Over and over in my mind, I was pondering, "Is it really this simple?" As my eye glanced out the picture window overlooking the lake at two thirty in the morning, I saw the northern lights explode into the night sky like never before or since. A colossal celestial celebration welcomed me into God's kingdom."[32]

The Father's love for his newborn baby boy in the Spirit, Ron Lindner, was so overwhelming that He sent to him a spectacular over-the-top sign through the northern lights of Minnesota! Ron felt the love of God that night for the first time. Love speaks.

To summarize these examples from Scripture and history, lightning, smoke, earthquakes, and the burning bush were all of the Father. Likewise, a loaf of bread, a well with water, a bird (dove), a fish, and a donkey were all signs of Father's love to Jesus and His disciples.

Revivalists throughout history have felt His love in creation.

His skylarks even have access to the lowest horrors of concentration camps, bringing moments of His love and glory.

He even sometimes welcomes new believers through signs in the heavens like northern lights.

Find Him today, speaking to you personally, in all of nature and creation! Worship and serve the Creator, who is blessed forever. Amen.

---

32 Al & Ron Lindner, *Reflections at First Light: A Fisherman's Devotional* (Eugene, Oregon: Harvest House Publishers, 2015), p. 155.

Very Common Ways

WAY		SCRIPTURE
1	The Established Word of Jesus	John 1:1
2	The Living Word of Jesus	Romans 10:17
3	The Inner Witness of the Holy Spirit	Acts 9:31
4	The Inner Voice of the Holy Spirit	Acts 8:29
5	The Desires of Your Heart	Psalm 37:4
6	Father Speaks Through All of Creation & Nature	Romans 1:19

Questions for Deeper Study:

1. How is Pantheism (the worship of Creation) reflected in our culture today?

_____

_____

_____

_____

2. How do all the elements of creation around you point to a Divine Creator?

_____

_____

_____

_____

3. What is the Creator saying to you in this place?

_____

_____

_____

_____

Keep listening!

NOTES:

_____

_____

_____

_____

Way #7: Providential Outward Signs & Circumstances

Prepare for Providence!

"**A**nd we know that God causes all things to work together for good to those who love God, to those who are called according to His purpose" (Romans 8:28).

It is a healthy exercise to pause every so often and ponder the Providence of the Father.

He really does love you personally.

He really does speak, every week, to help you learn what His best plans are for you.

He really does reach out from the eternal realm, into this temporal realm, and give you grace and strength to go on, no matter how hard the path.

The idea that His handiwork has led you to this very day, and oftentimes He has gone ahead of you, should lead you to praise and thanksgiving.

He is ahead of you now.

He is dwelling many years into your very future, and shifting and changing things so that when you arrive, you find your path made clear, and your heart's calling finds fulfillment.

Father Speaks through Providence, a simple definition: Your Father is speaking through His direct and indirect leadings of circumstances and outward signs. Often you will not notice His guidance through these outward circumstances, but later, when you look back, you recognize how everything worked itself out for your good, and it was He that was taking the initiative to bring His will to pass for you.

Some Old Testament Writings that Speak of God's Providence

"For the Lord is a God of knowledge, and with Him actions are weighed. The Lord makes poor and rich; He brings low, He also exalts. He raises the poor from the dust, He lifts the needy from the ash heap, to make them sit with nobles and inherit a seat of honor; for the pillars of the earth are the Lord's. He keeps the feet of His godly ones" (I Samuel 2:3-7, selections from Hannah's Song of Thanksgiving).

"Yours, O Lord, is the greatness and the power and the glory and the victory and the majesty, indeed everything that is in the heavens and the earth; Yours is the dominion, O Lord, and You exalt Yourself as head over all" (I Chronicles 29:11).

We also see God's providence reflected in the life of Joseph.

"Now, therefore, it was not you who sent me here, but God; and He has made me a father to Pharaoh and lord of all his household and ruler over all the land of Egypt. As for you, you meant evil against me, but God meant it for good in order to bring about this present result, to preserve many people alive" (Genesis 45:8 & 50:20).

In Ezekiel chapter 1 we find Ezekiel's vision of the Father's Providence as represented through the Holy Spirit as a "wheel within a wheel."

> "Now as I looked at the living beings, behold, there was one wheel on the earth beside each of the living beings; their appearance and workmanship being as if one wheel were within another. Wherever the Spirit was about to go, they would go in that direction. All the wheels rose close beside them; for the spirit of the living beings was in the wheels" (Ezekiel 1:15, 16b, 20).

This represents God's providence going forth everywhere for His people, all over the world, and His very personal Spirit leading them.

Madam Guyon, a 17th century Roman Catholic leader in France, had this to say,

"Ezekiel, the prophet, had a vision of wheels which had a living Spirit within and wherever the Spirit went, they went. They ascended and descended as the Spirit of life directed. We, in like manner, must move according to the life-giving Spirit within us and be cautiously faithful to move only when He moves.

"Therefore, your actions will not reflect on you but rather the Creator who made you and desires to lead you throughout your entire life.

"When your spirit is centered on God, all activities He initiates will be noble, full of peace, natural, and so spontaneous that it will appear to you there has hardly been any activity at all. God Himself draws us. He causes us to run after Him."[33]

So Ezekiel sees these giant wheels-within-wheels, and the activity of God is directed by the Father, and wherever He goes, His providential activity goes with Him (see Ezekiel 1).

Some New Testament writings that speak of God's Providence

> "Are not two sparrows sold for a cent? And yet not one of them will

---

33 From the writings of Madam Guyon, 17th Century French Mystic.

fall to the ground apart from your Father. But the very hairs of your head are all numbered. So do not fear; you are more valuable than many sparrows" (Matthew 10:29-31).

"And He made from one man every nation of mankind to live on all the face of the earth, having determined their appointed times and the boundaries of their habitation" (Acts 17:26).

"And we know that God causes all things to work together for good to those who love God, to those who are called according to His purpose" (Romans 8:28).

Commander Robert E. Lee, remarking on his achievements during the American Civil War, once said, "My trust is in the mercy and wisdom of a kind Providence, who orders all things for our good."

Can you begin to glorify God in realizing more and more and more of how He PERSONALLY loves you? Your Heavenly Father is reaching out everywhere, and it's almost like you "bump into Him" on a weekly basis in surprise!

You suddenly realize that a very personal God actually knows your name, your heart for Him, your passion, your weaknesses—and loves you anyway. He chose you, in Him, before the foundations of the world were laid.

He knows the number of the very hairs on your head, and if you are bald, don't worry—He knows everything else about you!

Let me share a few examples from my own life and also from my family.

License Plates & Stuffed Kangaroos

First off, can God actually speak to you through the Providence of a car in front of you and their license plate?

YES.

A number of years ago I was reading through a massive 2-volume set on the life of 18th century evangelist George Whitefield. Each volume

"And we know that God

causes all things to work together

for good to those who

LOVE

GOD

to those who are called

according to His purpose."

(Romans 8:28)

contained more than 500 pages so it was taking me some months to read through. At the same time, I was praying over an invitation to return to London and preach the gospel, and I needed to know if God's will was in this particular trip.

I finished reading one night in my book and put my marker down at the end of a particular chapter. It "happened" to be on page 498.

The next day I was running late for an appointment. I tend to drive a little fast when I am running late (which happens most of the time). One thing I hate when trying to go fast is when there is a slow car in front of me. This particular car I remember was green, and she was driving 40 miles per hour in a 45 zone. I nearly started honking. Suddenly I felt the Lord impress upon me to write down her license plate number. I looked at it, grabbed a piece of paper, and wrote down, GWF 499.

I thought nothing of it at the time, finally passing this car and arriving late to my appointment. I had stuffed the piece of paper into my pocket.

Late that night, I was sitting in my rocking chair in my study and praying, "Lord, do you want me to take this invitation to preach in London?" He said, "Look again at that license plate number."

So I pulled out the license plate info and pondered it. What could it mean? GWF...ah! A light bulb went off. Maybe that stands for "George WhiteField!" and the number, 499? Maybe the page number of the book?

So I quickly grabbed the volume of the book I had been reading, and opened it up to find my marker at exactly page 498. As I turned the page, I realized I would have the answer to my prayer on that page, if I was discerning correctly the Providence of God in sending that slow driver in the green car in answer to my prayers.

Sure enough, GWF, page 499, had a quotation of a letter that John Wesley had written to Whitefield, inviting him to come to London to preach!!!

So the moral of the story is, the next time you are behind a car with a license plate and the numbers jump off at you, write them down and look them up in Scripture or elsewhere! For that matter, God can use ANY-THING and EVERYTHING in your circumstances to speak to you. You just need to be aware that HE is there—a God who truly is, "ever-present."

—————◦•◦—————

Now what about Kangaroos? Back in 2012, I had been invited to preach in Australia and my trip was partly organized by some women who ran a ministry base in Melbourne. They really wanted me to bring Sarah, my wife, along. Normally, Sarah would not travel with me, as our children were little and required a lot of attention. Also, it was time consuming to fly to Australia (usually a two-week journey, minimum) and expensive to do so for two people.

All of these factors aligned themselves to make Sarah a little uneasy about traveling along with me. She has a missions background though, and loves to serve as a missionary, so she went to prayer about the invitation to join me. I did, too.

We gave the Father a deadline of 4:00 Monday afternoon to speak a confirmation, as we simply had to make the decision to either buy the plane tickets for her to accompany me, or not. Sarah was leaning towards not going as she was still concerned about being away from the children.

In a Providential circumstance, our middle-son Gideon went on a school trip that afternoon to a nursing home to play games with the older people there. In one of the games he won his choice of a prize, and of all the prizes, he "spontaneously" picked a stuffed Kangaroo.

Not just any stuffed Kangaroo, but this one was a mother Kangaroo with a baby in the pouch!

He brought it home at 3:45 p.m. and gave it as a gift to my wife. Sarah brought it to me, smiling.

An answer from Father to us! God was indeed sending Sarah with me and He would personally watch over our young ones as we ministered for Him.

A confirmation of guidance. Had it been any other animal in the world, we wouldn't have considered this an answer. But a kangaroo? Really, God, really?!

We booked the tickets and she came with me. And it was an awesome trip together. We ministered side by side and saw God's hand work in many situations to bring blessings to many people.

And now, for T-shirts! This story involves my oldest son Ethan.

Your Sons & Daughters Will Prophesy

A couple of years ago we had enrolled our oldest son, Ethan, in a summer kids camp that had an emphasis on praise, worship and prayer. His good friend, Micah, was spending the night here at our home before we brought them both to camp the next day.

On the morning of the camp I came down for my usual cup of coffee and this note was awaiting me. "Dear Dad and Mom, we were awakened by what we thought was GOD telling us to pray and worship God. You will find us in your office. 4:13 a.m., Love, Ethan and Micah."

Hmmm.

So the boys, age 11 at this time, "thought" they heard God's voice and so they went up into my office, which is actually my study and my prayer room combined.

Like the ancient Christian Celts did, who developed prayer rooms that they called "thin places" as the veil between heaven and earth was so thin, I believe in dedicating holy space to God. So this room is consecrated to Him. I have a CD playing with worship and praise music, 24 hours a day, 7 days a week, and my Bible is always accessible.

I found out that morning that indeed the two young boys went into my office to worship and pray, at 4:00 a.m.

When they arrived, there "just happened" to be a worship song by artist Chris Tomlin playing in the background titled, "How Awesome is the Lord

Most High."

As they began to sing that song, they opened my Bible on the desk and prayed, "Lord, give us a word from your word." Simple, right?

As they opened the Bible, it "fell open" to Acts chapter 2, and they began to read out loud and declare by faith, *"And it shall be in the last days, God says, that I will pour out My Spirit upon all mankind; and your sons and your daughters will prophesy"* (Acts 2:17-18).

They wrote these scriptures and some following ones out on paper. I still have that paper. Their note at the top reads, "Verses that spoke out to us as powerful verses."

The next day was the first day of this Christian camp. Towards evening a very excited Ethan came up to us after a session.

"Dad!"

"Yes, son?"

"Do you see the t-shirts? Do you see the shirts?"

I confess I hadn't looked at anyone wearing t-shirts but I suddenly looked around. The leaders of the camp all prayed each summer and asked God for a particular theme for the teachings of the camp and a particular scripture that would be the central theme of that week. They only revealed this theme on that day and passed out the t-shirts with the custom scripture printed on the back. Here is what they had printed, weeks ago, for the kids,

> *"And it shall be in the last days, God says, that I will pour out My Spirit upon all mankind; and your sons and your daughters will prophesy"* (Acts 2:17-18).

Ethan, again at age 11, smiled broadly and said, "Dad, you'll never guess the song that they opened with today in our first session? It was the same song that was playing in your study early this morning when we got that scripture from God. It was 'How Awesome is the Lord Most High.'

"I am hearing God's voice, right Dad?"

I smiled back and hugged him, exclaiming, "Yes you are son!"

So in God's Providence, the exact right worship song was playing in my study when they entered. They "flipped open" the Bible and landed on those pages and the Spirit encouraged them with those verses. Then the T-shirts, printed weeks in advance, "happened" to contain those same verses, even as the worship leader that night "happened" to open the singing with the song from my study.

So much for "happenstance!" How about instead, God Providentially leads you through your whole life and is shouting His love to you in your circumstances. Whenever you recognize Him, give Him glory. Praise Him.

He loves you and loves to speak in these ways. Prepare your heart for Providence!

Very Common Ways

WAY		SCRIPTURE
1	The Established Word of Jesus	John 1:1
2	The Living Word of Jesus	Romans 10:17
3	The Inner Witness of the Holy Spirit	Acts 9:31
4	The Inner Voice of the Holy Spirit	Acts 8:29
5	The Desires of Your Heart	Psalm 37:4
6	Father Speaks Through All of Creation & Nature	Romans 1:19
7	Providential Outward Signs & Circumstances	Romans 8:28

QUESTIONS FOR DEEPER STUDY:

1. When did God provide just the right thing at the right time...where He demonstrated His Fatherly care for you?

_____

_____

_____

_____

2. When have you encountered God's Providence in the form of a physical sign?

_____

_____

_____

_____

3. Has God ever used you to be part of His Providential hand for some-one else? How did that make you feel?

_____

_____

_____

_____

Keep listening!

NOTES:

_____

_____

_____

_____

7

COMMON
WAYS THE LORD SPEAKS

LOVE SPEAKS

8

WAY #8: THE PREACHING OF THE WORD OF JESUS

The Fire & the Hammer

"**A**nd for this reason we also constantly thank God that when you received from us the Word of God's message, you accepted it not as the word of men, but for what it really is, the Word of God, which also performs its work in you who believe" (I Thessalonians 2:13).

We begin now with seven common ways that the Father (reaching out through both Jesus and the Spirit), is speaking.

It remains part of the divine mystery that the Lord has chosen to share the work of announcing His plan of eternal redemption with us. He is complete in Himself. He needs no help from human hands to exist nor is He proud and needing people to acknowledge Him, as if there was some deep need in His being that craved the favor of man.

Yet He has chosen the simple things to confound the wise. He has shared the work of announcing the Kingdom with common men and women. And in His grace (His unmerited favor) He lets us take part in His grand plan of redemption. He offers callings and gifts and even appoints people to "offices" of responsibility in the Kingdom. He calls people to preach and teach His Word.

Through His anointed servants, His Word is proclaimed. As it is proclaimed, the Holy Spirit opens up hearts to receive it, and Jesus is made real. The Holy Spirit's power is made real. The Father's love is both known and also experienced.

> **The Preaching of the Word of Jesus, a simple definition:** It is the Established Word (*Logos*) and the Living Word (*Rhema*) coming forth from an anointed servant in preaching and teaching. The Holy Spirit is active and a community of believers is present in which to apply that Word, in love, to one another, and then to the unredeemed world around us.

Jesus is present in His Word as you study it, and in His Word as He brings it to you in personal devotion. Yet He is also everywhere His people are, as He has joined Himself within each person's heart that has trusted Him by faith.

Paul calls this "His Body" and shares the importance of meeting together with the Corinthian church, and how important each and every member of Christ's Body is. And the writer of Hebrews, likewise, gives us the importance of gathering together as believers.

> "*And let us not forsake our own assembling together, as is the habit of some, but encouraging one another; and all the more, as you see the day drawing near*" (Hebrews 10:25).

Now, whether that is in the context of an organized church structure, a community with various expressions or liturgy, a small group structure, whether it's 2 or 3 people or 2,000 or 3,000, it all works the same way: we are learning how to hear from Jesus (and both speak and listen to God) while doing life together.

The Word of Jesus comes to life inside and through His anointed servants whose job it is to proclaim that word to others. And if you tune your ears every time you hear the Word preached or taught, you can hear from Jesus Himself, and receive Fathers' love in that message.[34]

Jesus Speaks Through the Foolishness of Preachers

Paul writes, *"For since in the wisdom of God the world through its wisdom did not come to know God, God was well-pleased through the foolishness of the message preached to save those who believe"* (I Corinthians 1:21).

Charles Spurgeon put it this way, "If God calls you to become a minister, don't stoop to become a king."

In other words, God has called multitudes of weak men and weak women, many of whom will never earn a lot of money or prestige, to proclaim Christ. People who pray over the Word and "let the word of Christ dwell in them richly" and then proclaim that Word publicly. It is a lowly job to be called in ministry, but a heavenly reward awaits those who dare to speak in God's name.

Jesus Himself, upon His ascension, began to give gifts unto mankind. These gifts are, to put it frankly, other men and women into whom He has dwelt and commissioned, just like He commissioned His 12 to proclaim His Word.

They are often called into "offices" of apostle, prophet, evangelist, pastor and teacher. Paul writes,

> *"And He gave some as apostles, and some as prophets, and some as*

---

34 Note from the Author: The universal Church, the Body of Christ scattered among all Protestant, Roman Catholic, and Eastern Orthodox traditions, is like our very own "In-House Security System" for revelation and confirmation. Thus, starting here in Section 2, and throughout the rest of the book, remember the blessing of your fellow brothers and sisters in Christ, no matter what tradition they belong too.

I call other church members our "Security System" as they can help you in prayer and confirmation in the areas of guidance. There is security from both the Good Shepherd and the sheep around you so you don't misunderstand God's leadings. You might hear from God in the preaching of His Word, or as you will soon learn, through a myriad of other ways. And He often confirms His Word and His leadings through other members of His Body which He blesses you with in relationship all around you. Be a good listener and a lifelong learner from your peers, and you will have peace and security in the many ways the Spirit gives confirmation of direction.

"...the

WORD

OF

GOD

also performs its work in you

who believe."

(1 Thessalonians 2: 13b)

evangelists, and some as pastors and teachers, for the equipping
of the saints for the work of service, to the building up of the body
of Christ; until we all attain to the unity of the faith, and of the
knowledge of the Son of God, to a mature man" (Ephesians 4:11-13).

As a "good Lutheran boy" I had no idea of the relevance of hearing from Christ through His Word being preached. Most of the sermons (which were called "homilies") were dry and not very exciting. And they lasted about ten minutes.

I once heard it shared from the great English preacher John Stott, "Sermonettes breed Christianettes!" I was a good Christianette. Ten minutes was my absolute limit of listening.

That all changed once I started following Jesus. Now, every sermon I heard that preached the Word of God seemed to bring the Word TO LIFE inside of me. I realized how important it is to hear the Word being preached. Dietrich Bonhoeffer commented on this, too.

"Christians are dependent on the Word of God spoken to them. They are directed outward to the Word coming to them. Christians live entirely by the truth of God's Word in Jesus Christ."[35]

Let's return for a moment to John Stott. "We must speak what He has spoken. This is unique to Christianity. Of course every religion has its accredited teachers, whether Hindu gurus or Jewish rabbis or Moslem mullahs.

"Yet these instructors in religion and ethics, even if endowed with official authority and personal charisma, are essentially the expositors of an ancient tradition. Only Christian preachers claim to be heralds of good news from God, and dare to think of themselves as *His ambassadors who actually utter 'oracles of God'* (I Peter 4:11)."[36]

Paul is right, preaching seems to be "foolishness" to the lost, but it is also the "power and wisdom of God" to the believer.

---

35 Dietrich Bonhoeffer, *Life Together and Prayerbook of the Bible* (Fortress Press, 2004).
36 John R.W. Stott, *The Art of Preaching in the 20th Century* (Grand Rapids, Michigan: William B. Eerdmans Publishing Company, 1982).

The preacher himself or herself utters "the oracles of God." We need to prayerfully receive from God's ambassadors!

Jesus' Original Model: the "12" as Preachers of the Word

"And He called the twelve together, and gave them power and authority over all the demons, and to heal diseases. And He sent them out to PROCLAIM the Kingdom of God and to perform healing" (Luke 9:1-2).

Jesus shows us how important it is for Him to be present in His leaders. He sends out His original 12 and shares His authority and power with them, and they become His ambassadors to continue His ministry and multiply it. The preached Word went forth, and people responded in faith.

Let's let the Apostle Paul have the final word and then remember that every time we hear a sermon, God very well may be trying to speak to us.

"And for this reason we also constantly thank God that when you received from us the Word of God's message, you accepted it not as the word of men, but for what it really is, the Word of God, which also performs its work in you who believe" (I Thessalonians 2:13).

An Illustration from Australia

Two of my wonderful team of mentors, Alan and Dorothy Langstaff, were at a particular juncture of their ministry and seeking God's will and direction in Australia. Due to extenuating health circumstances in their family, they were requesting a year's rest from their Methodist denomination, which was granted them. However, this decision brought them no peace inside.

The following Sunday morning they prayed together, "Okay, God, we've had no peace about this decision to take a year's rest. If we're wrong, we need to take another pastorate instead. Would you please show us whether we are to stay or go? We need to know your will today!" After that prayer, they went off to their church. There was a guest speaker preaching that morning. Here's what they shared,

"We had a guest speaker visiting our little church and he was sharing from the Old Testament about Abraham. He began his message with the arresting words, "Go, and take little with you." Already an answer seemed to be arriving in our ears, delivered through the anointed preaching of the Word.

"We nudged elbows and glanced at one another excitedly," writes Dorothy. "This was God's answer to our dilemma. He wanted us to leave home and take an appointment. As the sermon progressed, it was as though the preacher had received a dossier on our specific circumstances and had prepared the sermon just for us. It was clear God was personally speaking to us through this message."[37]

This decision to go and not to stay and rest totally changed their lives. So in this case, God utilized the anointed preaching of His Word at a pivotal moment of decision. Alan and Dorothy's whole course of ministry opened up before their eyes as they "went forth" like Abraham once did.

So to summarize, the Word has power to speak to you. Jeremiah once declared the power of the Word of the Lord as it is preached.

> "Is not My word like fire?" declares the Lord "and like a hammer which shatters a rock?" (Jeremiah 23:29).

The Word of God when proclaimed through Jeremiah's mouth became a fire that devoured the chaff, and a hammer that smashed the stone of people's hearts and made way for change. Let it do so in you today.

The Father just might offer you some answers to your prayers through the anointed preaching of the Word, so be sure you are applying your faith every time you visit a church and prepare to hear it. His Word is a fire and a hammer.

So if you are a preacher, or perhaps can agree you are part of one of the offices of an apostle, prophet, evangelist, pastor or teacher, pray something like this every time you speak: "Father, I bow in your presence. May

---

37 Dorothy Langstaff with Alan Langstaff, *Called Together* (Duluth, MN: Published by A Christian Voice, 2008), p. 68.

your Word be my rule, your Spirit my teacher, and your glory my aim. In Jesus' name, Amen."

And if you are about to hear a message preached from a servant of God, pray something like this: "Jesus, speak to me through your Word by the power of the Holy Spirit. I humble myself before you and ask you to change me today by your Word, Amen."

So now we add another way of Jesus speaking, through His presence in the Trinity.

Very Common Ways

WAY		SCRIPTURE
1	The Established Word of Jesus	John 1:1
2	The Living Word of Jesus	Romans 10:17
3	The Inner Witness of the Holy Spirit	Acts 9:31
4	The Inner Voice of the Holy Spirit	Acts 8:29
5	The Desires of Your Heart	Psalm 37:4
6	Father Speaks Through All of Creation & Nature	Romans 1:19
7	Providential Outward Signs & Circumstances	Romans 8:28

Common Ways

8	The Preaching of the Word of Jesus	2 Thess. 2:13

QUESTIONS FOR DEEPER STUDY:

1. Why is it important to treat preaching with reverence?

_____

_____

_____

_____

2. How can you prepare yourself before hearing a message to hear more from God?

_____

_____

_____

_____

3. Record a time when the message being spoken seemed like it was just for you. What were the circumstances? How did it direct, confirm, instruct, or encourage you?

_____

_____

_____

_____

Keep listening!

NOTES:

_____

_____

_____

_____

WAY #9: OTHER BELIEVERS SPEAKING CONFIRMATION

Christic in Mouth of Friend & Stranger

> **"F**or where two or three have gathered in My name, there I am in their midst"_ (Matthew 18:20).

One of the greatest gifts that Christ has given to us is the change of our hearts, the change of our very natures, in the wonderful experience we call being _"born again"_ or _"born from above"_ (see John, chapter 3). In this mystery, Christ has multiplied His own nature and changed the nature of mankind. He has given to common, ordinary people an extraordinary gift: His glory within.

Now I can hear Him speak directly to me, and I can learn that He is also active speaking to me through other people who are also "born from above." The Body of Christ is thus both His actual, resurrection body and His Body of believers here on earth.

Other Believers Speaking Confirmation, a simple definition: Jesus affirming and confirming words of encouragement and direction, directly to us, through other members of His Body on earth.

This happens by the inspiration of the Holy Spirit in a very naturally supernatural way. This includes through the living, breathing members of His Body now, and through the departed saints who left behind their writing as records of God's dealings with them. The living and the dead in Christ thus speak every day if we are listening.

When Paul wrote about this mystery of Christ being multiplied in each of us, he shared, *"Christ in you, the hope of glory"* (Colossians 1:27).

A mystery, yes! So Paul also tells the Corinthians, *"Now you are Christ's body, and individually members of it"* (I Corinthians 12:27).

He then goes on to share in his illustrations about the various members of a body, and how they all must work together.

There's something beautiful in Jesus' own words about His presence being promised, *"Where two or three have gathered in My name, there I am in their midst"* (Matthew 18:20).

Christ blesses you through others.

And when it comes to guidance and learning to hear from Jesus in His body, we also are told, *"By the mouth of two or three witnesses, every fact may be confirmed"* (Matthew 18:16).

To put it simply:

Christ is in you, the hope of glory.

Christ is in your fellow believers.

Christ blesses others through you.

Christ blesses you through others.

And I am speaking of His voice and personal guidance. What does He sound like? He sounds like every person's voice who is called and anointed to speak His word to you. And sometimes, he sounds like your own voice, as you step out in faith and speak to others in encouraging ways.

Talk about naturally supernatural!

Jesus' Expanded Model: the "70"

> *"Now after this the Lord appointed seventy others, and sent them two and two, ahead of Him to every city and place where He Himself was going to come. He said to them, 'and whatever city you enter, heal those who are sick, and SAY TO THEM, "The Kingdom of God has come near to you."'* (Luke 10:1, 8a, 9).

In the previous chapter we looked at the idea of Jesus Himself being present in His word preached. He first sent out the 12 to preach it. Here, Jesus chose the 70.

Note, these were not the 12 apostles. The 12 were not included here. These were regular, run-of-the-mill disciples who were infused with the power of the Spirit and given the authority of the message of the Kingdom. And off they went and carried on the amazing work of the Kingdom. They fellowshipped with people and ate meals with them. They found out their "felt needs" and prayed for them to be healed. They spoke the word of God and announced that God's kingdom had come.

It always gives me hope to remember that if God can speak through a donkey (Numbers 22), He can speak through me! And He can speak through you, too. And he chooses two or three common people, usually in unrelated incidents, to speak and to help confirm His Word spoken to you, or to help you confirm His word to others. Thus, *"out of the mouth of two or three witnesses"* every word is established.

Hearing His voice is another reason to stay in fellowship with a group of believers who love one another. Whenever you pray together with others, or simply fellowship around a meal, you can listen for the voice of God speaking to your condition (the group size can vary between 2 or 20,000)!

Here, again, is Dietrich Bonhoeffer on this subject.

"God has willed that we should seek and find God's living Word in the testimony of other Christians, in the mouths of other human beings. Therefore, Christians need other Christians who speak God's Word to them."[38]

---

38 Dietrich Bonhoeffer, *Life Together and Prayerbook of the Bible* (Fortress Press, 2004).

Out of the Mouth of 2 or 3 Witnesses

The same kind of thing as the calling of the 70 happened after the cross, the resurrection, and the ascension of Jesus. In Acts chapter 6, seven faithful, common men were chosen to carry on the gospel work, and they are described as *"men of good reputation, full of the Spirit and of wisdom"* (Acts 6:3).

Throughout the book of Acts, we see believers in various places sharing words of counsel, advice, encouragement, and warning as everyday occurrences of the voice of God speaking. These were naturally supernatural moments of Christ speaking in and through His body to help each other make godly choices.

For example, when Jesus brought the mighty and proud Saul (Paul) to his knees in humility and surrender, through actual temporary blindness, He did not choose "one of the 12" like Peter or John to bring him a miracle of healing. No, he spoke to a common disciple named Ananias. Ananias even argued with the Lord about praying for Saul and the Lord had to explain that he was indeed a chosen instrument. Ananias then prayed and Saul received his sight and was filled with the power of the Holy Spirit. And all through the hands of this common disciple who spoke encouraging words of confirmation to him.

Jesus, you see, was speaking through him.

Fire and Ice

Let me also share a personal example. As I shared earlier in this book, many years ago the Lord led my wife and I to start a professional media company that specialized in wedding video. The vision the Lord gave us was that this company would be a means of support to help us support our missions work. We followed the leading of the Lord every step of the way and became very successful in the state of Minnesota, being named "Best Videographer" in our state five years in a row by a prestigious magazine.

In the midst of all the success, we were meeting for lunch with a couple, Gene and Bette, who had been mentors for us in the video production business for many years. Out of the blue, Bette shared, "Maybe you should consider opening up your company in a whole different market, in a whole new State perhaps. You have created something unique. I'll bet other brides and grooms in another market would be interested in booking you."

We began to pray about that. Then we went to visit my parents, who told us that after many years of spending their winters in Florida, they felt it was time to start visiting Phoenix, Arizona.

"Maybe you could visit us and film a few weddings down there?" they said.

Could this be God? Out of the mouth of two witnesses, right?

We started praying more, now praying about the state of Arizona. Less than a week later, the phone rang. It was a Minnesota bride, having a destination wedding in Scottsdale! "Do you travel?" she asked. "Yes we do!" we replied. She booked us for the wedding and even paid for our travel arrangements.

Less than another week after that, the phone rang again. This time the call came from Tucson, Arizona. "I just found you guys online and love your work. Nobody here in Tucson does what you do. Can I book you to come to Tucson and film our wedding?"

"Sure you can!" I replied.

Long story short, the Lord led us, through multiple voices in common people, all confirming His direction, to open our video business in Arizona. God even started to speak to me about running my business in two opposite, extreme climates simultaneously: the fire of the Arizona desert and the ice of the Minnesota lakes and rivers we were so accustomed to. Fire equals Arizona and Ice equals Minnesota.

Along the way, God's provision opened up many doors. This included my parents deciding quite independently to purchase a winter home in Phoenix to escape the Minnesota "ice" of winter. When I first arrived there to stay, they had purchased initial furnishings that included a beautiful, full-color portrait, hung upon the living room wall, of a night scene with both a campfire and a sky lit up with blue lightning. Red fire and blue ice in the atmosphere were represented in the same portrait. What a confirmation!

We ended up filming dozens of weddings down there over a five year period, and being nominated by a prestigious Arizona magazine as "Best Videographer" in the state of Arizona.

So, does God speak through other, common people? YES!

The Shield of St. Patrick

The Celtic Christians of ancient days who owe their original introduction of Christ and the gospel to St. Patrick, were very unique in their understanding of God's desire to speak through anyone and everyone in leading His children.

St. Patrick himself was an apostolic missionary, sent to Ireland to begin proclaiming Christ and building new communities of believers.

These believers became worshiping and praying monks. They sang worship songs and were in intercessory prayer from sunrise to sunset every day. Their prayer and worship lifestyles became legendary. One such famous monastery is located just south of Belfast and was renamed "Bangor" by the local inhabitants at the time of some monks there. "Bangor" means "The Vale of the Angels" and was named this because the presence of God and of actual angels was so strong at the monastery!

And Patrick had an amazing grasp on how his daily, passionate, and intimate relationship with Christ involved other believers, even writing, "Christ in mouth of friend or stranger."

Here's just a portion of Patrick's amazing poem, attributed to him and dating to the 5th century, called the "Breastplate of St. Patrick," or "Shield of St. Patrick."

"Christ be with me, Christ within me, Christ behind me, Christ before me,

Christ beside me, Christ to win me, Christ to comfort and restore me.

Christ beneath me, Christ above me, Christ in quiet, Christ in danger,

Christ in hearts of all that love me, Christ in mouth of friend and stranger." [39]

---

39 St. Patrick's Prayer text in public domain.

Isn't this beautiful? What a glorious experience to awaken every morning and pray like this. Put Christ at the center of every day, fully expecting His presence and personal touch to be near you. Recognize that He Himself is speaking, not just through His word, but through His Spirit in other people.

Any Christian person you may meet today, or if you read a portion of their life or testimony, can be speaking to you. Perhaps they will confirm your path, as Christ in them is communicating to the Holy Spirit in you. St. Patrick had this all figured out in the 5th century. I pray that you and I will apply our faith and understanding in this today.

Hence, Jesus Himself could boldly declare that He is very present whenever, *"two or three are gathered in His name"* (Matthew 18:20).

Very Common Ways

WAY		SCRIPTURE
1	The Established Word of Jesus	*John 1:1*
2	The Living Word of Jesus	*Romans 10:17*
3	The Inner Witness of the Holy Spirit	*Acts 9:31*
4	The Inner Voice of the Holy Spirit	*Acts 8:29*
5	The Desires of Your Heart	*Psalm 37:4*
6	Father Speaks Through All of Creation & Nature	*Romans 1:19*
7	Providential Outward Signs & Circumstances	*Romans 8:28*

Common Ways

8	The Preaching of the Word of Jesus	*2 Thess. 2:13*
9	Other Believers Speaking Confirmation	*Matthew 18:16*

QUESTIONS FOR DEEPER STUDY:

1. Read 1 Corinthians 12:12-26. How does this passage support the idea that the LORD will use other believers to speak His Word into your life?

_____

_____

_____

_____

2. What other scripture passages can you think of that support the fact that Jesus will use imperfect vessels to speak His Word and accomplish His will?

_____

_____

_____

_____

3. How have other believers (in your own lifetime) spoken the Word of the LORD into your life?

_____

_____

_____

_____

Keep listening!

CHAPTER

10

WAY #10: VISIONS

Conscious Pictures of the Holy Spirit

"*A*nd *your young men shall see visions*" (Acts 2:17b).

God has created so much variety in the expressions of His voice. He speaks through pictures because a lot of people are wired to learn visually and through visual stimulation. I am one of those people. I love images and pictures and so quite often I will hear God's voice through a picture in the Holy Spirit.

Thus, we find God uses visions and dreams, and both direct and indirect or symbolic interpretations to speak. The next three chapters all utilize visual imagery through which God speaks. They are: Visions, Dreams, and Symbolic Speech/Metaphors.

We'll start with visions.

Visions, a simple definition: The Holy Spirit originating a picture that flows from your inner spirit and out through your mind. They can be either literal or symbolic in nature, and either given to oneself for your own direction, or given for the edification of others. They can be "objective" or "subjective" in nature.

Within this experience, the person may either be very conscious or sometimes unconscious yet awake, as in a kind of trance or open vision that happens on occasion with these experiences. In either case, the person is awake, alert, and in full possession of their natural faculties, but the Holy Spirit is involved and actually the source of the picture in the vision.

In Scripture, we have multiple characters in both Old and New Testaments who experienced visions. Some were literal, and some were symbolic.

Literal (non-symbolic) visions include: Moses, Aaron, Nadab and Abihu, and the 70 elders, seeing Yahweh God and His glory.

"And they saw the God of Israel; and under His feet there appeared to be a pavement of sapphire, as clear as the sky itself. Yet He did not stretch out His hand against the nobles of the sons of Israel; and they beheld God, and they ate and drank" (Exodus 24:10-11).

Another moment with Moses came a few chapters later. *"Then Moses said, "I pray You, show me Your glory." But He said, "You cannot see My face, for no man can see Me and live!" Then the Lord said, "Behold...while My glory is passing by...I will put you in the cleft of the rock, and cover you with My hand...then I shall take My hand away and you shall see My back, but My face shall not be seen"* (Exodus 33:18-23).

So in Exodus chapter 34, he "sees" the Lord, and this was a visionary experience in operation through the power of the Holy Spirit upon him.

Ezekiel also saw the Lord. The same was true of Isaiah and Daniel in their experiences through visions.

Symbolic (Non-literal) Visions

Genesis 15:1 says, *"After these things the word of the Lord came to Abram in a vision, saying, 'Do not fear Abram, I am a shield to you; your reward shall be very great.'"*

Some of Ezekiel's visions also had symbolism, like in Ezekiel 1:13-14. *"In the midst of the living beings there was something that looked like burning coals of fire, like torches darting back and forth among the living beings. The fire was bright, and lightning was flashing from the fire."*

Matthew Henry comments on this passage, "The prophet saw these living creatures by their own light, for their appearance was like burning coals of fire; they are seraphim, or burners; denoting the ardor of their love to God, and fervent zeal in his service."[40]

Arise, Peter, Kill & Eat!

Perhaps my favorite vision that contained imagery that the Holy Spirit then interpreted for the person is found in the Book of Acts and happened to Peter.

He was visiting the house of a friend in Joppa at lunch time, and while they were making the food, he "fell into a trance." Now this kind of experience has happened to me personally, many times around dinner time, but none of them "in the Spirit" like Peter's! I usually start to picture the foods I love, like a good steak, medium-rare, right before dinner is served. That is NOT the same thing that is happening here, but I love the reality of this story and the details like this one!

Here's what Peter saw.

> *"And he beheld the sky opened up, and a certain object like a great sheet coming down, lowered by four corners to the ground, and there were in it all kinds of four-footed animals and crawling creatures of the earth and birds of the air.*

> *"And a voice came to him, 'Arise, Peter, kill and eat!'*

---

40 *Matthew Henry's Concise Commentary* (Hendrickson Publishers).

"But Peter said, 'By no means, Lord, for I have never eaten any-thing holy and unclean.'

"And again a voice came to him a 2nd time, 'What God has cleansed, no longer consider unholy.' And this happened 3 times; and immediately the object was taken up into the sky"
(Acts 10:11-16).

For some background to understand this better, we turn back to the dietary food laws in Leviticus. God had specifically ordained three different classes of animals and they represented (symbolically) three different classes of people:

Sacrificial Animals = Levitical Priests

Clean Animals = Jews/Nation of Israel

Unclean Animals = Gentiles/Nations outside of Israel

For centuries, God had been utilizing animals to symbolize His sacrificial system and how the Priesthood and the Jewish people would be set apart from the other nations. Certain animals were forbidden to be eaten by Jews.

To put it bluntly, Jews never ate bacon and eggs for breakfast! Pigs were unclean. They never mixed their "clean" system with the "unclean."

So you can imagine Peter's surprise in his vision, which was received after the resurrection of Jesus. Peter is a good Jew who would normally not fraternize with Gentiles.

And yet God chooses Peter as the one to whom He revealed, in a visionary form, that the "unclean animals" represented the Gentiles, and God was now opening the door of the gospel to all the nations of the world.

The Lord says through this vision, received as a kind of "open vision" that He no longer calls the Gentiles "unclean."

To put it bluntly once again, bacon and eggs are now okay to eat for breakfast for all Jews and Gentiles who are part of the new Kingdom of God!

Of course, this revelation from God to Peter via the vision was a game changer to all Jewish believers. They suddenly realized God's original intention in all those food laws was to separate, for a season, Jews and Gentiles. This was in place only until the New Covenant arrived with better promises. All Gentiles can now respond to the gospel and there is "One New Man" in Christ, composed of all Jewish believers and Gentile believers. The Jewish food restrictions are forever dissolved. That which they symbolized has now been fulfilled.

And the end of the story: Peter visits the house of Cornelius, a God-fearing Gentile, and preaches the gospel to him and a group of his friends.

They believe and trust in Jesus as their Savior, the Holy Spirit falls upon them in power, and then Peter baptizes them as new believers. Now, for the first official time, BOTH Jews and Gentiles are forever joined in the new Body, or church, of Jesus Christ. (See Acts 10 for the whole story.)

Visions Come Also in Praying For Others

I have been blessed to pray for many people, and sometimes I see visions that, when interpreted, mean something very special to the individuals I am praying for.

For example, I remember once praying for people in Ireland at a special service. I came to a man and as I prayed for him, I instantly saw him dressed in white and putting a tray of food into a hot oven.

As I shared what I was seeing, the people around me started laughing. I had no knowledge of this man, but as I shared this picture, he confessed he owned a bakery and he was the cook for the church! The Lord gave me more pictures for him and some scriptures that spoke to him, like the bread he was baking was a picture of his ministry to people, unpacking the Word and Jesus as the fresh bread of the gospel and relating it to people in a way they could understand.

Visions are very fun to get for yourself and others!

I named my ministry "Born to Blaze" many years ago. I would be a rich man if I had collected $1 from every brother or sister who came up to me, without knowing the name of my ministry, and saw a vision of FIRE over me. I love how God confirms our calling through others, and pictures of fires blazing have been seen over me more times than I can count.

So to summarize, visions are given as experiences with the cooperation of the Holy Spirit. They can be either literal or symbolic experiences. The person receiving this means of indirect communication with the Spirit is active with his/her mental faculties and consciousness.

Very Common Ways

WAY		SCRIPTURE
1	The Established Word of Jesus	*John 1:1*
2	The Living Word of Jesus	*Romans 10:17*
3	The Inner Witness of the Holy Spirit	*Acts 9:31*
4	The Inner Voice of the Holy Spirit	*Acts 8:29*
5	The Desires of Your Heart	*Psalm 37:4*
6	Father Speaks Through All of Creation & Nature	*Romans 1:19*
7	Providential Outward Signs & Circumstances	*Romans 8:28*

Common Ways

8	The Preaching of the Word of Jesus	*2 Thess. 2:13*
9	Other Believers Speaking Confirmation	*Matthew 18:16*
10	Visions	*Acts 2:17-21*

QUESTIONS FOR DEEPER STUDY:

1. Why do we need the Holy Spirit to help us understand visions & dreams?

_____

_____

_____

_____

2. Do you EXPECT that God will speak to you? Why or Why not?

_____

_____

_____

_____

3. Pray today and ask the LORD to give you a vision of His provision or call on your life! Record here anything you see.

_____

_____

_____

_____

Keep listening!

NOTES:

_____

_____

_____

_____

WAY #11: DREAMS

Sub-conscious Pictures of the Holy Spirit

"**A**nd *your old men shall dream dreams*" (Acts 2:17-21).

In Peter's proclamation of the beginning of the Last Days in his Pentecost sermon, he quotes the prophet Joel's ancient prophecy and unleashes the Spirit's activity for all who will call upon the name of the Lord to be saved. He opens with a barrage of symbolism, an all-encompassing few statements that include (of course!), both young and old, male and female. So don't take the "old men" here spoken literally. All people in God's new family in Christ are now invited to "dream dreams" inspired, at times, by the Holy Spirit.

There is an untapped reservoir of unconscious activity in everybody's brain, designed by God, and at night times during sleep many people dream vast dreams and the unconscious seems to become reality, at least until the alarm clock goes off.

Let's turn now to dreaming dreams.

Dreams, a simple definition: The Holy Spirit originating a picture or a "movie" that flows through your subconscious mind while you are asleep. They can be either literal or symbolic in nature, and either given to oneself for their own direction, or given for the edification of others, or even as warnings from God, or information about the future. They can be "objective" or "subjective" in nature.

Sometimes Scripture calls them "visions of the night seasons" and the key is that the person is fast asleep when they occur.

In Scripture, we have multiple characters in both Old and New Testaments who experienced dreams or "visions of the night."

Old and New Testament Examples

A literal (non-symbolic) dream example: Abimelech, a Philistine King, was directed by God in a dream not to touch Abraham's wife, Sarah.

> "But God came to Abimelech in a dream of the night, and said to him, "Behold, you are a dead man because of the woman whom you have taken, for she is married" (Genesis 20:3-18).

Basically God spoke fairly directly to him, not in symbolic language, and the king awoke and confronted Abraham and found out the truth, and returned Sarah, untouched, to him.

A symbolic (non-literal) dream happened a bit later in Genesis with Pharaoh. And God's man for the hour, Joseph, was right there to interpret it (see Genesis 41). "Now it happened at the end of two full years that Pharaoh had a dream" (Genesis 41:1).

In Pharaoh's two symbolic dreams, symbols included two different pictures that told the same story: He saw ugly and gaunt cows eating the sleek and fat cows, and he saw thin ears of grain eating up the fat ears of grain.

Joseph rightly interpreted these two dreams as wisdom from God to direct Pharaoh to prepare for the famine that was coming upon his lands.

The famine came, but Pharaoh had stored up enough food so that his people lived. Joseph got promoted, too. It was a win-win situation.

And of course, who can forget Jacob, who dreamed a dream and saw heaven opened and a huge ladder in the sky, with angels ascending and descending upon earth.

Thousands of years later, Jesus would utilize this dream event to relate that He, as the mediator between God and man, represents the ladder from heaven, *"And He said to them, 'Truly, truly I say to you, you shall see the heavens opened, and the angels of God ascending and descending on the Son of Man'"* (John 1:51).

There are many New Testament examples of the Lord speaking in both direct and indirect ways through dreams to His people.

For example, God gave Joseph (the earthly father of Jesus) four dreams around the time of the birth of Jesus to help him understand what was happening, and in one of those he warned Joseph to take the baby Jesus down to Egypt *(see Matthew 2:13-15)*.

Jesus appeared to Paul in a dream when Paul was facing opposition to his ministry in Corinth.

> *"Do not be afraid any longer, but go on speaking and do not be silent; for I am with you, and no man will attack you in order to harm you, for I have many people in this city"* (Acts 18:9-10).

The Holy Spirit is the Dream Interpreter

When my kids were small I wanted to give them a special memory of their Dad reading to them before bed. So they would snuggle up into their beds, and after trying to delay the bedtime (over and over) I would re-direct their attention to a very curious book: *The Pilgrim's Progress,* by John Bunyan. Arguably one of the most re-printed books in the English language.

Bunyan was a Puritan who used metaphors in his character names and certain objects to represent great gospel truths. He himself, as the Author, added some of his own interpretations on the side-notes of his manuscript to help readers understand.

I would read this every night to my kids, and try to dramatize the different characters and scenes and bring them to life. In one of the scenes, the lead character, Christian, is led to a particular house filled with unique objects, all of them symbolic and filled with wonder. The name of the house?

The House of the Interpreter.

Indeed, Bunyan himself recognized we all need to visit this House quite often: the Interpreter is the Holy Spirit. Bunyan's promise? "He will show you things that will be profitable for you."

———◦———

Adam Thompson and Adrian Beale have written a wonderful book with teachings and in-depth study on the subject of visions, dreams, and symbolic speech. Regarding dreams, they write,

"The proponents of the New Age and some schools of psychology have embraced dreams in their hunger for answers to life's questions. However, being without the Holy Spirit, who is the author (*see Acts 2:17*) and interpreter (*see Genesis 40:8*) of dreams, they are nonetheless still in the dark—blind leaders of the blind.

"Today, some churches are not even aware that God speaks through dreams. We obviously don't know the importance of dreams in the plans and purposes of God, and we have forgotten that the promise of the Holy Spirit brings with it God's prophetic guidance through dreams and visions. Sadly, we look at the equivalent of Nebuchadnezzar's magicians today and see them dabbling with dreams and interpretation and are turned off.

> We have forgotten the promise of guidance of the Holy Spirit through dreams and visions.

"We have thrown the baby out with the bathwater when God is calling for an army of Daniels to arise!"[41]

Dreams Can Become Reality

I have had both literal dreams, which God used to communicate fairly simply to me, and symbolic dreams, which He helped me interpret, or sent others to help me interpret, and which likewise spoke very strongly and beautifully to me. My wife, too, is actually more of a "dreamer" than I am. The Lord speaks to her in dreams much more often than with me.

I still remember a vivid dream I had when I was a very young Christian, perhaps only seven or eight months old in the Lord. It was in a time when God was wanting to direct my steps away from Hollywood, where I thought my best life would be spent in the film industry, towards the world of ministry.

In the dream I was on the center of a stage and there was a vast crowd before me. I remember the dream because I was preaching like a house afire, and scripture after scripture (from the King James Version, which was all I had at that time) was pouring out of me, somehow making sense and impacting all the people in the crowd.

Suddenly I awoke. And I wondered. Would I someday be called to a mission like that? And you know what? I was. This was a fairly literal dream as I have walked forward and since preached a bit like that in many settings around the world.

Steve Sampson, in one of his books, relates a dream that he had that contained symbolism, and only after a few days did he realize the full meaning.

He shares, "One night during my college years, I had a dream that I was giving birth to a baby. I could literally feel the birth pangs and was in a hospital delivery room, going through the whole process, until the baby came.

---

41 Adam Thompson and Adrian Beale, *The Divinity Code to Understanding Your Dreams and Visions* (Destiny Image Publishers, 2011), p. 24. Author's Note: I highly recommend their book as a great tool of teaching and interpretation for dreams, visions, and symbolic speech (metaphors).

"As I awoke from the dream (which was so real), I promised myself that I would never tell anyone that dream. Then a few days later, at 11:00 p.m. one night, there was a knock on my window. My good friend from high school wanted to talk to me. He had just had a big fight with his girlfriend. As we talked for the next two hours, I led him to Christ (and he is a Christian to this day). A few days later, it suddenly hit me—I did indeed have a baby! I had led my friend to Christ."[42]

A River Runs Through It

My long-time ministry colleagues and mentors, Alan and Dorothy Langstaff, share the story of their early years in Australia as they were planning a National Convention and seeking God's will for the right place to hold it. One night, their daughter Beth had a dream. She saw a map of a city with a river running through it. Dorothy relates the rest of the story,

"All we had to do was identify the city in her dream. But none of the maps of the cities we had already visited matched her dream. Then we visited Canberra. Alan visited the university and trusting he was doing the right thing, booked the auditorium and accommodation for the following January. He brought back some brochures and maps of the university with him. Our daughters Beth and Joy browsed through a couple of the spare copies, chattering. Then there was a stunned silence. I turned around. Beth's face was full of utter surprise.

"What's the matter?" I asked.

She looked down at the open map, which was an aerial view of the Canberra University.

"This is it!" she said. "It is exactly as I saw it in my dream. There is even a river running through it."

What a wonderful confirmation that this was the place!"[43]

---

42 Steve Sampson, *You Can Hear the Voice of God*, Ibid., p. 80.
43 Dorothy Langstaff with Alan Langstaff, *Called Together* (Duluth, MN: Published by A Christian Voice, 2008), pp. 206-207.

I'm sure you, too, could relate some of your dreams where you either felt God was speaking to you, in either symbolic or literal interpretation.

Now that you have more teaching on this, I hope you will begin to pray more actively that the Holy Spirit will choose to open up these lines of communication more often, in both visions and dreams, for you personally. And for those around you who need to know Him, or even for future events so you know better how to be in prayer and intercession.

Remember that in these last days, *"That I will pour forth of My Spirit upon ALL mankind; and your sons and your daughters will prophesy, and your young men shall see visions, and your old men will dream dreams"* (Acts 2:17-21).

As I mentioned in the start of this chapter, this is symbolic, visionary language quoted from the prophet Joel by Peter on the Day of Pentecost. It means that ALL people in God's family in Christ can possibly receive direct and indirect communication from God in both visions and dreams.

So start seeing. And start dreaming. And never stop.

Practical Applications

Here are a few practical applications.

1. First, from my friend, Steven Maddox and found in his excellent book, "The Dream Book":

   "After a dream, write it down immediately and ask yourself,

   "How does this dream fit in the context of your life right now? Including your education, training, desires, abilities and aptitude. Each dream you have will contain symbols and stories that are tailor-made for you. Remember, dreams are a language that's unique to each one of us just as we are unique to one another.

"Keep in mind the dream is only the beginning of the invitation for you to change, believe, move on..."

2. Pray about your dream and talk to the Holy Spirit about it. Search the Scriptures for confirmation.

3. Seek Godly counsel from individual trusted friends and mentors for further insights.

4. Praise, worship, and give thanks to the LORD of your dreams!

Very Common Ways

WAY		SCRIPTURE
1	The Established Word of Jesus	John 1:1
2	The Living Word of Jesus	Romans 10:17
3	The Inner Witness of the Holy Spirit	Acts 9:31
4	The Inner Voice of the Holy Spirit	Acts 8:29
5	The Desires of Your Heart	Psalm 37:4
6	Father Speaks Through All of Creation & Nature	Romans 1:19
7	Providential Outward Signs & Circumstances	Romans 8:28

Common Ways

8	The Preaching of the Word of Jesus	2 Thess. 2:13
9	Other Believers Speaking Confirmation	Matthew 18:16
10	Visions	Acts 2:17-21
11	Dreams	Acts 2:17-21

QUESTIONS FOR DEEPER STUDY:

1. Do you think God has been speaking to you and you have not noticed? Y/N Why or Why not?

_____

_____

_____

_____

2. Think of a dream you've had recently that was particularly vivid—one so vivid you remember every detail and feel it was from the LORD. Write it here and pray for the interpretation.

_____

_____

_____

_____

3. Think about some of your other dreams from the LORD. How did they build your faith, bring illumination and/or confirm direction?

_____

_____

_____

_____

Keep listening!

NOTES:

_____

_____

_____

_____

CHAPTER

12

WAY #12: SYMBOLIC SPEECH: METAPHORS FROM THE HOLY SPIRIT

Riddles in the Dark

"With him (Moses) I speak mouth to mouth, even openly, and not in metaphors and riddles" (Numbers 12:8).

Moses was very blessed. He spoke with God openly and God spoke to him openly.

He heard the Father's audible voice, which was very rare in his own day, and is even more scarcely discerned today. In these days of overspreading darkness, God's glory is seen and felt in the small ways of a day-by-day love relationship with Him, and He chooses far more often to communicate with you and me as He did with the children of Israel. In Numbers He reveals yet another way of talking.

It is not taught very often, but it is a common way of speaking.

Moses may get to have a full conversation with God at a coffee shop, but you and I must be more perceptive to speak with God while drinking our coffee. We must be keenly aware that He is reaching out in a special way of indirect communication all around us, possibly at all times; metaphors and riddles.

One of my favorite books of all time is J.R.R. Tolkien's *The Hobbit*. I remember reading this book as a kid, and then having the privilege of reading it to my two boys when they were younger. Of course, nowadays it's been created into a brilliant film series for the whole world to enjoy.

At one point, the Hobbit, Bilbo Baggins, is separated from a band of dwarves on an adventure to reclaim their treasure and defeat a dragon. In a dark, underground cavern, Bilbo confronts a rather interesting creature: Gollum.

I am borrowing Tolkien's account of Bilbo's encounter with Gollum for this chapter, as the riddles in the dark cave that the two characters recite to each other are a great illustration of a very ancient way of God's communication.

Remember this one?

"This thing all things devours;

Birds, beasts, trees, flowers;

Gnaws iron, bites steel;

Grinds hard stones to meal;

Slays king, ruins town,

And beats mountain down."

That riddle is solved by Bilbo and he wins the round.

In Scripture, this very unique way of God's communication with us is sometimes called "dark speech," or to put it in a plainer way, symbolic speech, or metaphors, or intriguing riddles.

The closest literary tool we have to this supernatural way of communication would be metaphors. God speaks in metaphors or word pictures that refer to, or point to, something else.

Until I realized the power of metaphors from the Holy Spirit, I was a bit like Jacob having that dream from the Lord where he saw the ladder reaching up to Heaven.

Here is what he remarked after he awoke, *"Surely the Lord is in this place, and I did not know it"* (Genesis 28:16b).

When I grasped the wonder of this unique category of the Holy Spirit reaching out, I began to recognize, with Jacob, that the Lord is in my "place" every week, and now I can "know it!" It's been quite an adventure in hearing from God since I discovered this.

As I mentioned in the previous chapters explaining visions and dreams, since many people are wired to think in symbols, pictures, and visual stimulation, the Holy Spirit utilizes the visual aspects of our comprehension more as an indirect way of communicating (symbolic, not literal).

Let me define symbolic speech and share some scriptures about it from both the Old and New Testaments.

Symbolic Speech, a simple definition: The most indirect and symbolic way of the Holy Spirit speaking. In this particular form, He utilizes common, everyday objects to teach us lessons. These objects are like the symbols in an abstract painting, symbols which need interpretation and point to something real. The "abstract" becomes "clear and real" as He brings the interpretation. They serve to paint words of knowledge for direction and encouragement. They are metaphors from God.

Definition of a metaphor: "Noun: a figure of speech in which a word or phrase is applied to an object or action to which it is not literally applicable."[44]

Think about all the imagery in that riddle from Gollum to Bilbo: birds, bees, trees, flowers and so forth. The answer to the riddle points all these to one single truth.

---

44 *Merriam-Webster's Learner's Dictionary*, online edition.

Throughout Scripture, God used these forms of communication to teach His people and lead them. They can be "objective" or "subjective" in nature.

Some Old and New Testament Examples

"I will utter an intriguing riddle from the past."

"Hear now My words: if there is a prophet among you, I, the Lord, shall make Myself known to him in a vision. I shall speak with him in a dream.

"Not so, with My servant Moses. He is faithful in all My household; with him I speak mouth to mouth (face to face), even openly, and not in metaphors (or riddles).

"And he beholds the form of the Lord" (Numbers 12:6-8).

The Psalmist tells us,

"I will utter dark sayings of old" or, as the Passion Translation puts it, *"an intriguing riddle from the past"* (Psalm 78:2b).

So He spoke most commonly and often to the people of Moses' day in these metaphors, and Moses himself seems to be the exception to the rule. He got real face time with God through intimate prayer. That is, even to this day, a lot rarer. Most of us receive symbols that we can learn to interpret and discover some great leadings of the Holy Spirit.

Consider for a moment the symbolism of the three objects contained inside the Ark of the Covenant that Indiana Jones once sought after.

In Joshua 3:3, that Ark actually contained three important objects, all of them objects that symbolized spiritual truths. They were:

— The stone tablets of the Commandments (symbolizing The Word),

— The manna (symbolizing God's provision), and

— The Rod of Aaron that had budded (the symbol of prayer and intercession of all believers through the royal priesthood).

"With him (Moses) I

SPEAK

mouth to mouth, even

OPENLY

and not in metaphors and riddles."

(Numbers 12:8)

In fact, once we arrive at the New Covenant and the life of Jesus Himself, the New Testament writers were able to discern, for the first time, that the Person of Jesus Christ and the Kingdom that He began to establish fulfilled all the Old Testament metaphors and prophetic utterances. Jesus changed everything!

The Good Shepherd Leads His Sheep

Just one example from so many throughout Scripture: the idea of Jesus as a Shepherd. First symbolized by David and his Kingship. Then symbolized by Jesus Himself declaring He was the fulfillment of this promise of a coming Shepherd. Finally, Jesus is still called a Shepherd by the writer of Hebrews.

Psalm 78, which contains the opening verse about God speaking through "intriguing riddles," ends with a few verses speaking first of David as a shepherd of his own sheep, learning in integrity and skillful care for the sheep, then, as a kind of metaphor became the "Shepherd of Jacob."

Here's how The Passion Translation puts it, as God made David, *"His prophetic servant. God prepared David and took this gentle shepherd-king and presented him before the people as the one who would love and care for them with integrity, a pure heart, and the anointing"* (Psalm 78:70b, 71, 72a,).

Later in the prophetic promises of the coming Advent of the Messiah, Isaiah cries out,

> *"Like a shepherd He will tend His flock, in His arm He will gather the lambs, and carry them in His heart. He will gently lead the nursing ewes"* (Isaiah 40:11).

Notice how this piece of prophetic literature is written to ensure that its readers know that this is a word picture, not a literal one: "Like a shepherd."

So the Psalmist reveals that the shepherd-boy David is a kind of metaphor for a Shepherd over Israel. And Isaiah goes the next step to reveal that the coming Messiah would be "like a shepherd."

So when Jesus appears and teaches us all how He wants to lead us, He fulfills this ancient word picture, or symbolic speech, or intriguing riddle. He calls Himself the Good Shepherd. And His sheep hear His voice and follow Him.

Finally, the writer of Hebrews carries this metaphor right down to present day by stating,

> *"Now the God of peace, who brought up from the dead the great*
> *Shepherd of the sheep through the blood of the eternal covenant,*
> *even Jesus our Lord, equip you in every good thing to do His will"*
> (Hebrews 13:20, 21a).

So Jesus is the literal fulfillment of what the Psalmist, the prophet Isaiah, and the writer of Hebrews declare. He is, in reality, exactly what the word pictures point to: He tends His flock, He gathers them, He leads them in gentleness, He carries them in His heart. And perhaps the most vital characteristic for this particular study: He speaks personally to them. He has continued to speak right down through today.

Remember, too, that one of the variety of ways of teaching that Jesus utilized was parables. Each parable, though it included loads of different details, usually was a teaching mechanism to teach or illustrate one main point or truth.

So, just for one example, in the three parables contained in Luke chapter 15, there is one central theme that weaves them all together.

The three parables are: the lost sheep, the lost coin, and the lost son (the "Prodigal Son" story). You have to read them closely, but you will find one main theme hidden within each one: JOY.

That's right, joy! The man that lost the sheep rejoices when he finds it; the same with the man who found the coin; and the end of the Prodigal Son story contains the word "rejoice!"

Jesus is teaching that there is joy in heaven when one person repents and humbles himself or herself and gives their heart fully to Him. Joy is a hallmark of the Kingdom of God!

Apocalypse Now

Scripture is full of these kinds of visual pictures that point to other realities. For example, there is even a form of writing in both Testaments called "apocalyptic" literature. It is a very ancient form of writing, and not very well known to us today.

Apocalyptic, a simple definition: "God discloses His purposes in visionary form. Symbolic figures and scenes indicate the relation of God's plan to history."[45]

The closest we can come in modern culture is to call it "poetic," as when a good poet writes a poem, you can translate the images of that poem and figure out that they can point to other realities.

In poetry, sometimes the poet rhymes the lines, like in a limerick, for example, which is a five-line poem with a rhyme scheme. Here's the start of a common limerick.

"There once was a man from Nantucket,
Who kept all his cash in a bucket," and so on.

There are specific passages of your Bible that are written in a poetic form (kind of like limericks).

I learned this from studying some great commentators on the Book of Revelation.

Now, before you open the Book of Revelation for study, always remember that, "all apocalyptic imagery in Scripture is basically rooted and grounded in either past Hebrew culture or in Hebrew history, both from the Old Testament."[46]

One of my favorite commentators is author and lecturer Vern S. Poythress. In his guide to Revelation he gives us several examples in the Bible

---

45 Vern S. Poythress, *The Returning King: A Guide to the Book of Revelation* (Phillipsburg, New Jersey: P & R Publishing Company, 2000).
46 From Dr. Lance Wonders, ACTS Bible College teaching course.

where God speaks to His people through symbolic communication. For example:

"Apocalyptic features are apparent in Numbers 23-24, Daniel, Ezekiel, Isaiah 24-27, 1 Thessalonians 4-5, 2 Thessalonians 1-2, the Olivet discourse (Matthew 24, Mark 13, Luke 21) and Revelation."

And as for the Book of Revelation itself, "Revelation is a Christ-centered vision.

> God speaks to His people through symbolic language and poetic imagery.

Christ is the way to God; He is the mediator of God's plan for history. Christ's death and resurrection introduce the great epoch of salvation. The gospel spreads to the nations and invites people everywhere to participate in salvation rather than remain under God's wrath. John was writing in an "apocalyptic" manner, a manner already as familiar to them as a political cartoon is to us today."[47]

You don't have to read very far into the Book of Revelation to discover the incredible symbolism. Chapter 1 includes a unique vision of the resurrected Christ based upon the Old Testament vision that Daniel saw (see Daniel 7 and 10). It's filled with vivid imagery and descriptions of Him including white hair, eyes a flame of fire, a sharp sword as His tongue, a brightly shining face, and other details.

"Jesus reveals Himself to John in the language of prophetic symbolism," writes Dennis E. Johnson in his excellent commentary on Revelation, "not in a literal description of his resurrection body as he now sits at God's right hand. The symbols seen by John in the vision reveal not what Jesus looks like but what He is like—His identity as the searcher of hearts, full of consuming holiness and boundless wisdom, the perfect priest standing for His people before the Father, the perfect king defending them against the devil by His invincible Word. Revelation's visions show us how things are, not how they look to the physical eye."[48]

So God can speak to us today like limericks or even political cartoons.

---

47 Ibid., Poythress, p. 47.
48 Dennis E. Johnson, *Triumph of the Lamb: A Commentary on Revelation* (P & R Publishing, 2001), p. 60.

Ready for a few real-life examples?

Rocking Chairs & Baseball Mitts

One thing you should know about me: I like to rock! God certainly must have had His hand in designing me to be a man on the move.

To put it quite simply, I am a man-in-motion. I am always wanting to move! For me, real rest is hard. I simply do not know what to do with myself on a day off and find it hard to slow down.

I currently have a rocking chair in nearly every room of my house. How did they get there?

There was this strange period in my life where everyone seemed to be giving me rocking chairs!

My Dad first asked me if I wanted my Grandmother's rocking chair after she went to be with the Lord and it was passed on to him.

"Sure!" I said.

I pray in that chair, and rock and read the Word, nearly every day. A friend called me up one day and said, "Carl, we are cleaning out a storage unit and the owner said we could give away or keep anything we found. We have a nice black leather rocking chair in here. Do you want one?"

"Sure!" I said.

Then my parents called me up, out of the blue, and asked if I wanted a rocker/glider with an ottoman as they wanted to give it away.

"Sure!" I said.

I suddenly had been given all these rocking chairs. What was God up to? Then one day we had a special prayer time with one of our employees.

She was praying for us and suddenly said, "The Lord says, 'I have given you these rocking chairs as they symbolize REST and PEACE in your life. I want you to know that every time I give you a rocking chair, I am inviting you to a new season of RESTING IN MY LOVE.'

She spoke this in prayer as a prophecy from the Lord. Awesome!

So, rocking chairs equal rest and peace.

In the same way, Shepherd equals David for Israel, and later, Jesus for His Church. Jesus gathers, leads, carries, and speaks to us.

Prayer Application: Find an Object as a Symbol & Then Give the Interpretation

I have a friend in Belfast, Northern Ireland, who leads some home groups. Sometimes he will pray over people and share words of knowledge for them of encouragement.

I once accompanied him on an afternoon before he went to a home meeting.

He took me to a thrift store and prayerfully walked around the store, buying several older items for a few dollars each that seemed completely unrelated (to me).

Then that evening I watched in awe as he went to pray for people. One by one, he took an item from his bag and handed it to the person. Each item was a symbol, or picture, of the word that he was ministering to that person, and he gave them a scripture to go along with the word.

At the end of the night he had given away all of the items he had purchased, and each individual took home that item and they had special reminders of the Lord's faithful word to them.

How special! You can do this, too! Try it, it works!

I once received an anonymous gift of an old catcher's mitt after a service where I was preaching. It was sitting on my chair, and after I preached I found the mitt and a note attached. It read, "Carl, God wants you to always know that you are His son and nothing could ever take that away. He wants you to go to Him as a boy to have the joy and faith of a child.

"He isn't just the Almighty God, but your Papa.

"When I picture a son with his father I imagine them playing catch, laughing, the Father giving his son advice and guiding and teaching him.

"Don't let go of that little boy inside playing and learning from his Daddy."

I still have that baseball catcher's mitt and note on the shelf of my study to help remind me of Papa-God's love for me personally.

1400 Monks

My final example comes from a dynamic minister named Shawn Bolz. He lives now in Los Angeles and is pastoring a unique church out there to help influence the film industry and media culture with the gospel. He has written several books, one of which is called "Translating God."[49]

In his book, he shares some wonderful illustrations of how to hear God's voice for the world around you.

I was once sitting in a meeting and Shawn began to pray for the crowd. He paused and heard a name and a date from the Holy Spirit and turned towards my section of seats.

"I am getting the name Ethan, and the birthday September 20th. Does that mean anything to anyone sitting over in this section?"

I was amazed and stood up. "Yes!" I said excitedly. "That is my oldest son's first name, and his actual birthday!"

He then went on to share a very specific word to me that was accurate and blessed me tremendously. I wondered how in the world he was able to share such specific details. He accurately called out my alma mater of U.S.C. Film School, my three children's names, their callings, and even my wedding anniversary. Yes, he had the actual date of my wedding day.

At another meeting I heard him share that God, as a loving Father, gives

---

49 For more info: Shawn Bolz, *Translating God: Hearing God For Yourself & the World Around You.*
www.bolzministries.com

details like this to people to let them know how much He loves them and has a plan for their life, and His plans were planned from all eternity.

Naming a person's college or school shows the person that the Father had a plan for their education and knew what He had dreamed about them doing for all eternity.

When Shawn gets wedding anniversary dates, the Father is reaching out to share His plan for marriage and how He created it as a blessing and wants the people to experience His love for each other and His love for them personally.

From what I have seen, the Holy Spirit often speaks to Shawn in visions and in symbolic speech and metaphors/pictures, which once translated, point to other very specific realities.

For example, I saw him pray over a woman in the vast crowd and the Lord gave him her first name, that she had two brothers, and the names of those brothers. He also saw she was receiving education and was a missionary. Then, he paused and said,

"I see 1400 monks surrounding you. Does that mean anything to you?"

The woman was so overwhelmed at the moment that she could not translate that picture for him.

Shawn paused, prayed more, and just left it there.

> God is creative, absolutely sovereign, and multi-faceted in His approach to speaking.

The people in the audience never heard the explanation, and Shawn had taken a bold step of faith to share that picture. He probably thought he had missed it, but he went on anyway and shared several more word pictures with people that really touched them.

Later that day I happened to catch a testimony on Facebook where the woman shared with Bolz the interpretation.

"I realized later that 1400 Monks was my address when I lived in St. Paul and was training as a missionary and I was in school.

My address was 1400 Monks Avenue!"

So the picture that Shawn saw in the Spirit of 1400 monks surrounding that woman was indeed a metaphor for her actual street address where she once lived.

How Does Symbolic Speech Differ from Prophecy?

An excellent question. The answer is: it is related to the gift of prophecy whenever you or I are personally ministering and seeing a picture, an object, or actually giving someone an object with an accompanying word of explanation.

In a later chapter I will share more on the gift of prophecy. It would be fitting here for you to know that whenever you personally share a word like these to people, you are flowing in the gift of prophecy.

It's also true that the Holy Spirit flows through all of God's creation and is reaching out to you at times through symbolic speech itself, rather than operating it as a gift through others to you or from yourself to others. He's creative, absolutely sovereign, and multi-faceted in His approach to speaking.

There are many blessings of prophecy, and pitfalls of prophecy, that I will cover in that later chapter, too.

Do you see the power and wonder of these "intriguing riddles" that God has always used to speak to His people? I hope and pray that reading this chapter will open you up to the many creative ways that the Holy Spirit is seeking to speak to you.

Keep on the lookout in your prayer time for symbolic speech and visual symbols that point to other realities, and receive these symbols and interpret them for yourself and others.

Pray for others and flow in the gift of prophecy so you can help them interpret these symbols. You will stand amazed at how God's love for you and for all the people around you speaks in symbols.

And remember: Jesus is still your "Good Shepherd" leading you forth and calling you by name.

So what did Gollum's riddle-in-the-dark to Bilbo actually mean? What possibly affects birds, bees, trees and flowers, slays a king, and brings down a mountain? The answer is TIME.

So let's try to "redeem the time," as Scripture tells us, and become very aware of our surroundings, looking for what everyone else is missing: the symbols and metaphors of the Holy Spirit that God is utilizing to speak.

Very Common Ways

WAY		SCRIPTURE
1	The Established Word of Jesus	John 1:1
2	The Living Word of Jesus	Romans 10:17
3	The Inner Witness of the Holy Spirit	Acts 9:31
4	The Inner Voice of the Holy Spirit	Acts 8:29
5	The Desires of Your Heart	Psalm 37:4
6	Father Speaks Through All of Creation & Nature	Romans 1:19
7	Providential Outward Signs & Circumstances	Romans 8:28

Common Ways

8	The Preaching of the Word of Jesus	2 Thess. 2:13
9	Other Believers Speaking Confirmation	Matthew 18:16
10	Visions	Acts 2:17-21
11	Dreams	Acts 2:17-21
12	Symbolic Speech: Metaphors from the Holy Spirit	Numbers 12:8

Questions for Deeper Study:

1. How do word pictures, parables or object lessons teach you a deeper spiritual reality?

_____

_____

_____

_____

2. Why is it important to have the "Interpreter" (Holy Spirit) give you the meaning of symbolic speech?

_____

_____

_____

_____

3. Has anyone given you a gift that you knew was actually or potentially a message or special blessing from Him? What was it and why was it special?

_____

_____

_____

_____

Keep listening!

WAY #13: DIVINE APPOINTMENTS FROM THE FATHER

Holy Coincidence, Batman!

"**A**nd as they went along the road they came to some water; and the eunuch said, 'Look! Water! What prevents me from being baptized?'" (Acts 8:36).

Through many years of walking with the Father and desiring to know His ways more intimately, I have stumbled upon a most wonderful outward manifestation of His love and His leading; what I like to call a "holy coincidence," or as some would term it, a divine appointment.

This theme relates directly to Father's Providence (which we delved into more back in Chapter 7). God arranges His divine appointments to display His love for us personally, and whenever you have one, you'll feel His love for you.

> **Holy Coincidences, a simple definition:** The idea that your Heavenly Father has gone before you on your journey and prepared a surprise person, people, or even objects in the normal circumstances of life to stumble upon.

I use the word *stumble* in the definition because that is how *we* perceive the situation; in the most incredible of odds against it, there in front of you is someone familiar, or an object that is a perfect answer to prayer, and you quietly wonder, *Was God involved in this moment?* To which you can enthusiastically answer, "Yes!"

The odds would be, in the natural, at one-in-ten-thousand or one-in-a-million that you would be in the right place, at the right time, with the right people and the right motivation to stumble upon a certain person that you have known in the past, or a certain object that exactly answers a prayer you have been praying.

So, divine appointment equals divine love!

Your Heavenly Father organized a special circumstance or arranged a meeting just for you, just for that unique moment. That is a Holy Coincidence, Batman!

> Every divine appointment is the handiwork of your Father so you will know His love.

These kinds of events happen consistently at least every month for me personally, and I always stumble away from them with a deep sense of awe at both the majesty of Almighty God, and the intimacy of Him as my Father.

From this day on, begin to recognize that in every divine appointment there is the handiwork of your personal Father making the situation wonderful so that you will know His love and direction for you.

Coincidence? No. There's no such thing outside of God.

Holy Coincidence? YES. They happen all the time. Let me share one example from Jesus Himself, who had many of these kinds of moments happen during His ministry. The most amazing one was just near the end of His sacrificial death upon the cross.

Be Not Far Off

Through the circumstances around Him and people that He met, Jesus Christ knew that His Father was with Him and leading Him, even in the darkest moments of His absolute obedience to the Father's will.

One day in prayer I asked the Lord to give me an example of how He knew the love of His Father.

I was reminded of the ancient practice that Rabbi's utilized in those days, of committing to memory whole passages of Scripture. The common practice then was to verbally speak the first verse of a particular passage, and then spend the next few minutes thinking deeply of all the following verses, and meditating in your heart on each verse that follows. Let's visit the cross itself.

Upon the cross, the single most important moment of all history, Jesus Christ bears the sins of all people. He who knew no sin became sin for you and I, that He might bestow upon us forgiveness of sins and His own righteousness. Death is the sentence for sin that all people must pay. He pays the penalty for us and in exchange, gives us eternal life. That is grace. That is *agape*. Divine love like no other. He laid down His life for His friends.

> *"Now from the sixth hour darkness fell upon all the earth until about the ninth hour. And about the ninth hour Jesus cried out with a loud voice, quoting the first verse of Psalm 22, saying, 'Eli, Eli, lama sabachthani?' that is, 'My God, My God, why hast Thou forsaken Me?'"* (Matthew 27:45-46).

In this very moment now, imagine Jesus beginning His quiet meditation of the whole of Psalm 22, which had been written over 1,000 years earlier.

Here are just some of the verses that begin to reverberate in His mind and heart, by the Holy Spirit, while right in front of Him, He sees them literally fulfilled, once and for all.

> *"My God, My God, why hast Thou forsaken Me? Far from My deliverance are the words of My groaning. Yet You are holy, O You who are enthroned upon the praises of Israel.*

"In You our fathers trusted; they trusted and You delivered them, a reproach of men and despised by the people.

"All who see Me sneer at Me; they separate with the lip, they wag the head, saying,

"Commit yourself to the Lord; let Him deliver him; let Him rescue him, because He delights in him."

"Be not far from Me, for trouble is near; for there is none to help. Many bulls have surrounded Me; strong bulls of Bashan have encircled Me. They open wide their mouth at Me,

"As a ravening and a roaring lion, I am poured out like water, and all My bones are out of joint; My heart is like wax; it is melted within Me.

"A band of evildoers has encompassed Me.

"They pierced My hands and My feet.

"They look, they stare at Me. They divide My garments among them, and for My clothing they cast lots."

Holy Coincidences Point to the Reality of God's Love

Right in front of the cross, Jesus sees these verses quite literally fulfilled.

He is reproached by those around Him, despised; they mock Him, crying out, *"He saved others, He cannot save Himself, He trusts in God; let Him deliver Him"* (Matthew 27:43).

He is surrounded by soldiers of the strongest army on earth, and they are encircling Him like strong bulls. He feels His very heart melting like wax, and His bones are all out of joint on that cross. His very tongue cleaves to His mouth in thirst.

His hands and feet have been pierced by this instrument of torturous death invented by the Romans as a most cruel form of suffering.

His bones are out of joint near His hands and feet.

The soldiers divide His garments and cast lots for His clothing.

Even one of the thieves next to Him mocks Him.

And yet, in the midst of this suffering, Jesus Himself feels the presence of His Father.

This experience will surely cause you to cry out, along with the centurion captain, *"Truly this was the Son of God!"* (Matthew 27:54).

And also a wonderful truth is revealed. Never once was the Father's face turned away from His Son, but instead, He remained connected in His love for Jesus (and I believe Jesus felt His love) even on the cross,

> *"For He (the Person of the Father in the Trinity) has not hidden His face from Him; but when He cried to Him for help, He heard"* (Psalm 22, selections).

And the last possible thought, from Psalm 22, as Jesus died in the presence of the Father and the Spirit.

> *"All the ends of the earth will remember and turn to the Lord, and all the families of the nations will worship before Thee."* (Psalm 22:27).

The circumstances that surrounded Jesus, as He became the sin-bearer, aligned themselves almost word-for-word with a scripture written more than 1,000 years before that moment.

This was the way that Father remained in love and connection with His Son upon the cross, even though God's wrath was being poured out upon the sinfulness of man in that paradoxical moment. God accepted the consequences for man's sin as He laid down His life in sacrifice.

Imagine that!

The Father never once left Jesus alone, but instead He showed Him, in bringing His mind a quickening memory of the passage of Psalm 22, that indeed the opposite was true in reality.

Do you see how Father spoke in these holy coincidences, through these outward circumstances, and through the very Word of God itself, to confirm His presence and love for Jesus even in His suffering on the cross?

Down to the very last detail of the moment.

All those actual people fulfilled that actual prophetic scripture, prophesied by King David some 1,000 years before the cross. Think of it.

Merely a coincidence? No. A Holy Coincidence? Yes.

Our Father Knows All About It

Now to church history to illustrate these divine appointments from the Father.

One of my favorite Revivalists of the 20th century was an Irishman named J. Edwin Orr. In the 1930s, the Father put a hunger for revival into this young man. With only a bicycle and a little money, but with a huge heart and massive faith in the provision of the Father, he set out upon a journey. His mission was to sow seeds of prayer for revival for all of the United Kingdom.

I would like to share a few words of testimony from Orr himself, and just one story of dozens that help illustrate the ways of God's leadings in the love of the Father through a Holy Coincidence.

"Retrospect should inspire confidence," writes Orr in his journal in 1933, "in the past the Lord helped us; the Lord will provide. To attest the Abounding Providence of God the Father, to affirm the Abiding Presence of our Lord Jesus, to advocate the Absolute Partnership of the Holy Spirit, as lasting joys.

Our beloved brother, Paul, once wrote, *"My God shall supply all your need."* Can God? Many folk think that money is the acid test. When I started out on my faith journey of 10,000 miles all over Britain, I had the equivalent of $10, yet the Lord has provided thousands of dollars; I had not the prospect of a single meal or a bed—I have not lacked either.

"Here is just once instance of countless to prove this:

"On the night of the 19th of March, we were approaching Edinburgh on our bicycles. I was traveling at the time with a brother, Stanley. We were singing the chorus as we rode, 'No, Never alone!' It was getting rather late, 10:30 p.m.

"Where are we going to sleep tonight?" Stanley asked suddenly.

"I'm sure I don't know," said I.

"What are we going to do about it?" he persisted.

"Why worry?" I replied. "Our Father knows all about it."

"Quite so! But I'd like to know too!"

"Very well. We'll ask Him then!"

So we free-wheeled, and prayed simply that the Father would provide us with bed and breakfast.

> Merely a coincidence? No. A Holy Coincidence.

"Now, Stanley," said I, "we have asked Him, and His word tells us that he hears us. Are you quite sure that you believe?"

"I do," said Stanley, "praise the Lord!"

"Well," said I, "it is rather late to expect hospitality, but I feel that Father will provide it. We'll visit a few certain acquaintances of mine at Merchiston Grove and see if the Father gives us an exceptional sign, and if so we'll know that we are not imposing in accepting hospitality."

"When we arrived at the house, we made a remarkable discovery.

"These friends, who had seen me only once before, had THAT DAY received from South America a letter inquiring for me. They decided to write to me at my Belfast address and the letter was lying on the table when I turned up at their front door. Delightful hospitality was offered and enjoyed."[50]

---

50 J. Edwin Orr, *Can God? 10,000 Miles of Miracles in Britain* (London: Marshall, Morgan, and Scott Publishers, 1937).

Do you see the wonderful faith, and this true Divine Appointment? That was an exceptional sign and a quiet indicator that the Father had gone ahead of them.

Orr spontaneously decides to visit someone he had only met once before, and that ON THAT VERY DAY, they had received correspondence about Orr that had taken months to arrive, and they were going to invite him to come, and their letter was lying on the table when he turned up at their front door.

Wow.

There is simply no explanation for that; a one-in-a-million Holy Coincidence that Father used to let Orr know, "My son, you are on the right track here; I will of course provide for your every need."

Let me close this chapter with one more example, this one from an experience Philip had in the Book of Acts.

Join This Chariot!

Sometimes God chooses to speak in multiple ways utilizing all three Persons of the Trinity. The reason for that is to provide us with confirmation that it is, indeed, Him that is speaking and leading. The Father, Son and Spirit are always fully unified with each other, too. Unity in Divine diversity!

Philip was one of the earliest missionaries, a young convert who showed great promise as one of the first seven who were commissioned by the original apostles to missions.

The young evangelist first travels down to Samaria and exercises a mighty evangelistic ministry. He combines powerful preaching with signs and wonders, and those signs were confirming the word preached with healings and deliverance.

This was a massive revival, and you might think that Father would want him to stay awhile in the midst of this success. But indeed, Father had gone ahead of Philip in his ministry, and saw the need for the gospel of His Son to reach Africa.

So as a good Father does, He secretly sets up the circumstances to match perfectly His plans.

In Acts chapter 8, Philip is suddenly directed by an angel to *"Arise and go south to the road that descends from Jerusalem to Gaza"* (literally, "this city is deserted.").

Philip might have thought to himself, *"Why do you want me to leave a real revival in the midst of its awesome power and go to a deserted road? Really, God?"*

So many times, the spontaneous flow of God's direction actually leads us in a direction that makes no sense to our natural thinking; and at the time, He doesn't allow us to ask, "Really, God?" but only to obey, in faith.

Here He is sending his revivalist from the midst of the revival to a deserted place where no one has ever heard of him.

Off he goes, and let's see how the fullness of the Trinity is in operation. Leaving aside the fact that God did (and still does, at times) use an actual angel to get Philip moving (we will study angels a bit more closely later in this book, as they are a means of the Father speaking), let's watch how the story unfolds.

> *"So he got up and went; and there was an Ethiopian eunuch, a court official of Candace, queen of the Ethiopians, who was in charge of all her treasure; and he had come to Jerusalem to worship, and he was returning and sitting in his chariot, and was reading the prophet Isaiah.*
>
> *"Then the Spirit said to Philip, 'Go up and join this chariot.'*
>
> *"Philip ran up and heard him reading Isaiah the prophet, and said, 'Do you understand what you are reading?' And he said, 'Well, how could I, unless someone guides me?' And he invited Philip to come up and sit with him. Now the passage of Scripture which he was reading was this:*
>
> *"'He was led as a sheep to slaughter; And as a lamb before its*

shearer is silent, So He does not open His mouth. In humiliation His judgment was taken away; who will relate His generation? For His life is removed from the earth.'

"The eunuch answered Philip and said, 'Please tell me, of whom does the prophet say this? Of himself or of someone else?'

"Then Philip opened his mouth, and beginning from this Scripture he preached Jesus to him. As they went along the road they came to some water; and the eunuch said,

"'Look! Water! What prevents me from being baptized?'

"And Philip said, 'If you believe with all your heart, you may.'

"And he answered and said, 'I believe that Jesus Christ is the Son of God.'

"And he ordered the chariot to stop; and they both went down into the water, Philip as well as the eunuch, and he baptized him. When they came up out of the water, the Spirit of the Lord snatched Philip away; and the eunuch no longer saw him, but went on his way rejoicing" (Acts 8:27-39).

So here we have all three members of the Trinity active in this leading of Philip and this most amazing incident of the first seed of the word being deposited for the continent of Africa through this man's conversion.

Here is the multi-faceted approach God takes with all 3 Persons of the Trinity:

1) **Father is present.** He alone timed the circumstances of Philip and the Ethiopian leader on that road. Had Philip arrived ten minutes late this exchange never would have happened! A Holy Coincidence.

   Father provided the timing of the eunuch reading that exact passage of Scripture at that exact moment of time. A Holy Coincidence.

Father also provided water in the desert. It was an oasis at the right place at the right time; so much so that the eunuch cries, "Look! Water!" Another Holy Coincidence.

2) **Jesus Christ is present in His Established Word, proclaimed from Isaiah.** In fact, that passage from Isaiah 53 was the perfect passage on which to start preaching Christ and Him crucified!

3) **And the Holy Spirit Himself spoke:** *"The Spirit said to Philip."* I used this same example earlier in the book as we looked at "The Inner Voice of the Holy Spirit."

Your Father is in the Details

Now to a true story of a kind of "Divine Appointment" not with a person, but with an object. God ordains circumstances ahead of time so that sometimes you "stumble upon" answers to your prayers in perfect timing.

One of our good friends, Sally, relates a recent story to help illustrate.

"My husband and I have been in a season of furnishing a new home. We have not only seen the Lord's provision of material things, but a demonstration of His love and interest in the smallest details of our life including interior design. We had multiple instances where we would identify something that we needed or wanted and then the Lord would provide it in a very cost effective way.

"One example is when we needed a fireplace tool set for our living room. The need was not only practical as it was a wood burning fireplace, but it also needed to be beautiful and large, as the fireplace was the focal point of a great room with 20 foot ceilings.

"We had started online at Home Depot and after extensive searches found one we both liked. It even came in two sizes. We knew we needed the larger one which was more than we planned to spend at $139.00. We agreed to both keep shopping to see if we could find one we liked just as much, for a cheaper price. A couple days later I was at a thrift store and there it was!

"The exact same set in the right size at $19.99.

"It looked like it had been used only a couple times. I knew a quick touch up was all it needed and I already had the right paint product. I couldn't help but think about how my Heavenly Father must have enjoyed seeing my shock and delight when I saw it, and knew that He put it there just for me."

So, always remember, divine appointment with people or objects equals divine love!

Your Father, who is a personal Father to you directly, went ahead of you to organize a special circumstance or arrange a meeting with someone special, just for you for that unique moment. Give Him praise today!

Very Common Ways

WAY		SCRIPTURE
1	The Established Word of Jesus	John 1:1
2	The Living Word of Jesus	Romans 10:17
3	The Inner Witness of the Holy Spirit	Acts 9:31
4	The Inner Voice of the Holy Spirit	Acts 8:29
5	The Desires of Your Heart	Psalm 37:4
6	Father Speaks Through All of Creation & Nature	Romans 1:19
7	Providential Outward Signs & Circumstances	Romans 8:28

Common Ways

8	The Preaching of the Word of Jesus	2 Thess. 2:13
9	Other Believers Speaking Confirmation	Matthew 18:16
10	Visions	Acts 2:17-21
11	Dreams	Acts 2:17-21
12	Symbolic Speech: Metaphors from the Holy Spirit	Numbers 12:8
13	Divine Appointments from the Father	Acts 8:27

Questions for Deeper Study:

1. Think about some "coincidences" in your own life. What made them extraordinary or special?

_____

_____

_____

_____

2. How does it feel knowing the Father has already visited your tomorrow and provided for you?

_____

_____

_____

_____

3. What can the truth of the Father going before you and never separating Himself from you do for your outlook on any potential suffering that may come into your life?

_____

_____

_____

_____

Keep listening!

NOTES:

_____

_____

_____

_____

CHAPTER

14

WAY #14: FATHER SPEAKS THROUGH ALL FORMS OF MEDIA & CULTURE

Every Man A Braveheart

"*You alone are the LORD, You have made the heavens, the heaven of heavens with all their host, the earth and all that is on it, the seas and all that is in them and the heavenly hosts bow down before you*" (Nehemiah 9:6).

This chapter follows our theme thus far of the Father and His unique, and virtually indirect, outward ways of leading.

He hides Himself cleverly everywhere, and loves it when you discover Him and sense His love for you as a result. In fact, He is hidden away in all man-made or woman-made media and cultural creations, all over the world. And He might just choose to speak or inspire you today through media that someone has created.

Father Speaks through All Forms of Media and Culture, a simple definition: His reaching outwardly in all areas of media and culture is an extension of His love and grace. This literally includes all modern mass-media within nine forms: books, blogs/blogging, the Internet, magazines, movies, newspapers, radio, music recordings, and television. Added to this are all advertising, like billboards for example, and all areas of a particular culture that are unique to that culture.

Why an extension of His love and grace? Because the Triune God is complete in Himself. He does not need to create or redeem, and never has, since before He even created the world or chose to redeem it through His Son. "Creation and redemption are acts of sheer grace, expressions of God as free eternal love."[51]

Can God, in His grace and love, speak through movies? How about music? How about advertising like billboards or television? The answer is a resounding, "YES!"

Think of a time in your not-too-distant-past when you really identified with a certain character in a TV show or movie. Or perhaps when you listened to the lyrics of a love song, or felt the presence of God reaching out to you during a worship song, or a thought from a book or magazine article really resounded with your heart. ALL of these are simple examples of your heavenly FATHER reaching out to you through the media of this world.

You might remember my usage of the film *"Inception"* in the earlier chapter, "Holy Spirit Inception," or even the scene from both the book and film of *"The Hobbit"* for my chapter, "Riddles in the Dark: Symbolic Speech & Metaphors." Both of these are examples of including the Father's Presence within those film examples, as He is the One who is reaching out through books and films and many other means.

---

51 Bruce Milne, *Know the Truth: A Handbook of Christian Belief* (Downers Grove, Illinois: InterVarsity Press, 1998).

Man Creates Media & Culture, God Speaks Through It

Now with mobile phones and small devices there is instant access to these forms of media 24/7.

It is information overload every day—but it need not be overwhelming if one is trained to pray through the information and be alerted by the Spirit when the Father is utilizing it to speak.

The design of media to the masses is to "reach to those far-removed in time and space from the producers."[52]

God, in one sense, has the same purpose as the producers of all media: to reach His people, far-removed in time and space from His eternal realm, with His leadings and voice.

He reaches into our temporal realm through media and His voice must be discerned, welcomed, and expected.

Now, in one sense, all of His creation is dependent on Him as He alone is the Source of all life.

At the same time, since media within creation is independent of Him (man's free will produces it), He does not necessarily become an advocate for media.

In fact, Satan is known as *"the prince of the power of the air"* (Ephesians 2:2), and that certainly extends to his control over the airwaves and media. He is actively inspiring spiritual darkness that meanders its way through much of the broadcast world. There is so much that is pure evil that is only one or two clicks away for the masses.

Much of our entertainment industry completely twists the nature and character of God.

Man seems to re-make God into his own image and worships this image apart from Him.

And yet, God seems to work through this media to reach out.

---

52 Quoted from sociologist John Thompson of Cambridge University, 2015.

Just because fallen man and a fallen angel twist the usage of media for their own evil devices, does not leave God out of the means of expression within it.

Oh the wisdom and knowledge of God! The verse quoted at the beginning of this chapter from Nehemiah states, *"You alone are the Lord, You have made the earth and all that is on it"* (Nehemiah 9:6).

Note the phrase *"all that is on it,"* which includes, of course, all media!

So why not actively seek the Lord as you consume media today?

Perhaps when you watch your next movie the Lord will apply that character or situation and speak right to you. The same can be true of anything around you in your culture. You just need eyes to see and ears to hear and be actively looking and listening.

And, it doesn't make any difference what the actual producer was intending for that media. Their history, their religious beliefs, and their personal agendas are all secondary to the intention of the Father, who can bypass all of that to speak directly to your mind and heart. Let me share just a few examples.

Every Man Dies. Not Every Man Really Lives.

I can still remember my first experience seeing the medieval epic war film, *"Braveheart."* It was 1995, and I was a 25-year-old evangelist starting out in full-time ministry to the nations. The uplifting and inspiring character from Scottish history, portrayed brilliantly by Mel Gibson, spoke volumes to me.

I can also remember the final scenes where the character of William Wallace is tied to a wooden cross and killed. I was weeping and I left the theater in tears, being greatly impacted by the story. It was, to me, almost like watching the sacrifice of Jesus at the crucifixion.

Wallace was, in one sense, a martyr and symbol of freedom for the people of Scotland, and indeed for all people of all times. His story, for me, mirrored the true story of Jesus Christ, who in a very real sense became the first martyr of the new faith. Jesus' life and death brought the gift of eternal freedom to all who have and will call upon Him, for He rose from the dead in victory.

Even though Wallace himself dies at the end, he showed by his courage and leadership that he had really lived out all his days. The people of Scotland, inspired by Wallace, fought and gained their freedom from tyranny.

I remember being so impacted by the film that I saw it dozens of times. My friends began to call me Braveheart as I identified with the character and even learned the freedom speech that Wallace used to inspire the Scots warriors to fight the enemy.

To this day, I am still inspired by the film, and I know it is the Father who is behind the scenes, inspiring me to greater courage and action in serving His Kingdom. All who aspire to preach the gospel can learn a thing or two from someone like William Wallace. In the film he says, "Every man dies. Not every man really lives."

You see, it might have never been the intention for the writer of that script to influence actual gospel ministry through a piece of entertainment.

Maybe the intention was purely to make money. Maybe the intention was just to put Scotland on a pedestal or make heroes out of common men. There are plenty of historical inaccuracies in the film.

But for me, none of these things matter. I know that my Father is reaching out to me to speak encouragement to me through the film and the character of William Wallace. Every man can be a Braveheart and fight for freedom in their own right.

Sometimes a Song is Worth a Thousand Words

I mentioned in my Introduction that I have been going through a particular trial for the past several years. One day, in the midst of that trial, I got a very high fever and was actually hospitalized with continual observation. At one point I began to get the chills and shake uncontrollably. I could not stop the shaking no matter what I tried. My fever was rising and soon peaked at 104 degrees.

In the middle of the shaking, I remembered I had my mobile phone that had access to a music station with my favorite worship music. I turned to this form of media to try and get my mind off of the shaking and the fever.

A song came on, and the lyrics of the song seemed to leap out of my phone's tiny speaker and penetrate my heart. It was sung by a worship leader named Jeremy Camp. Here are the words from that moment.

> *"I know the journey seems so long*
> *You feel you're walking on your own*
> *But there has never been a step*
> *Where you've walked out all alone*

> *"Troubled soul don't lose your heart*
> *Cause joy and peace he brings*
> *And the beauty that's in store*
> *Outweighs the hurt of life's sting*

> *"But I hold on to this hope and the promise that He brings*
> *That there will be a place with no more suffering."*[53]

As I heard those lyrics, especially that I was not alone in the circumstance in that hospital bed, I felt the love of the Father reaching out to me personally.

I realized I was not alone! And that I would make it through this day and through this trial! Father was with me! Jesus was there. The Holy Spirit helped me that day.

I began to cry. Tears of joy streamed down my face.

The nurse on duty saw me crying, and misunderstood my moment of experiencing not sorrow, but joy in the presence of God. She came in and offered to give me more drugs. I replied, "No thank you. I don't need any more drugs right now. I am experiencing my Heavenly Father's deep love for me. I sense His presence through this song and know that He loves me."

---

53 Song by Jeremy Camp from his album: *Speaking Louder Than Before*, 2008.

Then the nurse, herself sensing the presence of God, also began to cry, and she left the room as I put my hands up in surrender and worship to your Heavenly Father.

So, He uses all things. All forms of media are at His disposal to reach out and speak to you. You just need to activate your faith and expectation that He can and will speak. All mass media, all elements surrounding you in your culture, are at His disposal.

This wraps up our final "Common Way" of the Lord speaking through His presence in the Trinity.

Very Common Ways

	WAY	SCRIPTURE
1	The Established Word of Jesus	*John 1:1*
2	The Living Word of Jesus	*Romans 10:17*
3	The Inner Witness of the Holy Spirit	*Acts 9:31*
4	The Inner Voice of the Holy Spirit	*Acts 8:29*
5	The Desires of Your Heart	*Psalm 37:4*
6	Father Speaks Through All of Creation & Nature	*Romans 1:19*
7	Providential Outward Signs & Circumstances	*Romans 8:28*

Common Ways

8	The Preaching of the Word of Jesus	*2 Thess. 2:13*
9	Other Believers Speaking Confirmation	*Matthew 18:16*
10	Visions	*Acts 2:17-21*
11	Dreams	*Acts 2:17-21*
12	Symbolic Speech: Metaphors from the Holy Spirit	*Numbers 12:8*
13	Divine Appointments from the Father	*Acts 8:27*
14	Father Speaks Through All Forms of Media & Culture	*Nehemiah 9:6*

QUESTIONS FOR DEEPER STUDY:

1. How can you use your unique perspective to communicate your faith to your circle of friends, family and culture?

_____

_____

_____

_____

2. How does hearing about God the Father being active in the past give you hope that He is active now, even when you cannot sense it?

_____

_____

_____

_____

3. How does knowing the LORD will speak to you through media change the way you listen for His voice?

_____

_____

_____

_____

Keep listening!

SECTION III

7

UNCOMMON

WAYS THE LORD SPEAKS

CHAPTER

15

WAY #15: THE REVELATORY GIFTS: THE GIFT OF PROPHECY

Fighting Well in the Lord's Battles

"**N**ow there are varieties of gifts, but the same Spirit. And there are varieties of ministries, but the same Lord. And there are varieties of effects, but the same God who works all things in all persons. But to each one is given the manifestation of the Spirit for the common good. For to one is given—prophecy" (I Corinthians 12:4-7, 10).

We begin this section with four very special chapters, each one a description of a unique gift that relates directly to the theme of communication with the Father through the Son and the Spirit.

The apostle Paul gives us this unique list of nine "gifts of the Spirit" in I Corinthians 12, and four of them relate in special ways to the voice of God. You will be happy to know that each of these four gifts have been in operation since the early days of the world, and will continue in operation until the coming "last day on earth" as Jesus Christ returns in both salvation and judgment.

These four chapters will be new to some of you, in particular if you have been raised in more of an evangelical background as I was. Our particular Evangelical Lutheran church simply neglected the spiritual gifts as a topic of study or experience.

I place four of them in this section on uncommon ways of God speaking only because they are simply not commonly taught in many churches today. They are in operation every day, everywhere. It's just that we need to be both taught more and practice their use more to appreciate the value that Jesus places upon them in leading and directing His Body. Faith will lead to action, and the action of these gifts leads to us to the Father's love and the edifying of the Body of Christ.

There are a total of nine gifts listed if you read the whole passage of I Corinthians 12:1-11. The four gifts that are linked to God's communication with us are: prophecy, the word of wisdom, the word of knowledge, and the discerning of spirits.

They are known as revelatory gifts as a category because they allow the believer to see, to understand, and to know a portion of the Lord's heart and heaven's perspective and purpose for an individual's journey.

Thus, the next four chapters will highlight each of these four revelatory gifts. They are all inspired by the Holy Spirit to reveal to us information from the Spirit to help us in the natural.

<hr />

We're starting with a look at the gift of prophecy.

The Inspired Gift of Prophecy, a simple definition: "It is an inspirational gift, and is speaking to another as the Spirit gives utterance. It is an inspired utterance, often with a beauty of expression. It is also a gift which Paul encourages us to, 'earnestly seek' for the edification of believers."[54]

---

54 Howard Carter, *Questions and Answers on Spiritual Gifts* (Tulsa, OK: Harrison House Publishers, 1976).

This gift was widely utilized in both the Testaments. In the Old Testament, one only has to consider the books of Isaiah, Jeremiah, Ezekiel and so many others. In the New Testament, you can see this inspirational gift from the Spirit being used to bring the word of Jesus to many people.

As a "good Lutheran boy," I simply had no idea that the gift of prophecy even existed. I attended church services with my parents for 18 years and I was never exposed to prophecy or taught it. If you would have told me that one of the gifts of Jesus to His Church was prophecy, I would have told you to check yourself into an insane asylum.

Yet this gift, though overlooked and undervalued by some groups, carries with it something wonderful. It combines the Person of Jesus and the Person of the Holy Spirit. Paul teaches that the gifts of the Spirit are part of the down payment of our inheritance; we will someday receive the full measure, but for now, we can "earnestly desire" spiritual gifts for the betterment of others.

As we saw from Paul's letter to Corinth, we are part of the Body of Christ (His mystical Body on earth, made up of every Christian and each member having a function). So Jesus in me can speak to you, by the operation of the gift of prophecy, and Jesus in you can speak to me by that same Spirit and gift.

I love the prophecy of Simeon found in Luke's gospel as a confirmation of the calling and destiny of Jesus Christ. *"Simeon came in the Spirit into the temple, and when the parents brought in the child Jesus, then he took Him into his arms, and blessed God, and said, 'Now Lord, you can let your bondservant depart in peace, according to your word, for my eyes have seen Your salvation'"* (Luke 2:27a, 28-30). Simeon prophetically witnessed and confirmed that the child Jesus was indeed the light of the whole world to both Jews and Gentiles.

Let me share a few personal examples of how I stumbled onto the amazing confirming power of this gift, and how every time I have received from it, it causes me to worship the Father deeper and also reach out to others to encourage them.

I Have Marked You

During my early time in Los Angeles as I was pursuing the film industry (and was a brand-new Christian), I had an amazing encounter with someone who moved powerfully in this gift. She was a guest speaker invited to our church for a special Sunday night service.

During her ministry time, she walked right over to me and laid her hands on my head. I felt something like anointing oil being poured over my red-haired head. She began praying for me, and her prayer turned into, *"The Lord says, 'My son, I have marked you, and you will never be the same again. That longing and hunger you have found for Me will never be satisfied in the old life. You must go on.'"*

I remember writing down those words. I was shaking because God's power was so real. She moved on to other people in the congregation and told them things that were impossible for her to know about them except that God Himself was speaking to her and through her.

I wrote down the words "I have marked you," and researched that in Scripture. A blessing indeed, as to be marked is to be branded with a new name. The picture is like a hot iron branding a sheep with the owner's marking.

I had been struggling then with the idea of turning back to my old Lutheran ways, and this word came as a wake-up call that I needed to abandon all of my old religious ways and seek God in fresh ways. I am not saying that everybody in the Lutheran church is religious, but I sure was.

Fast forward nine months later. I arrived in Israel for a ten-day tour. The tour was made up of about 25 Christians from all over America who had never met one another. We were traveling to Jerusalem to be present during the historic Feast of Tabernacles.

My first night I tried to go to sleep, but my roommate, a gentle, giant man who hailed from New York, was an intense snorer, and I simply couldn't fall asleep!

So I meandered down to the lobby of the hotel and sat down in one of the over-stuffed chairs. A man came and sat down next to me. He had recognized me from dinner and was from Canada and on a different tour.

He introduced himself to me and asked me if I would like to pray with him. "Sure" I said.

We closed our eyes, clasped hands, and began to pray. Suddenly he stopped, put his hand on my shoulder, and said, *"The Lord says, 'My son, I have marked you, and you will never be the same again. That longing and hunger you have found for Me will never be satisfied in the old life. You must go on.'"*

You can't write this stuff!

For real?

Yes, for real. The Lord spoke through another common servant of His, some 5,000 miles away, in completely different circumstances, the same word!

And the word of prophecy had shaken my world.

Gifts That Keep On Giving

Many people don't realize that in fact, seven of the nine gifts in the list found in I Corinthians 12:8-11 were all in operation, by the same Holy Spirit, in all of the Old Testament. They were never meant to die out with the original apostles as some churches teach today. As Paul wrote in the first chapter of this letter,

> *"So that you are not lacking in any GIFT awaiting eagerly the revelation of our Lord Jesus Christ, who shall also confirm you to the end, blameless in the day of our Lord Jesus Christ"* (I Corinthians 1:7-8).

In other words, the gifts, such as prophecy, are available and meant to be in full usage in the Kingdom during this present dispensation, while we await the second coming of Christ. After Jesus returns, it will no longer be necessary to operate in these gifts, as He will bring with Him the fullness of the Kingdom of God for all eternity.

Until then, the gifts are here and we are called upon to utilize them, for both the tearing down of the kingdom of darkness (dismantling Satan's workings), and the edifying and building up and encouraging and comforting of believers.

This includes the gift of prophecy, and this particular gift is awesome because it is Jesus Himself, the living Word and the eternal One, whose very nature is inhabiting the person flowing in the gift, and by the mechanism of the gift, is making Himself real to both the one speaking and the one receiving. Awesome.

> "For the testimony of Jesus is the spirit of prophecy"
> (Revelation 19:10b).

The New Testament understanding of prophecy usually refers to two things: foretelling and forthtelling. First, a foretelling of future events (as when Agabus, a disciple-turned-prophet in the Book of Acts, warned Paul that if he visited Jerusalem he would be bound in chains; see Acts 21:11).

Second, it can mean anointed utterances that are inspiration from the Holy Spirit and revelatory to people. This would be, forthtelling.

The gift of prophecy is a valid way of Jesus speaking (through others or through you) and the Holy Spirit, too. They both originate from the Father so you can receive His love! Love Speaks!

Both foretelling and forthtelling are wonderful uses of this gift, when kept in balance, and with proper order and confirmation from the Holy Spirit.

Paul writes of prophecy and its power to bless others in I Corinthians. *"Pursue love, yet desire earnestly spiritual gifts, especially that you may prophesy. The one who prophesies speaks to men for edification, and exhortation, and consolation"* (I Corinthians 14:1, 3).

So the parameters around this particular gift is that it will edify, exhort, and comfort people. Again, this is the forthtelling element of the gift.

The blessing of this gift within the parameters of Paul is that you *"seek to abound for the edification of the church"* (I Corinthians 14:12).

There are multiple means of flowing in this gift: for example, through song! Praise and worship can often lead to prophetic singing, like the ancient "song of Moses" that Miriam sang after the deliverance by the Red Sea (see Exodus chapter 15). I have visited many churches where the worship leader or one of the singers moves out in faith, and there comes forth a beautiful prophetic song of the Lord. Also, remember that in prayer and intercession for others, often you can begin to flow naturally into this gift. Be bold in your prayers of edification, exhortation, and comfort over people. Proclaim the good word of the Lord over them!

The Most Common Pitfall of Prophecy

I know that for many years, on the other side of the religious spectrum, people in many settings have been exposed to a kind of mistreatment or even abuse of this gift. This happens when people step outside of Paul's three parameters or boundaries of the gift. That doesn't nullify its authentic place in the Body of Christ worldwide. We need more of the genuine expressions of this gift!

The Lord, by His very nature as our Father, is an encourager. He also is our corrector and sends us nudges by the Holy Spirit and sometimes circumstances that make us aware of our behavior that may need to change.

Repentance is a common and often daily feature of the Kingdom of God, especially as you grow in maturity. The closer you get to the Lord, the more often He allows you to be aware of certain areas where you need to change.

The problem arises when we, as people, seek to utilize the gift of prophecy to point out areas in other people that they need to change.

In some circles I have heard it said, "God has not called you to be a Corrector of the Brethren." This is absolutely true. God Himself is the only one to whom you and I are accountable to on Judgment Day.

Now I am not speaking here in the context of relationships where areas of character are brought up between two people, or in a group context, and behavior is potentially harmful to others.

What I am mentioning here is just a reinforcing of the parameters that surround this gift. It is utilized for three areas, and three only as a boundary: edification, exhortation, or comfort.

This means that you are never called to begin a "Thus Says the Lord" and then have it contain something negative about a person, or point out some areas that they need to fix or change in order for God to be more fully pleased with them.

So God will never give you a word for someone that echoes something like, "Job, this is all your fault, and the boils upon your skin are judgments from God to teach you a lesson," as Job's friends did!

> The testimony
> of Jesus is
> the spirit of
> prophecy.

When this gift enters this pitfall, I have seen it split marriages, split friendships, home groups, and sometimes even a whole church, when "one side" seems to have the word of the Lord about what the "other side" is doing wrong.

Quite simply, if you think you are sensing something negative, shut up. Don't speak it. Just like you would want the courtesy if someone else was about to open up their mouth and quote scripture or say something to you that was negative. Perhaps you are wrong in what you are sensing. Or perhaps you are called simply to pray in private for that situation to change.

The Holy Spirit is holy. On the receiving end, He will never operate this gift to bring embarrassment to you or cut you down in any way, and He expects you to always follow His protocol for the gift of prophecy: edify others, exhort others with Godly exhortation, and comfort others in their times of sorrow or trial.

If you have ever received a negative word from someone, first off please forgive them. Secondly, pray about it, too. If you need to change, take it up in repentance with the Father in Jesus' name and make better choices in the future. If they need to change, pray a blessing over them and leave it with God.

Wage a Good Warfare with Your Prophecies

Now for a positive spin on the gift. Just by way of personal application of this particular chapter, Paul shared with Timothy something very key.

> "Timothy, my son, here are my instructions for you, based on the prophetic words spoken about you earlier. May they help you fight well in the Lord's battles" (I Timothy 1:18, New Living Translation).

I love this very practical advice. Paul was kind of telling Timothy, "Align yourself with the truths of the prophetic words that God has spoken over you. God believes in you. I do too. Wage a good warfare by speaking forth and believing and trusting in the prophecies spoken over your life."

You see, there is power in agreement. There is power released in the Spirit realm when you stand forth and boldly speak out the prophetic words that have been spoken over you.

Many times in my life, I feel discouragement.

That's when I bring forth the decree of the Lord's word that He has spoken over me. In fact, in my study I keep a stack of some of the prophecies I have personally received and I have them ready.

Whenever I need personal encouragement, I pick up one or two and I DECREE them, out loud, as if they are fact in my life, even if my current circumstances are not lining up with what they say. If these prophecies are edifying, encouraging, or comforting, then they will help me fight well in the Lord's battles.

Try it!

Prophecy is one of those gifts that keep on giving.

Try praying this: "Thank you, Lord, for using me to prophesy to others. Thank you, Lord, for using others to prophesy to me. Amen."

Very Common Ways

WAY		SCRIPTURE
1	The Established Word of Jesus	John 1:1
2	The Living Word of Jesus	Romans 10:17
3	The Inner Witness of the Holy Spirit	Acts 9:31
4	The Inner Voice of the Holy Spirit	Acts 8:29
5	The Desires of Your Heart	Psalm 37:4
6	Father Speaks Through All of Creation & Nature	Romans 1:19
7	Providential Outward Signs & Circumstances	Romans 8:28

Common Ways

8	The Preaching of the Word of Jesus	2 Thess. 2:13
9	Other Believers Speaking Confirmation	Matthew 18:16
10	Visions	Acts 2:17-21
11	Dreams	Acts 2:17-21
12	Symbolic Speech: Metaphors from the Holy Spirit	Numbers 12:8
13	Divine Appointments from the Father	Acts 8:27
14	Father Speaks Through All Forms of Media & Culture	Nehemiah 9:6

Uncommon Ways

15	The Revelatory Gifts: The Gift of Prophecy	1 Cor. 14:1

Questions for Deeper Study:

1. Why is it important to seek the LORD for yourself rather than seek a "word" from a prophet?

_____

_____

_____

2. Why do you think at times God communicates His desire for your life and then waits to see how you will respond?

_____

_____

3. Why is it important to look for the confirmation of a prophetic word and to make sure it aligns with Scripture?

_____

_____

_____

4. Write out one of the prophecies you have received and decree it out loud every day this week!

_____

_____

_____

Keep listening!

NOTES:

_____

_____

_____

_____

WAY #16: THE REVELATORY GIFTS: THE WORD OF WISDOM

Blueprints from Heaven

"**B**ut to each one is given the manifestation of the Spirit for the common good. For to one is given the word of wisdom through the Spirit" (I Corinthians 12:7, 8).

Continuing now on the journey of discovery, Paul leads us to yet another dimension of the unique gifts that Jesus has blessed His church with in the New Testament. These gifts are available to everybody in the Kingdom! And these gifts keep on giving. Century after century now, some 20 centuries later, they are still blessing people.

The next of these is called the revelatory gift of the word of wisdom.

I love that word, *revelatory*. I think it's a great way to look at the life of the Holy Spirit and the adventure of discovery of all of the Trinity's ways of communicating to you. Each and every day, as you seek the Lord, you can begin to expect that He will reveal Himself to you. By faith, you can begin to better recognize the beauty of these revelatory gifts and in fact develop a revelatory lifestyle.

As you might discover in these chapters, the gifts of the Holy Spirit by themselves are multi-faceted, and often work in tandem with each other.

> **The Word of Wisdom, a simple definition:** "A supernatural revelation of the mind and purpose of God communicated by the Holy Spirit. When the Lord specifically reveals His purpose to an individual, that person receives it through a word of God's wisdom. It is His wisdom flowing to you."[55]

"In Old Testament Scripture, the whole law and precepts, as well as the detailed structure of the Tabernacle, were given to Moses in Mount Sinai by means of this gift.

"The whole range of Messianic prediction, and predictions concerning nations, cities, and individuals came to the prophets by the word of wisdom.

"In New Testament Scripture, the glorious new covenant truth with the order and rules of the church of Jesus Christ, as well as the predictions of Agabus (in the Book of Acts) and the Revelation of John on the Isle of Patmos, came through this gift.

"This gift is the basis of all heavenly leadings. Through it Adam knew the extent of his privileges and the consequences of his disobedience; Noah learned of the coming world judgment; Abraham of a promised land; Joseph of the coming devastating famine to Egypt; and so many more like Moses, Joshua, and Jeremiah.

"The word of wisdom transports one to the very council chamber of the Almighty."[56]

---

55 Howard Carter, *Questions and Answers on Spiritual Gifts* (Tulsa, OK: Harrison House Publishers, 1976). I am indebted to this Pentecostal pioneer, Howard Carter, for insights about these gifts. His book is the clearest explanation I have found, and extremely practical.
56 Ibid., pp. 13, 23.

The Blueprint of Future Plans

Consider this beautiful passage from Exodus of the Lord speaking to Moses.

> *"Tell the sons of Israel to raise a contribution for Me; from every man whose heart moves him you shall raise My contribution. And let them construct a sanctuary for Me, that I my dwell among them, according to all that I am going to show you, as the pattern of the tabernacle and the pattern of all its furniture, just so you shall construct it"* (Exodus 25:2, 8-9).

Notice those words, "according to...the pattern." THAT is the wonderful Word of Wisdom gift. The word of wisdom is like the blueprint, or pattern, of answered prayer that lies ahead of you. In the case of Moses, what follows in Exodus is a complete and direct word from God, as the Holy Spirit operates the word of wisdom, with the blueprint for the tabernacle that was built.

The word of wisdom comes into practice often when you are in prayer for your future plans. As you consider all your options, and you are honestly seeking the Lord for His best for you, you will find the wonder of this gift. It will help you put together a "pattern" that is like a heavenly plan, filled with God's wisdom, and fitted just for you.

I look at the word of wisdom like the piece of the puzzle that is the linking piece.

Sometimes in life, as you are seeking God's will, it's like you are putting together pieces in a puzzle. In front of you is the picture, and the detail, of the portion of the puzzle you are fitting together. But perhaps you are lacking a key piece. And then, suddenly, you have eyes to see that one key piece. The moment you fit it in place, it unlocks five or ten more pieces instantly, and together the part of the picture you are working on is complete and perfect.

The word of wisdom is that key piece that unlocks a number of others and helps you move forward into your destiny and fulfilling God's will for your life by His direction.

Exciting, yes?

In fact, some scholars believe that because Paul lists this gift first, it is the foremost of the nine gifts; that is, it outshines the other gifts in splendor. If you thus approach the full list of gifts in this manner, you'll find prophecy and even the gift of tongues more toward the bottom of the list, yet most Pentecostal churches today focus nearly all of their teaching and practice on these two "lower" gifts and nearly none on the word of wisdom. Time to start operating in the greater gifts like this one.

> A word of wisdom is like the blueprint of a future answered prayer.

You can apply your faith today and ask the Holy Spirit to impart the operation of this heavenly wisdom to your situation.

Why wait?

The actual operation of the gift will vary from circumstance to circumstance. In fact, the Holy Spirit will bring newness and freshness each time this gift is in operation. Sometimes the "blueprint" will come to you in pieces, through various means and interpretations, and sometimes it will come all at once. In either case, you will "know that you know that you know" that God Himself is imparting His wisdom to you.

"This gift is PRACTICAL," writes Dr. Lance Wonders, one of my colleagues in ministry, "and it shows HOW TO GO FORWARD with God's purposes, not so much telling us what those purposes are."

"The Most Startling of Guidance"

Let me turn to an example from Loren Cunningham, founder of one of the world's best known missionary organizations, Youth With A Mission. YWAM, as it is known, began through a vision that God gave Loren while he was in prayer many decades ago. It has grown to a staggering world-wide impact and is still on the cutting edge of modern missionary endeavors.

His book, *Is That Really You, God?* has become a classic on the subject of hearing God's voice. Loren tells many compelling stories of both success and failure in the process of listening, obedience and guidance. Here is an excerpt from a pivotal time in Loren's ministry where God gave a word of wisdom to impart a blueprint. This blueprint brought much fruitfulness to the ministry of YWAM. Loren himself calls this, "the most startling of guidance stories to date" in his book.

The "startling guidance" happened in this way: Loren and his wife, Dar, had just settled into the creation of a small school and training base to help prepare young missionaries for the call of short-term missions in Hawaii. They had fulfilled some amazing vision up until this point, but were waiting upon the Lord for guidance as to what His plans were for their future.

"The breakthrough started one amazing night. I had decided to stay up all night and pray, asking three of the school staff to join me. The four of us walked to a small, wooden annex about 10:00 p.m., turned on the light and went in. We knelt down on the rough floor beside some folding chairs. We followed 3 steps in hearing God which I had first learned from Joy Dawson in New Zealand.

"First, we took Christ's authority to silence the enemy.

"Second, we asked the Lord to clear from our minds any presumptions and preconceived ideas.

"Third, we waited—believing He would speak in the way and in the time which He chose.

"All night long we waited and listened to God. In essence, God spoke in several ways: through His word, through visions, and through impressions. Here is some of what came forth from the Spirit.

— The word *Kona*. Kona was a place on the Big Island, but I, Loren, had never been there

— The idea of founding a University.

— A white ship anchored in a bay."[57]

---

57 Loren Cunningham, Ibid., *Is That Really You, God?*

So the four of them received this "guidance" from their all-night prayer, and then, later that morning, Loren went in to a classroom of 92 students and asked them all to wait upon God in silence. He was praying for confirmation to some of these words.

"Here is what the students, led by the Holy Spirit, saw.

— The letter K and then the word, KONA.

— A picture of a "big place," like a University.

— A picture of a white ship anchored in a bay."[58]

I know what you might be thinking. "You can't write this stuff!" I know. It sounds almost too amazing to be true, but it is true. Apart from some other details, all of this actually came from God as confirmation and happened exactly as it is written.

What's the end of this story? These words and guidance came forward as a kind of blueprint for the future days of Loren's ministry and the destiny of YWAM.

In the coming years, they moved to Kona, founded a University that is still impacting thousands of youth in over 100 nations, and they obtained a white ship called the *Anastasis*. Upon this actual ship, my wife Sarah Elizabeth originally received her training, through YWAM, for missions when she was only 19 years old.

And it all began in that all-night prayer meeting and morning "waiting upon the Lord" session as a word of wisdom from the Holy Spirit!

Loren concludes these remarkable stories with a good admonition to always keep our focus on the glory of God, and not on the seeking of the guidance itself,

"We have to be especially watchful when He is leading us toward tools, such as a ship or a university. There is nothing wrong with tools. But it's a sad day if the tools ever supersede the Lord Himself.

---

58 Loren Cunningham, Ibid., *Is That Really You, God?*

"Guidance is first of all a relationship with the Guide," writes Loren. "The first goal of guidance is to lead us into a closer relationship with Jesus. All other goals should be subservient to that."[59]

So, begin to believe that when you are sincere in seeking the Lord about guidance, you can see the guidance arrive through the remarkable gift of the word of wisdom. It may take different forms as we have seen, but the amazing power of God's wisdom is inexhaustible in His eternal resources and is available to you right now.

In the next chapter we'll look at how another remarkable gift, the word of knowledge, works in tandem with the word of wisdom and other gifts. And in the Fourth Section of this book, I will return to some of Loren's practical teaching on guidance to help you put into practice the art of listening to God and receiving words of wisdom.

For now, begin to pray, *"Lord, show me Your patterns and blueprints to my life! Guide me, O Lord, for your glory!"*

---

59 Loren Cunningham, Ibid.

Very Common Ways

WAY		SCRIPTURE
1	The Established Word of Jesus	John 1:1
2	The Living Word of Jesus	Romans 10:17
3	The Inner Witness of the Holy Spirit	Acts 9:31
4	The Inner Voice of the Holy Spirit	Acts 8:29
5	The Desires of Your Heart	Psalm 37:4
6	Father Speaks Through All of Creation & Nature	Romans 1:19
7	Providential Outward Signs & Circumstances	Romans 8:28

Common Ways

8	The Preaching of the Word of Jesus	2 Thess. 2:13
9	Other Believers Speaking Confirmation	Matthew 18:16
10	Visions	Acts 2:17-21
11	Dreams	Acts 2:17-21
12	Symbolic Speech: Metaphors from the Holy Spirit	Numbers 12:8
13	Divine Appointments from the Father	Acts 8:27
14	Father Speaks Through All Forms of Media & Culture	Nehemiah 9:6

Uncommon Ways

15	The Revelatory Gifts: The Gift of Prophecy	1 Cor. 14:1
16	The Revelatory Gifts: The Word of Wisdom	1 Cor. 12:4-11

Questions for Deeper Study:

1. Read the "blueprints" in Genesis 6 and Exodus 26. What does the detail of these passages tell you about the mind or purposes of God?

    _____

    _____

    _____

    _____

2. Describe a time when you needed a Word of Wisdom and received one (if you haven't, are you willing to begin to pray and ask for one?):

    _____

    _____

    _____

3. List some isolated words or ways in which the multi-faceted voice of God has been speaking to you.

    Ask the Lord to help you put them together for fresh direction.

    _____

    _____

    _____

    _____

Keep listening!

NOTES:

_____

_____

_____

_____

WAY #17: THE REVELATORY GIFTS: THE WORD OF KNOWLEDGE

Puzzle Pieces That Fit Together

"But to each one is given the manifestation of the Spirit for the common good. For to...another is given the word of knowledge by the same Spirit" (I Corinthians 12:7, 8).

And now to another remarkable gift, very widely found throughout the world, but not very often utilized to its full extent. Here is a definition and some explanation, again from Howard Carter, in his wonderful presentation of questions and answers on spiritual gifts.

> **The Word of Knowledge, a definition:** "A supernatural revelation of the existence, or nature, of a person or a thing; or the knowledge of some event, given to us by the Holy Spirit for a specific purpose.

"It is a participation, to some infinitesimal degree, in the omniscience of God. If the Lord who knows all things, is pleased to reveal to us by His Spirit any fragment of His unlimited knowledge, then we can claim to have this manifestation of the Spirit designated, "the word of knowledge."

Examples in Scripture

"In Old Testament Scripture, you might remember Elijah, hiding in the cave and thinking that he alone was left among the people of God who had not bowed their knee to Baal. But God gave the prophet some interesting statistics, of which Elijah was evidently ignorant. The Lord said that He had still 7,000. This was the operation of the word of knowledge (1 Kings 19:7).

> We have received the Spirit of God that we may know the things freely given to us by God.

"In the life of Jesus in the New Testament, you'll remember the woman at the well. When the woman requested that she might receive the living water, the Lord told her to call her husband, to which she replied, "I have no husband." Then was manifested the word of knowledge, for the Lord Jesus said, *"You have well said, 'I have no husband' for you have had five husbands, and he whom you now have is not your husband; so you spoke truly"* (John 4:18).

"The revelations received might be small or they may be vast; yet, whether little or great, they are equally divine in origin. When the Spirit shares in His omniscience, He allows the believer to partake of this enlightenment that will equip him for service, or direct him in his travels, and generally to glorify the One who has filled him with His Spirit."[60]

Here is an excellent scripture to remember when considering this gift.

> *"For to us God revealed these things through the Spirit; for the Spirit searches all things, even the depths of God. For who among men knows the thoughts of a man except the spirit of the man, which is in him? Even so the thoughts of God no one knows except the Spirit of God. Now we have received, not the spirit of the world, but the Spirit who is from God, that we might know the things freely given to us by God"* (I Corinthians 2:10-12).

---

60 Howard Carter, Ibid., pp. 29, 37.

A Word of Knowledge is a Word of Divine Love

This is wonderful revelation, and by the operation of the gift of the word of knowledge, you and I can both give and receive words that are the thoughts of God. These thoughts are always positive. These thoughts are always life-giving. These thoughts are always full of Divine love.

"When God gives a word of knowledge," writes Steve Sampson, "it is always creative. The knowledge is from the mind of God; it is something He intends to do. His word always has creative power accompanying it. Whatever the word is, it already exists in His mind. This is exciting because whenever we hear the Lord speak to us in this way, His creative power is released. Our only role is to agree with Him."[61]

Isn't this exciting? Words of knowledge are powerful. My first time I ever witnessed this gift was an evening at John Wimber's original Vineyard Church in Anaheim, California. Wimber was a pioneer in introducing *naturally supernatural* ministry of the Spirit, and his primary message was that the Kingdom of God that Jesus introduced is very much an ongoing force in this world. The Kingdom is here, and the ministry of Jesus in healing the sick, delivering from occult powers, miracles, signs and wonders are continuing to this day. These signs include the gifts of the Spirit.

I was invited into Wimber's church one night and what I experienced rocked my world. There were two men ministering that evening. They were flowing in the prophetic gifts and they were calling people out of the audience and sharing "words of knowledge" about their lives. These words were very accurate and only things that God Himself knew about these people.

As I grew in my own understanding of the Spirit and began to mature in His gifts, I recognized that as I was praying for something, I, too, could receive words that were the actual knowledge of God. They could help me in my discernment as to certain courses of action that I was to take, or they could be amazing words of confirmation, that as I took certain courses of action, I was on the right path.

---

61 Steve Sampson, Ibid., p. 45.

You might recall from my previous chapter's teaching that the Word of Wisdom is like a heavenly blueprint or a key puzzle piece that helps fit together a number of other pieces. The Word of Knowledge is like the specific portions of that same blueprint that are fit together towards a common vision, or like the individual pieces of the puzzle that the Word of Wisdom helps assemble.

Moving to Avalon

Some years ago, my wife and I were praying together about the possibility of moving house. We lived in our first home together for about five years. As our family was expanding and we brought two sons and a daughter into this world, the neighborhood in which we lived was also growing and the automobile traffic was increasing. It was just too busy and noisy for us, and we wanted to move to a place that would give us some privacy and peace and quiet.

As we prayed, we both felt a green light (the inner witness of the Spirit) in our decision to sell our home and buy something else.

But where to move to? And what kind of home do we look for?

These are very common questions, and I am sharing this example of the word of knowledge in operation with you as you yourself might be facing similar life changes that require discernment like this. We obviously wanted to be led by the Holy Spirit in our move.

Through about a month of praise, worship, prayer, and waiting upon God, I received some words of knowledge that came in the form of scriptures, visions/pictures, and actual words. For example, I saw the following:

— A picture of a small wooden man-made bird's nest, near water.

— A scripture from the prophet Joel: *"And it will come about in that day, that all the hills will flow with milk, and all the brooks of Judah will flow with water; and a spring will go out from the house of the Lord, to water the valley"* (Joel 3:18).

— A picture of prayer and intercession that came as an old metal saw that lumberjacks used to cut down trees in the pioneer days in Minnesota where we live; the motion of the saw and the cutting of the lumber represented the action of prayer and faith.

We hired a real estate agent and began looking. Note: sometimes in the action of faith you need to be on the move. It has been often said that God can't direct a parked car; you have to be off in motion for the direction to happen.

We must have looked at 30 houses within a range of 30 miles. Both Sarah and I felt that our new home would be somewhere outside the city of Minneapolis, in the west, maybe on the edge of the suburbs. Close enough to be a 40-minute drive to downtown, but far enough away to have privacy and be out in the country.

None of the properties really were lining up with the words of knowledge I had received. Then on a Sunday morning our agent excitedly rang us. "I think I have a property you are going to love" she said.

We set up the showing for just after church. That morning, during the worship service as we were singing songs of praise, the Lord whispered another word to me. One word, which I confess I didn't understand.

"AVALON."

Along with the word I saw in the Spirit a pathway or driveway with a curve. And I was coming around the curve and into a new destiny for my life.

In the car ride on the way out to our showing of this property, I looked up the word Avalon on Google. I found that it literally means "the place of the apple trees," and is a reference to the island that was the supposed home of King Arthur in southern England, where he had his knights of the round table. A legend, yes, but the name stuck.

I wondered what that meant?

As we approached the home, the first thing I noticed was that the driveway was lined with trees, and took us over a small, flowing stream. It also was a curved driveway, and you had to go around the curve to see the actual house.

The home itself was beautiful, a Victorian more than 100 years old, situated on a wonderful piece of several acres of land.

As we got out of the car, we realized the trees that lined the driveway were apple trees. We had indeed arrived at "Avalon."

I walked the land, and down by the stream was a man-made bird's nest, exactly like the one I had seen in the vision.

Inside the house, upstairs in one of the bedrooms, was a huge antique saw that the lumberjacks used to use to cut down trees. And the name of the kid who occupied that bedroom was also on the wall. His name was JOEL. That's right, the same name of the prophet where I had received the scripture!

And just outside this bedroom window, in the field between this house and the next, is a spring of water that never runs dry. In fact, this spring waters the valley that the home is located in.

And the next-door neighbor later told me that he has nicknamed the valley Paradise Valley as it feels a bit like living in paradise out here!

And across the street, the farmer raises cows for milk. That's right, the "hills (literally) flow with milk!"

So here is a summary of all the words of knowledge that led us to this home.

— The small wooden man-made bird's nest, near water.

— A scripture from the prophet Joel: *"And it will come about in that day, that all the hills will flow with milk, and all the brooks of Judah will flow with water; and a spring will go out from the house of the Lord, to water the valley"* (Joel 3:18).

— The old metal saw that lumberjacks used (literally in JOEL's room!)

— The flowing brook on the property, the spring on the property to water the valley, and the hills "flowing with milk" (a symbolic phrase to mean the cow's milk).

— The curved driveway lined with apple trees: our "Avalon."

We made an offer that very day and bought this home, and I made my study that upstairs room that belonged to Joel with the lumberjack saw on the wall. I pray and intercede daily in this room, and I am literally writing this chapter of this book from inside this room! I feel like my prayer and intercession in the Spirit are like the action of faith when you cut down a tree with a saw.

Can it really be this exciting to flow in words of knowledge and grow in expectation of the gifts of the Spirit? Yes it can! God has your "Avalon" waiting, just around the corner.

A final word about prophecy: throughout this book I talk a little about the counterfeit voices (with a much more thorough explanation of the counterfeits in my Appendix at the back). A note to remember the next time you turn on your television and see a psychic in operation, they are using the Satanic counterfeit to the gift of prophecy. They have always been around (psychics are mentioned in both the Old and New Testaments) and their source for their information can sometimes appear genuine and be accurate, when it pertains to people's past and present. But that's as far as they can go.

Where the gift of prophecy far surpasses all that Satan can share about a person is in the authentic ability it provides to disclose God's own heart and will and purpose to people and their situations.

When praying for others, it takes a surrendered life to Jesus Christ, and an openness and ability to work solely with the Holy Spirit, to bring genuine supernatural information to people through this gift.

When utilized properly and in order, in prayer for someone you can read and share God's promises and intentions for their life, right from His heart to theirs. It's beautiful!

Words of knowledge are ready and waiting from God's eternal mind to flow into your redeemed mind today, through the Holy Spirit.

Expect. Believe. Receive. This gift is waiting for you to tap into.

Very Common Ways

WAY		SCRIPTURE
1	The Established Word of Jesus	John 1:1
2	The Living Word of Jesus	Romans 10:17
3	The Inner Witness of the Holy Spirit	Acts 9:31
4	The Inner Voice of the Holy Spirit	Acts 8:29
5	The Desires of Your Heart	Psalm 37:4
6	Father Speaks Through All of Creation & Nature	Romans 1:19
7	Providential Outward Signs & Circumstances	Romans 8:28

Common Ways

8	The Preaching of the Word of Jesus	2 Thess. 2:13
9	Other Believers Speaking Confirmation	Matthew 18:16
10	Visions	Acts 2:17-21
11	Dreams	Acts 2:17-21
12	Symbolic Speech: Metaphors from the Holy Spirit	Numbers 12:8
13	Divine Appointments from the Father	Acts 8:27
14	Father Speaks Through All Forms of Media & Culture	Nehemiah 9:6

Uncommon Ways

15	The Revelatory Gifts: The Gift of Prophecy	1 Cor. 14:1
16	The Revelatory Gifts: The Word of Wisdom	1 Cor. 12:4-11
17	The Revelatory Gifts: The Word of Knowledge	1 Cor. 12:4-11

QUESTIONS FOR DEEPER STUDY:

1. Think about an area of your life where you need a "fuller picture." List some of the pieces below and ask the LORD to give you (or someone else for you) words of wisdom and words of knowledge.

_____

_____

_____

_____

2. Why would the enemy take the genuine gifts and twist or counterfeit them?

_____

_____

_____

_____

3. Why is paying for a gift of knowledge or information about the future (from a spiritualist) an indication of a counterfeit voice?

_____

_____

_____

_____

Keep listening!

NOTES:

_____

_____

_____

_____

WAY #18: THE REVELATORY GIFTS: THE DISCERNING OF SPIRITS

X-Ray Vision

" **B** *ut to each one is given the manifestation of the Spirit for the common good. For to...another, is given the distinguishing (discerning) of spirits, by the same Spirit"* (I Corinthians 12:7, 10).

As we continue to the fourth of the unique gifts of the Spirit that have to do with God's direct communication with us, we come to one that, quite frankly, is also not taught very often and yet is most remarkable.

When I was growing up, my favorite super hero was Superman. I loved all his powers, and especially awesome to me was his ability to see things that no one else around him could see.

X-ray vision.

That is so cool. I wanted that.

Then, when I became a follower of Jesus, I realized that He is way cooler than Superman. He operated in His own version of X-ray vision (He saw

Satan fall from Heaven like lightning!) and He then passed along His gift to us who follow Him.

You can have X-ray vision! Well, sort of. In the list of gifts it is known as "discerning of spirits."

The gift of discerning of spirits is the last of the four revelation gifts. Sometimes this gift works in tandem with other gifts, and sometimes it stands alone, depending on the circumstance of the Holy Spirit operating this gift through a person. Here again is how Howard Carter defines it.

The Discerning of Spirits, a definition: "A supernatural enablement to see into the spirit world. By this insight he/she can discern the similitude of God, or of the risen Christ, or the Holy Spirit, or cherubim, or seraphim, archangels or the hosts of angels, or Satan and his legions.

"It may also be used to discern if demonic power is the origin of any particular sickness or affliction. By the discerning of spirits we see beyond the sphere for which we have been created, since we are natural beings. It is only by the revelation of the Holy Spirit that we can perceive the beings that live in the spirit world.

"In Old Testament Scripture, we have Ezekiel by the river Chebar, who saw the overwhelming revelation of the glory of God, and the similitude of the God of Israel, with the cherubim beneath His throne. Later, while Ezekiel was sitting in his house in Babylon with the elders of Israel before him, he was carried in the Spirit to Jerusalem, and saw the things that were taking place in that city. Those around the prophet in his house saw nothing (Ezekiel chapters 1 and 10).

"In the New Testament, Jesus Himself saw, '*Satan fall from heaven like lightning*' (Luke 10:18). Stephen, as he was being stoned, being full of the Holy Spirit, '*gazed intently into heaven and saw the glory of God, and Jesus standing at the right hand of God*' (Acts 8:55). And John the Revelator, on the Isle of Patmos, on the Lord's Day, saw the glory of heaven and the heavenly beings (Revelation 1).

"The telescope may reveal the galaxies of space, and the microscope the mysteries of the minute, but only the discerning of spirits can introduce us to the spirit world."[62]

"Use the Force, Luke."

I myself have learned to appreciate this gift. To be honest, there are different manifestations of it and different people operate in it differently. I have met people around the world in my travels who regularly see either the angelic realm and angels, or the demonic realm and demons, or both. Some see visually, others hear in their spirit, and still others sense the spirit realm.

To simplify this with yet another modern-day example, you could say the Star Wars revolutionary films with their world of "The Force," could illustrate the reality of the spirit realm around us.

The key difference between the reality of this gift and the made-up world of "The Force," is that we come to understand the spirit realm is not a kind of impersonal force that can be manipulated by people. In fact, the spirit realm is very real and the demons there are attempting to manipulate us, and the angels there serve and fully surrender to a very personal God.

The point here is simply that the spirit realm can be accessed instantly and sensed by a believer. Just for the sake of this illustration, instead of you saying, "The Force is strong with this one," you can actually say, "The anointing of the Spirit is strong with this one!"

Thus, there is another dimension, not accessible through natural faculties that is discernible only as the Holy Spirit brings it to light. (In some cases, people who choose to work with demonic spirits can also have access to the spirit realm. See the Appendix for more teaching on the "Counterfeit Voices.")

In the case of the gifts of the Spirit, all believers in Jesus can access the spirit realm, by faith, through the operation of this gift for the common good. All the gifts are given so that we, as the extension of the ministry of Jesus through His expanding Kingdom on earth, can mutually benefit one another.

---

62 Howard Carter, Ibid., *Questions & Answers on Spiritual Gifts.*

For example, when operating in the gift of discerning of spirits and seeing or hearing in the world of the spiritual, combining this gift with prayer is a powerful force. Prayer power while utilizing this gift can help set people free. You can intercede properly for whole regions, cities, and sometimes, nations themselves through it.

The Army of Darkness Cannot Win Their Battles

Here's an example from a remarkable man, Dr. John G. Lake. Lake was a pioneer healing evangelist in the early days of the Pentecostal revival, and after seeing countless miracles, signs and wonders, and healings through evangelism in South Africa, moved to Portland, Oregon to start a mission base there.

Before he was able to open his healing rooms, he first had to do battle in intercession, and one night he went for a prayer walk and the Lord opened up the spirit realm for him.

Here is his description of that evening as the gift of discerning of spirits went forth in operation during his prayer walk. He began to see in the spirit realm above his own church building. This happened on an evening in May, 1920, in Mount Tabor Park.

"Through the park is a footpath coming down through the trees that leads out to the street where we live, and in my vision I was seemingly out in the street, at the foot of this footpath, and then shown my church building.

"To my amazement, on seeing the building, high in the atmosphere a half a mile or more, I discerned millions of demons, organized as a modern army. There were those who apparently acted as shock troops. They would charge with great ferocity, followed by a wave, and yet another wave, and yet another wave.

"After a little while I observed there operated a restraining influence that constituted a barrier through which they could not force themselves. With all the ingenuity of humans at war, this multitude of demons seemed to endeavor to break the barrier or to go further, but were utterly restrained.

"In amazement, I prayed, "What does it mean?" Through an angel, the Lord said to me, "Such is the care of God for those that strive in unselfishness for His best."[63]

Open Our Eyes, Lord

Now I know some of you reading this true story, like me, are equally as amazed as Lake must have been, and are wondering, "Does this prayer experience of the gift of discerning of spirits line up with Scripture?"

A very good question to ask, and in fact, I have tried to include enough scriptural examples in each of the 21 ways of recognizing God's communication so that you would know that situations like this are, indeed, in the Bible.

Think for a moment in the Old Testament, when Elisha was facing a situation with an army who had surrounded is house; and in encouragement he spoke to his servant, *"Do not fear, for those who are with us are more than those who are with them." Then Elisha prayed and said, "O Lord, I pray, open his eyes that he may see." And the Lord opened the servant's eyes, and he saw; and behold, the mountain was full of horses and chariots of fire all around Elisha"* (2 Kings 6:12-17).

And in Ephesians, the Apostle Paul writes some amazing revelation of what is going on in the spirit realm all around us, as *"the prince of the power of the air"* as he calls Satan, our enemy, is in active operation.

> *"For our struggle is not against flesh and blood, but against the rulers, against the powers, against the world forces of this darkness, against the spiritual forces of wickedness in the heavenly places"* (Ephesians 6:12).

It's almost as if Paul is listing a kind of army of darkness, an organizational structure of wickedness and teaching us that this kind of realm really exists, and we are all fighting in it at all times and in all places.

This, to me, is what God allowed John G. Lake to see, through the oper-

---

63 *John G. Lake: His Life, His Sermons, His Boldness of Faith* (Kenneth Copeland Publications, 1994).

ation of this gift, so he could discern better how to pray. It's important to know what is happening in the spirit realm at times.

Keep God's Perspective

X-ray vision is pretty cool, or as my teenage son would say, it's "sick." But let's keep this gift, along with all the gifts, in perspective. Let's "strive for the greater gifts" but remain humble.

Let's develop our character in Christ, and keep all the gifts flowing for the sake of other people.

Let's keep prayer as a priority, and serving the poor and the weak and utilizing these kinds of gifts to bring God the glory.

A final word from Howard Carter. "If one covets the greater gifts, and the Lord is pleased to bestow them, he will be led still deeper into his spiritual heritage, and will witness the gracious, yet unlimited, power of God in operation; or he will have revealed to him the will and purpose of God.

"The things of Christ will be seen in the light of the Spirit, and things to come will amaze the spiritual explorer. The Bible, which must ever be the guide and sure anchor of the man or woman of God, will yield its treasures more readily, and its truths more fully.

"The experience of the believer filled with the Spirit and seeking for the best gifts will be one of untold and unimagined glory. A consciousness that he has become truly united with God in His work, able in some small way to continue the beneficent ministry of his Master which commenced 2,000 years ago.

"This great and sacred heritage of the Spirit is before us; let us go up at once and possess it."[64]

Some Final Comments on the Revelatory Gifts

I also have seen all four of these gifts working in tandem with each other, and almost simultaneously.

---

64 Ibid., pp. 98, 108, 127.

For example, I have received a prophesy or two, and also a word of knowledge, then the word of wisdom comes in operation helping me to apply that word of knowledge in a practical way, and then the discerning of spirits operates to help me see into the spirit realm, if I need to, in relation to that particular situation.

It happens especially in times of prayer, and oftentimes, in intercessory prayer for others.

The more information God supplies you with, the more effective can be your prayers.

Some practical moments for us have been times of prayer over our media company. There were so many choices as to where to spend our advertising budget, for example. Year by year, Sarah and I would set aside times of prayer, and seek the wisdom and knowledge of the Spirit for our business. He would always speak.

As to other times of ministry, in many nations I have asked the Spirit for prophetic words or words of knowledge about healing, and when I have given those words, many people have been healed of various diseases, sometimes miraculously, and sometimes instantly.

And in the discerning of spirits, I have been with many people in many places that have seen, and described, both angels and demons, or have even seen Jesus or His glory manifested, or described the enemy's movements or intentions.

In the latter case, the Spirit gave us burdens of intercession and we felt our prayers for people and areas were more directed and fruitful. In the former cases, seeing the Lord always brought us to deeper moments of thanksgiving, praise, and worship.

And in particular, since through the operation of the gift of discerning of spirits you are allowed to see and sometimes converse with real angels, the next chapter will share on the subject of angels as God's messengers and another way of His speaking to us.

So go on, Superman or Supergirl, exercise your X-ray vision! And now we add the fourth "Uncommon Way" of the Spirit speaking, through His presence in the Trinity.

Very Common Ways

WAY		SCRIPTURE
1	The Established Word of Jesus	*John 1:1*
2	The Living Word of Jesus	*Romans 10:17*
3	The Inner Witness of the Holy Spirit	*Acts 9:31*
4	The Inner Voice of the Holy Spirit	*Acts 8.29*
5	The Desires of Your Heart	*Psalm 37:4*
6	Father Speaks Through All of Creation & Nature	*Romans 1:19*
7	Providential Outward Signs & Circumstances	*Romans 8:28*

Common Ways

8	The Preaching of the Word of Jesus	*2 Thess. 2:13*
9	Other Believers Speaking Confirmation	*Matthew 18:16*
10	Visions	*Acts 2:17-21*
11	Dreams	*Acts 2:17-21*
12	Symbolic Speech: Metaphors from the Holy Spirit	*Numbers 12:8*
13	Divine Appointments from the Father	*Acts 8:27*
14	Father Speaks Through All Forms of Media & Culture	*Nehemiah 9:6*

Uncommon Ways

15	The Revelatory Gifts: The Gift of Prophecy	*1 Cor. 14:1*
16	The Revelatory Gifts: The Word of Wisdom	*1 Cor. 12:4-11*
17	The Revelatory Gifts: The Word of Knowledge	*1 Cor. 12:4-11*
18	The Revelatory Gifts: The Discerning of Spirits	*1 Cor. 12:4-11*

Questions for Deeper Study:

1. What do the Scriptures reveal about the ability to see or sense the spirit realm?

2. How will your life and the lives of others be transformed when you increase your ability to operate in the gifts of the Spirit?

3. When was the last time you clung to the LORD until something happened? What was the result?

Keep listening!

NOTES:

_____

_____

_____

_____

19

WAY #19: ANGELS (BY DREAMS OR IN REALITY)

Angels On Our Shoulder

"**A**bout the 9th hour of the day he clearly saw in a vision an angel of God who had just come in to him" (Acts 10:3).

As we journey further along with our final three ways out of 21 to recognize the Lord speaking, we find that the list begins to enter the least common and most direct characteristics.

The probability that you will ever encounter a real angel who will direct you in some course of action is small in comparison to you recognizing the Father in nature, for example, or Him encouraging you through a movie or a song. It's small in comparison to Jesus speaking to you in the Bible, or to hearing that "still, small voice" of the Holy Spirit within.

And that's okay! We are always walking a balance here between the intuitive and the reasonable. So, I maintain a posture of seeking the Lord, not seeking for certain experiences. I continue to worship the Father, and the Son, and the Spirit.

My focus is always upon the Trinity and the glory of God.

So if Father chooses to send an angel to my path, I will, of course, welcome that! Though I continue to seek Him, not His angels, who are His *"ministering spirits, sent out to render service for the sake of those who will inherit salvation"* (Hebrews 1:14).

To look at this subject from a practical standpoint, I want to remind you of the gift of discerning of spirits in our previous chapter. We are told in Hebrews 2:4 that, *"God is bearing witness with His people by signs and wonders, and by various miracles, and by gifts of the Holy Spirit according to His own will."*

So, discerning of spirits is one of the gifts and can and should be sought after for your own life. As mentioned previously, this gift enables the person to see into the spirit realm and behold, depending on the operation of the moment, either the demonic forces of opposition, or the angelic forces of God's power.

That is the only way for you to see an angel (unless, of course, that angel has taken human form and looks like one of us). This, too, is possible, as later in Hebrews the writer surprises us with, *"Do not neglect to show hospitality to strangers, for by this some have entertained angels without knowing it"* (Hebrews 13:2).

I often wonder if I personally have entertained an angel.

Father Speaks Through Angels, a simple definition: Through the operation of the gift of discerning of spirits, and possibly in tandem with other means of God's communication like visions and dreams, actual angels can and do appear to people. They sometimes speak and carry on dialogue with people, or open a person's spiritual eyes to behold new dimensions of God's love and the spiritual battle that is all around us.

In the Old Testament, many of the saints had encounters with them. Abraham, Jacob, Joshua, Daniel, and Gideon, just to name a few.

In the life of Jesus, we find that after His successful encounter against

Satan in the wilderness, *"angels came and ministered to Him"* (Matthew 4:11).

That must have been a powerful ministry time!

In the Book of Acts, God utilized angels in multiple encounters. You might remember me sharing earlier in this book about Cornelius from Acts chapter 10. There, an angel appeared and spoke directly to him. *"Your prayers and alms have ascended as a memorial before God. Call for a man named Peter"* (Acts 10:4).

Here, an angel directly intervened with a word of knowledge about the whereabouts of Peter, and when they followed his instruction, the revival broke out and Cornelius and his friends came to faith and were filled with the Holy Spirit through Peter's ministry.

Angels are sent into creation to carry out the sovereign plans of the Father and intervene in the affairs of men.

As we saw previously, Paul gives us insights that there are levels of demonic forces (he calls them *"spiritual forces of wickedness in the heavenly places"* in Ephesians 6) and thus, there is a kind of battle waging in the spirit realm at all times, involving angels and demons.

When Gabriel, a high-ranking angel of Heaven, appeared to Daniel after Daniel had been fasting 21 days, he shared insight that he had been in a spiritual struggle in the spirit realm against *"the prince of the Kingdom of Persia"* and he needed the aid of another high-ranking angel, Michael, to withstand these spiritual forces *(see Daniel chapter 10)*.

The Real Always Has a Counterfeit

Always remember that there is also a counterfeit out there. Satan himself is described in Scripture as a fallen angel, and he masquerades once in a while to try and fool people and lead them to deception. He appears as an "angel of light."

Paul writes in Corinthians, *"Satan disguises himself as an angel of light"* (2 Corinthians 11:14).

For example, an angel was said to appear to Muhammad, which led to the establishment of the world religion of Islam. In fact, Muhammad claimed it was Gabriel himself who called him out as an apostle.

Another angel appeared to Joseph Smith, and out of that experience came a mixture of doctrine and yet another powerful world religion, Mormonism. Both Islam and Mormonism have spiritual forces of evil behind them and are full of demonic influences.

I would call both of these "angels" NOT angels, but an appearance of Satan or one of his demons, disguised as an angel. They both helped the free will of fallen man create world religions that have turned countless people towards the darkness and away from a personal relationship with Jesus Christ.

Personally I think it's far more likely to look at the mixture in the religion of Islam and the cult of Mormonism and discern that it was Satan, not an angel sent from God, who appeared. He was masquerading as an angel. Demonic forces are real and people who work with them are receiving all sorts of mixed signals and lead many people astray.

The key: always seek the Lord and operate in the Holy Spirit with discernment! Know the Source of eternal salvation and always seek Him, Jesus Christ!

Escape From Alcatraz

On the real side, apart from counterfeits, there are some truths to learn about angels from a scriptural perspective.

First of all, there seems to be a connection between the intensity of the need for an angel to appear, with the rarity of this kind of appearance. In other words, if you really need an angel (and this is also true of the Audible Voice that we will look at soon) then God the Father has the prerogative to send you one to help direct you.

Take, for example, the case of the Apostles Peter and Paul, in two separate occasions in the Book of Acts. In Acts 12, Peter gets arrested and is

"About the 9th hour of the day

he clearly saw in a

VISION

an

ANGEL

of God who had just come in to him."

(Acts 10:3)

likely to be martyred for his faith. But it was not his time to die. God sends an angel who opens his prison cell, removes his chains, and leads him out. In fact, the scripture leaves open the idea that perhaps the two of them were invisible too, as they walked right past the first and second guards and Peter escaped from the prison.

Talk about escape from Alcatraz!

In Paul's case, Acts 27 shares that he was on board a ship that seemed by all accounts destined to be shipwrecked with death and casualties because of a fierce storm they encountered while on his way to Rome. An angel appeared personally and spoke to Paul that indeed the ship itself would suffer shipwreck, but Paul, along with the whole crew, would be spared and they would all live. It happened exactly as the angel spoke.

Do you see the rare and intense cases of both of these instances? God most often speaks through many other means, but in both of these, His angels on assignment were absolutely needed to bring deliverance and life instead of death to these men.

I am borrowing from Steven Spielberg's World War II epic, "Saving Private Ryan," for this chapter's title. His protagonist, Captain Miller, lies dying upon a bridge near the end of the film. Just then, American bombers fly over and help aid in the rescue of these men.

"They're tank-busters, sir. P-51s" says Private Ryan.

"Angels on our shoulders" replies Miller.

Angels are kind of like massive bombers sent from the Father in Jesus' name to your service. You might remember the Portland vision that John G. Lake received in May, 1920. In that vision, as the gift of discerning of spirits began to operate, he discerned a real angel was walking with him. That angel talked to Lake and shared from Scripture some truth with him. Here's some more of that unique moment.

"As I looked up in the park I was attracted by a quite brilliant light far up in the park. It was very slowly coming down the pathway to the street. I stood somewhat surprised, supposing it was some night man on some duty in the park, probably searching for something or somebody. As it approached I discovered that, instead, it was an angel presence, and the brilliance was an illumination surrounding him. He stood a few feet from me, and said to me, "I have come to answer your prayers. Come with me."[65]

And the evening continued with a prayer walk of unusual company: he walked in the company of an angel!

And the angel showed him that through the power of prayer, the power of the name of Jesus is kind of like a bomber airplane that opens up new breakthroughs in the realm of the Spirit.

Sometimes angels bring words of formation and encouragement, too. Some good friends of mine, Andy and Sharron, are Irish missionaries planting a new church in the south of England. When their son was just a boy, an angel visited him one night and shared that one day, he would be a preacher to a specific island in the South Pacific. He showed the boy a supernatural map with this particular island on it where God would one day send him. It was such a powerful experience that the boy grew up knowing the reality of angels.

Remember to keep on praying, keep on discerning, and keep your focus on the goodness of God. And sometimes, you might just have a visitation from an angel, either through a vision, in a dream, or in reality. As evangelist Jesse Duplantis shares in some of his experiences, you might just have "a real close encounter of the God kind!"[66]

---

65 Ibid., *John G. Lake*, Portland Vision.
66 Title from a series of messages that Duplantis has preached, sharing some of his unique experiences with angels and the Lord, even being taken to heaven in prayer one day and speaking with the Lord, all through the operation of the gift of discerning of spirits.

Very Common Ways

WAY		SCRIPTURE
1	The Established Word of Jesus	John 1:1
2	The Living Word of Jesus	Romans 10:17
3	The Inner Witness of the Holy Spirit	Acts 9:31
4	The Inner Voice of the Holy Spirit	Acts 8:29
5	The Desires of Your Heart	Psalm 37:4
6	Father Speaks Through All of Creation & Nature	Romans 1:19
7	Providential Outward Signs & Circumstances	Romans 8:28

Common Ways

8	The Preaching of the Word of Jesus	2 Thess. 2:13
9	Other Believers Speaking Confirmation	Matthew 18:16
10	Visions	Acts 2:17-21
11	Dreams	Acts 2:17-21
12	Symbolic Speech: Metaphors from the Holy Spirit	Numbers 12:8
13	Divine Appointments from the Father	Acts 8:27
14	Father Speaks Through All Forms of Media & Culture	Nehemiah 9:6

Uncommon Ways

15	The Revelatory Gifts: The Gift of Prophecy	1 Cor. 14:1
16	The Revelatory Gifts: The Word of Wisdom	1 Cor. 12:4-11
17	The Revelatory Gifts: The Word of Knowledge	1 Cor. 12:4-11
18	The Revelatory Gifts: The Discerning of Spirits	1 Cor. 12:4-11
19	Angels (by Dreams or in Reality)	Acts 12:7-10

Questions for Deeper Study:

1. Have you ever felt like you were ministered to or protected by an Angel? Y / N   If yes, what were the circumstances and what was supernatural about it?

_____

_____

_____

_____

2. What are some areas in your life that need Divine protection?

_____

_____

_____

_____

3. What is your part to get Angels on the job?!

_____

_____

_____

_____

Keep listening!

NOTES:

_____

_____

_____

_____

WAY #20: JESUS HIMSELF SPEAKS
(BY DREAMS OR IN REALITY)

He Moves Among the Candlesticks

"*A nd behold, Jesus met them and greeted them. And they came up and took hold of His feet and worshipped Him*" (Matthew 28:9).

Venice Beach, on the Pacific coast just a few miles from Los Angeles, California, U.S.A., is known worldwide as a place to meet some very strange people. I used to walk that beach and pray during my time at film school.

I once met Jesus on Venice Beach.

Really?

No, not the real one. But he thought he was the real one! He had on blue jeans and a tee shirt, with long, straggly hair and a beard. He told me he was Jesus.

"Jesus? THE Jesus?" I replied?

"Yes. I am Jesus."

After several minutes of questioning him, I could discern he was missing a few brain cells, probably from drug use.

So, I closed my eyes and began to pray, out loud, and praise the real Jesus.

He immediately became upset and started shouting obscenities at me, and walked away speaking to himself in disgust and shaking his head.

This counterfeit Jesus did not quite have the character of the King of Kings!

Thus far we have seen how, every week, you can begin to expect to encounter Jesus Himself, and His Presence in the Trinity, multiple ways.

You can objectively study His word, and encounter Him in the established body of truth.

You can be in devotional inquiry in His word, and encounter Him in the Living Word.

You can listen to a sermon preached, and encounter Him in His spoken Word.

You can speak with one or two other people, friends or strangers, and you can encounter Him as they share in His Body and are His ambassadors for sharing His thoughts.

You can go to pray with another person, and through the operation of the gift of prophecy in them, you can encounter His voice to you.

This chapter will unveil the final, and least common way, of Jesus the Word speaking to you—a personal encounter with Jesus Himself.

Jesus Himself Speaks, a simple definition: Jesus Christ, risen and anointed Son of God, can appear to you in a vision, in a dream, or in reality. He is Lord of all. He can choose to appear directly and speak with you, or share insights into the Bible or speak to you about your calling.

Jesus Himself is Lord. He is risen! He has forever stepped into His new resurrection body, and He ascended to the right hand of the Father, and in this current dispensation, lives to offer intercessory prayers to the Father on your behalf. Amazing!

I share this toward the very end of the book, as I am attempting to place these in order of most common to least common. This chapter, and chapter 21 (the Audible Voice of the Father) are the two least common of all the ways of God communicating.

He Doesn't Often Risk Direct Contact

Because He is Lord, Jesus has the divine right to choose whether He will risk direct contact with you. Why is this one of the rarest ways? My hypothesis is simple: God (either in His Person of the Father or the Son) does not often risk direct contact with people, because we, as His children, are still flesh and blood, and enough of pride and the old ways are still at work in us.

Because of this, if He were to appear to us individually and speak directly, we would most likely misinterpret it, especially if it happened too often. Our mind and more natural ways of thinking would misdirect His intentions.

So, my theory here (and it is only a theory) is that unless you are personally in a very intense situation that almost would require a Divine intervention from Jesus Himself, or the Father, to change the outcome of that particular situation, you must be content to seek the Lord and let Him help you in any way that He chooses.

Nevertheless, this actual blessing of Jesus Himself appearing has been taking place, in secret, all of the church age, and I have uncovered just a few stories to make the hair stand up on the back of your neck. He comes in visions, He visits in dreams, and He appears in reality.

My intention for sharing these simple stories of real people in real history, is simply to alert you to the fact that, at anytime and anywhere, if HE so chooses, Jesus may appear—to you—or someone you know.

If He does, it is a rare blessing. Like John the Revelator, who had a personal encounter with Him and received seven outrageously vivid visions that still captivate millions of people (and out of which came the Book of Revelation). In John's case, he bowed low to worship Him.

Jesus Appeared to People in the New Testament

> *"And while they were telling these things, HE HIMSELF stood in their midst. But they were startled and frightened, and thought that they were seeing a spirit. And He said to them, "Why are you troubled, and why do doubts arise in your hearts? See My hands and My feet, that is I Myself"* (Luke 24:36-39a).

Jesus also appeared to the common disciples. Paul wrote, *"After that He appeared to more than five hundred brethren at one time, most of whom remain until now"* (I Corinthians 15:6).

We have multiple appearances of Jesus in the Book of Acts, too.

And, as already mentioned, He appeared to John the Revelator.

In John's case, He sees a most amazing vision of Jesus in Revelation chapter 1. In the opening vision of the book, He sees seven golden lampstands, and *"One like a Son of Man" (Jesus) moving in the "midst of the seven golden lampstands (or candlesticks)"* (Revelation 1:12-13).

Here is a very encouraging thought. One possible interpretation of this vision is that these candlesticks each represent an individual church, and that Jesus Himself is moving among the Church, and actively involved in the day by day details and activity in His churches. The churches are all different and all have their struggles and successes, and Jesus in the next few chapters of Revelation seems to be very personally involved in all of them.

In the old dispensation (the Old Testament), God had ordained one lampstand containing seven lamps. This symbol represented the Jewish church-state (if you will) in the midst of the pagan cultures around it. There was one group of believers only, known then (and now) as the spiritual descendants of Abraham.

In the new dispensation (the New Testament), He has now multiplied Himself by spreading out His presence within His Body everywhere. So now, the vision is changed. There is no longer one lampstand with seven candles; we now have the seven lampstands (candlesticks) representing true spiritual unity in His church-state, which is now scattered among all the nations of the world!

Paul calls the church-state the "One New Man" comprised of both believing Jews and Gentiles (see Ephesians chapter 2). There is now, *"One body and one Spirit, just as also you were called in one hope of your calling; one Lord, one faith, one baptism, one God and Father of all who is over all and through all and in all"* (Ephesians 4:4-6).

We are still the light in the midst of the darkness, but now we are not located in the Middle East as one nation surrounded by pagans; we are everywhere. And Jesus is still actively moving among His churches.

He is appearing among the candlesticks!

He brings Himself by the operation of the Holy Spirit. Though each church may have a unique variety of ministries and backgrounds, we are all one in the same Spirit and Jesus is on the move among us, anywhere in the world.

Jesus Appeared in Church History

And what of church history? In most cases, the history books are fairly silent on this issue, though my hunch is, He has been appearing, here and there, to various saints throughout the ages.

There is never a guarantee that He will appear. In fact, He challenges us that we who have never seen Him personally (and I myself fall into this category, as of the time of this writing) are those of great faith, which He said to Thomas after dear old "doubting Thomas" realized Jesus was really Jesus.

"Because you have seen Me, have you believed? Blessed are they who did not see, and yet believed" (John 20:29).

Jesus Appears to Muslims Today in Dreams & Visions

"There is an end-time phenomenon that is happening through dreams and visions" writes author Christine Darg. "He is going into the Muslim world and revealing, particularly, the last 24 hours of His life—how He died on the cross, which Islam does not teach—how He was raised from the dead, which Islam also does not teach—and how He is the Son of God, risen in power."[67]

Darg also reported that compiling a report of the visions is often difficult because of how often they are happening.

In another report from a different website, a Saudi man gives his account of a dream that started with a "horrible" scene.

"One night, while I was asleep, I had this horrible dream of me being taken into hell. And what I saw there brought me real fear, and these dreams kept coming to me almost every night. At this point I was really wondering as to why I should be seeing hell in this manner.

"He said Jesus appeared to him and said, 'Son, I am the way, the truth and the life. And if you would give your life to Me, and follow Me, I would save you from the hell that you have seen.'

"This came as a surprise to me, for I did not know who this Jesus was. Of course, He is mentioned in the Quran and in the book Surah Mariam. He is stated as one of our prophets, but not as a savior who could save us from hell. So I started looking out for a Christian who could give me some advice about this Jesus I have seen."

"He said he had to reach out to an Egyptian Christian, because Christianity is 'totally banned in Saudi Arabia and if a Christian is caught witnessing to a Muslim, [it is] almost sure that he would be beheaded.' He went on to give his life to Jesus."[68]

Once again, let me point out that these instances seem to be the exception and not the rule in terms of guidance, perhaps because of the intense

---

67 Christine Darg, *The Jesus Visions: Signs and Wonders in the Muslim World* (Quoted from a report on CBN News, The Christian Broadcasting Network, 2016).
68 Read more at http://www.wnd.com/2014/11/rising-number-of-muslims-reporting-dreams-about-jesus.

anti-Christian conditions in these nations and the scarcity of individuals who can bring the gospel to these people.

Out of the Limelight into the Lamplight

I'd like to close this chapter with a most remarkable story from fairly recent history. This is an eyewitness account. You probably have never heard this story before, as this brother's name is not to be found in Google searches or in your Christian library. His name was Paul Munson.

Paul was a simple shoe salesman in the 1940s following World War II. He had a desire to be used mightily by God in the work of the gospel after his conversion.

In 1949, the same year of the breakthrough crusade of Rev. Billy Graham in Los Angeles that set Graham's ministry in full motion, one night Munson was in prayer about his own calling. Would he be an evangelist like Graham? The Lord spoke to his heart, "I am calling you out of the LIMELIGHT and INTO THE LAMPLIGHT."

For Billy Graham and many others, limelight awaited, as that was their calling. Evangelicalism in America began to flourish in the 1950s and beyond.

Paul Munson consecrated himself to the secret calling of God in 1949 to begin a hidden ministry of intimacy and intercession before the Lord. This ministry lasted faithfully, every single day, from that day in 1949 for exactly 49 years. He decided to engage the Lord in relationship in four areas every day.

1) Confession of his sins before the Father in Jesus' name

2) Meditation of the Word of God

3) Prayer and Intercession

4) Worshiping and Praising the Lord in song

Those indeed were the four daily pillars of discipline that Munson had practiced. They are simple and yet still excellent reminders of a strong and intimate relationship with God that each soldier of the Cross needs to practice.

Munson was encouraged by the Lord to balance his time in the Word, in prayer, and in praise. So if he chose on a particular day to read the Word for three hours, he also had to pray for three hours and worship and praise for three more.

Next to his piano in the little basement where he sought the Lord was a stack of hymnals that he had literally worn out over the years of praising and singing. The papers hardly stayed in the bindings.

He was also told to assemble 12 disciples and teach them these simple and powerful principles, which he did, and over many years he saw personal revivals and the birth of powerful prayer ministries in the lives of each of these 12.

One of these 12, a man named Scott, was a mentor to me personally in the areas of prayer and intercession, and it was from him that I compiled the following eyewitness account, published here for the first time.

Let me share just one story with you about Paul's experiences, as this pertains directly to an encounter he had with two very important characters in this section: Satan and Jesus Himself.

On one occasion, Paul was spending about eight hours of his day in the Word, prayer, worship, and waiting on the Lord. His house was a typical 1940s rambler, with a kitchen door adjacent to a door with stairs leading down to the basement.

There was a knock on his kitchen door, and his wife, Martha, answered the door. Paul heard some talking and then this man came down the stairs to the basement prayer room. He was dressed in a fine suit with expensive shoes, Paul remembered. He identified himself as Satan!

After a few brief words of discouragement towards Paul, Jesus Himself walked through the wall of the basement, proceeded to rebuke Satan on behalf of Paul. He stood, in Person, between Satan and Paul.

At that moment, instantly Satan disappeared and Jesus walked on through the room and disappeared, but His glory and manifest Presence remained for several days in the room!

What an incredible moment with the operation of the gift of discerning of spirits. Both Satan and Jesus Himself appeared in Munson's basement.

And how does the story of Paul end? Well, this simple shoe salesman maintained this season of the glory of the Lord, out of the limelight of public ministry and platforms, shining in the lamplight for 49 years.

The year of his passing, 1998, the Lord spoke to Paul and said that He had heard every prayer and that He knew that never a day had passed where Paul had not exercised the four spiritual disciplines of confession of his sins, study of the Word, prayer, and worship, and that he always kept them in balance.

Paul asked the Lord if there were more people, like him, that had secretly been called and chosen to not be on the front lines as it were, but to remain on the supply lines and help pray for the witness of the gospel in the nations.

The Lord told Paul to go find his phone book. Paul did so. The Minneapolis phone book was filled with hundreds of thousands of names and phone numbers. As he opened the phone book, the Lord highlighted three different names of people Paul had never met and knew nothing of.

Of course, you recognize the names as the gift of the word of knowledge in operation.

Then He gave Paul a word of wisdom (a plan with what to do with the words of knowledge). He said, "Call them, Paul."

In blind obedience and simple faith, Paul Munson picked up his phone and called one by one the three random names that Jesus had told him to call.

He introduced himself to each person, and to his utter amazement, they were all the same age as Paul. Upon talking with each one, he discovered a stunning truth: all three had secretly been called by Jesus to a life of prayer and intimacy in the "lamplight," in the same year of 1949!

All four of these prayer warriors died the same year after 49 years of faithful intercession!

So do not ever feel that a calling from the Lord to the "lamplight" of intimacy, worship, Bible study, and hearing His voice is a lower calling than say, a pulpit ministry. In fact, a "lamplight" calling of prayer and intimacy is a greater calling.

To summarize, many of you reading this will never meet Jesus personally in this realm in life. It won't be until after your death that you enter His presence and bow low to worship Him, though it has happened in both Scripture and in history, and it is happening today somewhere in the world. He is appearing somewhere through a vision, through a dream, or in reality.

He truly is Lord of all.

Oh, and if you run into Jesus on Venice Beach near Los Angeles, California, please tell him I send my love and greetings.

Remember, "One like a Son of Man" is on the move today. He is in the midst of the candlesticks.

Let's add number 20, a very uncommon way of Jesus speaking.

Very Common Ways

WAY		SCRIPTURE
1	The Established Word of Jesus	John 1:1
2	The Living Word of Jesus	Romans 10:17
3	The Inner Witness of the Holy Spirit	Acts 9:31
4	The Inner Voice of the Holy Spirit	Acts 8:29
5	The Desires of Your Heart	Psalm 37:4
6	Father Speaks Through All of Creation & Nature	Romans 1:19
7	Providential Outward Signs & Circumstances	Romans 8:28

Common Ways

8	The Preaching of the Word of Jesus	2 Thess. 2:13
9	Other Believers Speaking Confirmation	Matthew 18:16
10	Visions	Acts 2:17-21
11	Dreams	Acts 2:17-21
12	Symbolic Speech: Metaphors from the Holy Spirit	Numbers 12:8
13	Divine Appointments from the Father	Acts 8:27
14	Father Speaks Through All Forms of Media & Culture	Nehemiah 9:6

Uncommon Ways

15	The Revelatory Gifts: The Gift of Prophecy	1 Cor. 14:1
16	The Revelatory Gifts: The Word of Wisdom	1 Cor. 12:4-11
17	The Revelatory Gifts: The Word of Knowledge	1 Cor. 12:4-11
18	The Revelatory Gifts: The Discerning of Spirits	1 Cor. 12:4-11
19	Angels (by Dreams or in Reality)	Acts 12:7-10
20	Jesus Himself Appearing (by Dreams or in Reality)	John 20:19

QUESTIONS FOR DEEPER STUDY:

1. How does it make you feel to know that Jesus is praying for you?

_____

_____

_____

_____

2. What are you seeing and hearing in your church that is evidence that Jesus is at work?

_____

_____

_____

_____

3. How would increasing your own confession of sin, meditation in the word, prayer of intercession and songs of worship impact your relationship with Jesus?

_____

_____

_____

_____

Keep listening!

CHAPTER

WAY # 21: THE AUDIBLE VOICE OF THE FATHER

Some Said It Thundered

"*And a voice came out of the heavens: 'You are My be-loved Son. In You I am well-pleased'*" (Mark 1:11).

We arrive at the end of our journey of discovery of recognizing how God speaks and leads through the unique Persons of the Trinity.

As we pause here, do remember that the following is what I will call the least common of all the 21 ways I have outlined in this book. It is rare. You might have never heard the audible voice of God. I never have.

This does not mean that God somehow loves a person more just because they have heard Him speak in His audible voice. It also means that He doesn't love you less if you haven't heard it. Instead, a person who has experienced the true Father speaking, as Jesus did, will most likely be humbled and walk in a spirit of humility.

The Father's Audible Voice, a simple definition: God the Father, in all His majesty and glory, may choose the most direct means of communication by speaking with His voice. In Scripture He is called a Spirit, and "no man has ever seen the Father" except the Son who helps reveal Him to mankind.

In the Old Testament, the Psalmist wrote of the majesty of the voice of the Father.

> *"The Lord also thundered in the heavens, and the Most High uttered His voice"* (Psalm 18:13).

> *"The voice of the Lord is upon the waters; the God of glory thunders. The voice of the Lord is powerful. The voice of the Lord is majestic"* (Psalm 29:3, 4).

The Father's voice is so rare that we only have three instances of Him speaking in the New Testament. Two of them were to Jesus Himself (spoken by a true proud Father out of love for His Son), and one to the disciples who had accompanied Jesus up the Mount of Transfiguration.

I love that when He spoke, He always called His son "beloved." And by the spirit of adoption, by which we can actually call God, Father, you and I can receive that same affirmation. You are "beloved" sons and daughters of the Almighty.

What did HE sound like? We are not told exactly.

In the account in John 12, "some said it thundered" and in Matthew 17 it was a voice from the clouds.

In Matthew's account, Father added this powerful phrase, "LISTEN TO HIM!"

So, it's a good thing to listen to Jesus and His Word today!

The voice of the Lord

is powerful. The

VOICE

of the Lord is

MAJESTIC.

(Psalm 29:4)

Rebuild My Church

In history, there are a few examples here and there of this direct contact with God, as He has chosen to speak audibly in every generation. Many times, the hearer of the audible voice chose to put into literal fulfillment what they heard, only to realize later that the original intention of the direction was not being fulfilled. The audible voice was, and is, usually short, direct, and to the point.

In my Introduction to this book, I cited a historical example of St. Francis of Assisi. He is known widely as a Roman Catholic priest who made a huge impact. Early in his life, young Francis was deep in prayer outside the chapel of San Damiano. He heard and testified of an audible voice of God speaking directly to him, saying,

"Francis, repair my church." Some translations say "rebuild."

He heard the audible voice of the Father!

In order to fulfill this request, he sold some of his father's goods and began to rebuild that particular church with his own hands.

He did not realize that God did not mean the church at San Damiano to be physically rebuilt, but rather the *universal* church that was suffering from inside scandal and avarice, as well as outside heresies.

Thus, St. Francis stopped actually building a church structure and set about to build the spiritual church of God. He became the founder of the Franciscan Order and lived a righteous and holy life.

God's intention was for St. Francis to go forth and preach and rebuild the Church of Jesus Christ!

He went forth in a most amazing ministry that has impacted many thousands in the Catholic Church for centuries.

This is exactly why God does not choose to speak in His audible voice very often. God's intention was not for Saint Francis to physically build a church building, but to spiritually build His Church around the world.

Thus the Father seems to love and value the indirect means available far more often than the direct ones. I am sure St. Francis had a vibrant relationship with all three Persons of the Trinity and enjoyed hearing from God and receiving His love in many other ways than this instance early in life.

Field of Dreams: the "Voice" as Himself

One of my favorite movies is "Field of Dreams." In this unique film, a young Kevin Costner plays a character who seems to hear an audible voice that, in the film, is almost a whisper. The Voice leads Costner's character to build a baseball field in the middle of his farm's corn field in Iowa. The Voice promises, "If you build it, he will come."

The film gets a little off in its theology when his own father appears as a young man and plays baseball on the field along with the other deceased players from his team from many years ago. But hey, it's Hollywood!

Not all of the theology is correct about the afterlife, but it sure makes for an original story and a heartfelt ending when Costner ends up fulfilling his lifelong dream that had never been realized: playing a game of catch with his own dad.

As the credits roll, we find them listing The Voice as *Himself*.

I do love that! Was it God's audible voice? Is THAT what He sounds like? Well, He did in this movie. But you won't want to seek for that kind of "Voice" unless you are Kevin Costner and acting in a film.

The Apprentice

Billionaire Donald Trump once starred in a hit television show for years called "The Apprentice." Here's a little-known fact about me: ten years ago I applied for that hit Mark Burnett show and after four personal interviews by casting directors in three different cities, I was invited to an all-expense paid week in L.A. as a finalist.

Yes, I was nearly one of the most embarrassing potential apprentices on NBC.

I could have personally heard the words, "Carl, you're fired!"

I endured a fun and grueling week of interviews and exams. One of the exams was an intense questionnaire, and a common psychological test, which contained the question, DO YOU HEAR VOICES? Circle Yes or No.

How would you answer that one? Most people, if ever faced with that question, would answer "NO!" I mean, who wants to be locked up in a straight-jacket in a room with rubber walls for the rest of their life, right?

Well, needless to say, I am not "most people."

And as I have endeavored to show forth in the simple teachings of this book, there are at least 21 unique ways that God might get in contact with you.

So, if you were taking a psychological exam, how would you answer that question?

I answered "Yes!" and I still would. I hope you would, too, after reading this book (though not necessarily in this Way number 21).

As you now know, you can hear voices in most of the 20 other ways of God speaking much more often than with Father's audible voice.

Slow Down

When Father does actually speak, every so often, He is usually direct, to the point, and helpful in instructions. These instances appear to remain a little more on the extreme side.

When He risks direct contact with people, He is wanting to intervene and His voice is directive.

I remember talking to a friend of mine who ended up being a missionary to Ireland. He shared that one time in his life, he did hear the audible voice of the Father.

He was driving around a stretch of highway and was just about to come around a curve. He was going the speed limit. In a flash, he heard the direct voice say, "SLOW DOWN!"

He instantly obeyed, put his foot on the brake and slowly rounded that curve, only to find an accident had just occurred. Had he not slowed down exactly when the Voice spoke, he probably would have been severely injured or even killed. But God had other plans!

He Has Sealed You with His Name

I would like to leave this chapter and section with a thought: as you seek to get to know God the Father deeper, begin trusting and believing that He alone knows your name. He knows how He created you, and He knows how to best communicate with you. And you share His name and identity with Him, too.

Put your faith forward to hear from Him in any of the 21 ways that He is seeking you and reaching out in His arms of love for you.

Remember He loves you, and His desire in these Last Days is to continue to show you His love in multitudes of special ways and very personal ways.

You are His beloved son, or His beloved daughter.

In the Book of Revelation we are given an incredible vision of Jesus Himself, with all of His people, sealing *"His name and the name of His Father" upon their foreheads* (see Revelation 14:1). And right after that, John hears His voice *"as a voice from heaven, like the sound of many waters and like the sound of loud thunder"* (Revelation 14:2).

Amazing! You and I are "sealed," which means we have a promise of personal relationship with God *(the promise: the Lord knows them that are His)*. And His voice is speaking! It may not be audible or in the form of thunder, but it is real, nonetheless.

Also, through your receiving the Father's love every day, you can show that same love that He has to the people around you who so desperately need it.

We'll now look more at some practical ways of prayer and outreach for this purpose in Section 4.

Very Common Ways

WAY		SCRIPTURE
1	The Established Word of Jesus	John 1:1
2	The Living Word of Jesus	Romans 10:17
3	The Inner Witness of the Holy Spirit	Acts 9:31
4	The Inner Voice of the Holy Spirit	Acts 8:29
5	The Desires of Your Heart	Psalm 37:4
6	Father Speaks Through All of Creation & Nature	Romans 1:19
7	Providential Outward Signs & Circumstances	Romans 8:28

Common Ways

8	The Preaching of the Word of Jesus	2 Thess. 2:13
9	Other Believers Speaking Confirmation	Matthew 18:16
10	Visions	Acts 2:17-21
11	Dreams	Acts 2:17-21
12	Symbolic Speech: Metaphors from the Holy Spirit	Numbers 12:8
13	Divine Appointments from the Father	Acts 8:27
14	Father Speaks Through All Forms of Media & Culture	Nehemiah 9:6

Uncommon Ways

15	The Revelatory Gifts: The Gift of Prophecy	1 Cor. 14:1
16	The Revelatory Gifts: The Word of Wisdom	1 Cor. 12:4-11
17	The Revelatory Gifts: The Word of Knowledge	1 Cor. 12:4-11
18	The Revelatory Gifts: The Discerning of Spirits	1 Cor. 12:4-11
19	Angels (by Dreams or in Reality)	Acts 12:7-10
20	Jesus Himself Appearing (by Dreams or in Reality)	John 20:19
21	The Audible Voice of the Father	Matthew 17:5

QUESTIONS FOR DEEPER STUDY:

1. How is every believer called to "build the Church?"

_____

_____

_____

_____

2. What are you doing to, "build the Church?"

_____

_____

_____

_____

3. How can increasing your ability to hear the Trinity help you be more effective?

_____

_____

_____

_____

Keep listening!

NOTES:

_____

_____

_____

_____

SECTION IV

PRACTICAL
APPLICATIONS
10 UNIQUE PERSONAL &
OUTREACH-ORIENTED APPLICATIONS

LOVE SPEAKS

PRACTICAL APPLICATIONS

10 Unique Personal & Outreach-Oriented Applications

Now that you've read through all 21 possible ways that the Father, through His Son Jesus and the Holy Spirit, may be in contact with you this week, you can begin to apply faith and increase your contact.

This will, I pray, increase your sense of the love of the Father for you. And this, I pray, will increase your ministry of that same love to others.

Some of the 21 ways were probably already familiar to you, and perhaps you have already been in contact with God through them. Others were probably brand new to you.

For those that were brand new, or areas where you had never received actual scriptural examples and teaching on them, I would encourage you to go back and read them again. Open your Bible and find the stories and passages for yourself, and re-read certain chapters until both you and the Holy Spirit within you are excited to attempt some new contact with God in that particular way.

All of our life and growth in the Kingdom requires God to be sovereign and you and me to act. God's grace, plus our sweat and effort, equal success in the Kingdom.

This section will include a wide variety of practical suggestions to begin to activate your faith in both hearing God's voice and sharing His love with others. I do not cover all 21 ways here, but there is a wide enough number of choices for you to prayerfully consider.

Your unique life and the context of your culture and maturity will all help guide you into the applications that make the most sense for you.

One of the keys to this book and its unique message is that I have endeavored to help you begin to recognize more and more ways that God Himself may choose to speak with you personally. But if recognizing God's voice for yourself was the end of it, what purpose would that fulfill in the eternal Kingdom? In other words, whenever the Lord speaks TO you, He then gives you the responsibility to go forth and speak FOR Him.

If my children had only learned to hear the sound of my voice, but I never required them to grow up and learn responsibility and move forward in helping others, the world would call them spoiled kids! And God doesn't want any more spoiled kids in His Kingdom.

If any of you only want to learn to recognize His voice for your own blessing, then you are missing out on the wonderful calling of blessing others and telling them of the great salvation in Jesus Christ and the love of God the Father for this fallen world. That which you have freely received, you now must freely give!

So here are Ten Practical Applications from a wide variety of the 21 ways. The first six deal mainly with personal applications, and the last four deal directly with outreach applications to share the love of God and His Word and voice with other people for an eternal impact of the gospel.

Let's give it a go! God is Love, and Love speaks!

Practical Application #1:
Meditate on the Established Word of Jesus

*"Were not our hearts burning within us while He was speaking
to us on the road, while He was explaining the Scriptures to us?"*
(Luke 24:32).

This application comes after a time of objective study, where you will gain insights in the word that lead you to knowing His revealed will, and conforming your life in action to it.

I'd like to more clearly illustrate this application through a true story from the life of Dietrich Bonhoeffer. Hitler sought to seduce the church leaders of his day into conformity to Nazism. Bonhoeffer would have no part in it.

This illustration comes from an annual retreat he often held in the late 1930s for his theology students. In this particular case he brought the students away from the city to the edge of the sea.

They were probably expecting a great weekend, filled with sessions of strong teaching from the gifted theologian. His intellectual grasp of the doctrines of Christ went far deeper than most people of his day.

Instead, he surprised them all by a unique announcement on the Friday night, as they all gathered by the sea and sat upon the sand to listen.

His challenge?

Each student was to walk along the shores that evening with their Bible, and select one passage, either a single verse or a small collection of verses, and memorize that verse or verses. The context of the verse was important, too.

They were to find, perhaps, a Bible character that was going through a similar circumstance as themselves, and see how what they found out about God's faithfulness would relate personally to their own circumstance.

The next day, instead of a day filled with activity, teachings, and camaraderie, it was to be a silent day: no talking was allowed! Each student's only mission was to meditate on the scripture they had memorized the night before.

He wanted them to do a little research, of course, into the context of that scripture. Meditation of the word was the key.

Prayer brought the Person of Jesus Himself into their hearts, as in invitation to teach them personally. Remember the disciples on the road to Emmaus? Just after the resurrection, Jesus appeared to them, *"And beginning with Moses and with all the Prophets, He explained to them the things concerning Himself in all the Scriptures."*

After He revealed Himself to them and disappeared in front of them, they testified, *"Were not our hearts burning within us while He was speaking to us on the road, while He was explaining the Scriptures to us?"* (Luke 24:26, 32).

Bonhoeffer was trying to apply the truths of what he knew about the power of meditation.

> *"This book of the law shall not depart from your mouth, but you shall meditate on it day and night, so that you may be careful to do all that is written in it: for then you shall make your way prosperous, and then you will have success"* (Joshua 1:8).

Here's another confirming scripture of the beauty of meditation on the Word.

> *"What delight comes to those who follow God's ways! Their pleasure and passion is remaining true to the Word of "I Am," meditating each and every moment in the revelation of light"* (Psalm 1:1a, 2; The Passion Translation).

Jesus is the great "I Am," and meditating on His Word is the same as meditating on Him. He is light, and the revelation of light.

On the Sunday morning, Bonhoeffer built a fire on the beach, and invited each student, one by one, to share the scripture they had memorized, and what Jesus was saying to them through it.

He slowly added logs to the fire as each student shared their verses.

Then Bonhoeffer himself expounded briefly upon those scriptures. He shared the strong doctrines that each one helped reinforce, and then how to live those doctrines in the midst of a culture that was growing anti-Christian.

And like the logs in the fire, soon a blaze of God's glory was glowing both upon the beach and within the hearts of all the students.

Practical Application #2:
Discipline Yourself to Listen, then Test the Voice

Let me start from an example from church history. Evan Roberts was a Bible school student from a poor family living in Wales. He became one of the evangelists God used mightily in the 1905-1906 Welsh Revival.

"As Roberts was praying one day and listening to Jesus, he received guidance. God's Spirit kept speaking into Roberts' mind the suggestion that Roberts would one day effectively preach in the schoolroom of his village, to his old friends and to the young people of the village.

"As he heard these suggestions in his thoughts, he could picture all of this occurring. He could picture all of these people sitting in rows while he preached to them.

"Roberts was at first afraid that these thoughts were from Satan. They needed to be tested to see if they are really from God."[69]

Question: How do you KNOW it's God speaking?

Answer: We need to TEST everything, because there are other voices trying to speak to you.

69 Graham Fitzpatrick, *How to Recognize God's Voice* (Spiritual Growth Books, 1984), pp. 43-44.

Note: the Appendix in this book teaches more on the subject of the "Counterfeit Voices." You may wish to turn there and read that Appendix before continuing, or read it after you finish this application. The Appendix deals primarily with Satan and his demonic forces, which imitate the voice of the Spirit and indeed, the whole Trinity.

Here in this application we'll look at how Satan's voice of doubt and fear, and sometimes even your own mind and thoughts, will try to stop you from hearing God's voice clearly, and what you can do about it.

The counterfeit voice of Satan brings doubt, fear, shame, guilt, rejection, condemnation, pride, and selfishness.

First off, learn by obedience to resist your enemy!

Satan spoke to Jesus in the wilderness and tested Him. He will be actively trying to test you, too. He is crafty. He puts questions in your mind, and you can begin to think thoughts that do not align themselves with the Word of God. So Peter tells us to "Be on the alert!"

The counterfeit voice of Satan brings doubt, fear, shame, guilt, rejection, condemnation, pride, and selfishness.

The real voice of the Spirit brings truth, joy, grace, love, acceptance in the beloved, peace, humility, and submission to God's will and ways!

How do well-trained agents recognize a counterfeit bill when they see it? By studying the original. The Holy Spirit is the original, and He speaks inside of you.

The letter of 1 John gives us some practical wisdom. First, we are told to not put our love or focus on the world (one of the "other voices") for *"all that is in the world, the lust of the flesh, and the lust of the eyes, and the boastful pride of life, is not from the Father, but is from the world"* (1 John 2:16).

Then he shares practically, *"And as for you, the anointing which you received from Him abides in you, and you have no need for anyone to teach you;*

but as His anointing teaches you about all things, and is true and is not a lie, so you abide in Him" (I John 2:28).

He is not saying here that we should not seek the wise counsel of others, or that we should not listen to our teachers. On the contrary, we have received the Holy Spirit and His anointing is internal and should always be our FIRST WITNESS. You and I need DISCERNMENT from the Spirit. Then, after we have that, it is good for us to seek the witness of the direction and TEST the Voice.

TEST #1: Test through the Word, the Bible! The Spirit will always speak and lead you in full agreement with Jesus in His Word. If the direction you are receiving lines up with the Word, you are good-to-go onto the other tests.

TEST #2: Test through the Inner Witness! How do you feel intuitively, as you pray about a certain direction, or as you ask the Holy Spirit to confirm His word to you? Is there a tightness or a "No" inside, like that red light? Or is there peace and joy inside, like that green light?

So John goes on to tell us, *"It is the Spirit who bears witness, because the Spirit is truth"* (I John 5:7).

TEST #3: Test Through the Wisdom of Counselors!

> *"Beloved, do not believe every spirit, but test the spirits to see whether they are from God; because many false prophets have gone out into the world"* (I John 4:1).

> *"And if one can overpower him who is alone, two can resist him. A cord of three strands is not quickly torn apart"* (Ecclesiastes 4:9).

So, it is always wise to surround yourself with mature Christians, those who have walked the path ahead of you, and those whom you trust are actively praying for you and trying to listen to God on your behalf.

Get counsel and test it by the word and the Spirit, and always move out only by the fresh direction of the Voice Himself! Two people can join spiritual forces to defeat the enemy.

If you are married, your spouse has been strategically designed by God to be a primary witness in areas of discernment. Respect and love your spouse and trust that the Holy Spirit inside of them is joining in union with Himself inside of you. Your husband or wife is one discerning spirit with you, and it is wise to open your ears and listen to what God is saying through them, especially if you two are very different kinds of people. My wife is very unique, and very different from me.

I have learned (and am still learning) over the years that often, in the little things and small conversations, God is shouting answers to my prayers to me through her voice!

Confirmation from 2 or 3 Witnesses

Back to Evan Roberts in Wales. "As Roberts prayed about his impressions of preaching in his village, he tested them by the Word, and found them in agreement. Jesus commanded His followers to preach! And these suggestions were not contrary to other teachings in Scripture."

These suggestions passed the second major test to see if they were from God: Roberts didn't have a sense of uneasiness or lack of peace in his spirit as he prayed about this over some months. During those months, the Holy Spirit woke him in the early hours of the morning, and he got on his knees and prayed for revival in Wales. The power of the Spirit of God came every morning for three months, and his bed literally shook under the Presence.

Roberts went to his Bible school teacher and asked him for a wise confirmation. He told him he felt he was being called to preach, and asked for some time off from his studies to go back to his village. His counselor wisely replied, "The Devil never gives orders like that. You can have a week off!"

Roberts returned to his village and walked forward in faith, obedience, and action according to the leading of the Holy Spirit. The revival that broke out through his direct style of preaching (which was exactly what the Spirit had showed him to do) reached tens of thousands of people in Wales and all over the British Isles![70]

---

70 Graham Fitzpatrick, Ibid., p. 44.

So test every word and look for confirmation from two or three witnesses. Likewise remember your adversary is trying to speak to you through contrary voices and you must resist him.

> *"And he will speak out against the Most High and wear down the saints of the Highest One...And those who have insight will shine brightly like the brightness of the expanse of heaven, and those who lead the many to righteousness like the stars forever and ever"* (Daniel 7:25 and 12:3).[71]

Practical Application #3:
Train Yourself to Live in "Code Orange" like Bourne

Code Orange. What is that?

Let me illustrate with one of my favorite movies, The Bourne Identity.

In the film series, Jason Bourne has an identity crisis. He finds out he is a "30 million dollar malfunctioning weapon" for the government in Special Ops. He realizes, through experiences, he has tremendous gifts and special abilities, and comes to the realization that he no longer wants to use his training in hurting people, but helping them.

In one of the earliest scenes of the first film in the series, he is sitting in a booth of a restaurant talking to a girl he had just met, and trying to figure out why he had so much situational awareness, but he did not even know his own name.

He explains that he can tell her the numbers of the license plates of all the

---

71 Warning note from the Author when it comes to "thinking by faith that everything is just going to be fine" without testing it and getting confirmation. Satan has been around a very long time and has an effective tactic that has worked for him countless times. It is this: he sometimes gives a feeling of euphoria to people that, "all is well," "I am right," "I am going to win out here!" "God is on my side" even when none of these things are true. You need to sharpen your discernment, and really learn to test everything you hear, by the Word, the voice of the Spirit, and through trusted counselors. By the way, God is ALWAYS ON HIS OWN SIDE so learn how to walk in humility and train yourself to listen in fresh ways every time you are seeking fresh direction!

cars parked out front (he had instinctively memorized them in a flash on his way in), he knows where the best place is to hide a gun, and he knows how far he can run at that altitude before getting short of breath. Wow!

Jason Bourne is truly situationally aware. He was trained that way. This is known as Code Orange. It is a heightened awareness of your surroundings. Bourne lived every moment in Code Orange. It was as natural to him as breathing. I have met some Special Ops soldiers who likewise are trained this way, and as a result of their completion of the training, they realize the huge responsibility it is to carry a gun out in public. Soldiers become situationally aware just like Bourne was.

Code Orange can be defined (in the sense of this teaching on hearing God's voice) as a heightened awareness of God's presence, sensitivity to His direction, and spiritual alertness at all times, in all places, with all people.

He can speak through nature, He can speak through license plates or t-shirts or situations. Just become aware that He is near you, and suddenly you'll find His love pouring out to you in ways you had never thought possible.

To really apply this section's teachings, you will need to prayerfully change the way you are interacting with the Holy Spirit on a daily basis. You will need to become aware of His instant access to your life and His presence in any situation, through any means or person, all the time. You will need to expect that He is everywhere.

Try praying something like this, every day, to live in Code Orange:

> "Father, in the name of Jesus, I invoke Your presence today. I activate my faith through the name of Jesus and the access of the Holy Spirit. I give you permission to speak to me through any means you choose. I will listen to you today, Father, everywhere I go. I choose to hear your voice and respond. Speak, Father, for Your servant is listening."

Practical Application #4:
Prayer, Fasting, & Expectation!

Jesus instructed His disciples with the staggering words, "WHEN you fast." He did not say, "IF you fast." Prayer and fasting is one of the least practiced, yet most powerful spiritual disciplines available to us. Prayer and fasting humbles you. Prayer and fasting tells your body, your flesh, to shut up and obey. Prayer and fasting brings your spirit into alignment with God's Spirit, and puts you in a place to be able to listen to God's voice more attentively.

On my travels around the world, a lot of people ask me what I think the most powerful fast is in the Bible.

My answer?

The so-called "David Fast" of 24 hours: sundown to sundown. I believe that David fasted in this way very often, and as a result, he walked in such an intimacy with the Father that He was able to express so many various Psalms of praise that we still use today. He fasted sundown to sundown.

Here's simply how it works (try this sometime in the next week if you can!):

On the evening of day one, you can eat a normal breakfast and lunch. Your fast technically begins in the late afternoon. As the sun sets that day, no dinner (or food of any kind, if you are physically able to do this) that evening. Just drink water. Drink lots of water throughout this fast.

The next morning, you eat no breakfast. At mid-day, you eat no lunch. Keep drinking water.

That evening, as the sun sets, you can begin eating food again. I would advise you to make that first meal a bit lighter on the protein (so perhaps no steak dinner on that evening).

You have now successfully fasted a full 24 hours.

Simple. Yet profound. I always take extra time to pray and seek the Lord in the midst of these fasts. And I almost always find that the morning after I have broken the 24-hour fast with a meal, the Holy Spirit is very active and speaking with me.

I find my spiritual sensitivity is heightened and I am on full alert and living in Code Orange for several days after the fast. I am reaching out in faith, of course, towards many of the 21 ways that God might just choose to reach out to me.

As to the idea of expectation, especially after prayer and fasting, Loren Cunningham (whom I already quoted from in his great book, *Is That Really You, God?*) shares this,

"When you are trying to listen to the Holy Spirit, expect Him to speak, and don't make it too complicated. Expect an answer. After asking the question that is on your mind, wait for Him for an answer. Allow God to speak to you in the way He chooses. Don't try to dictate to Him concerning the guidance methods you prefer. He is Lord—you are His servant (1 Samuel 3:9).

"Practice hearing God's voice and it becomes easier. It's like picking up the phone and recognizing the voice of your best friend—you know his or her voice because you have heard it so much. Compare young Samuel with the older man Samuel: (1 Samuel 3: 4-7, 8: 7-10, 12: 11-18).

"So listen with a yielded heart; there is a direct link between your yieldedness and hearing."[72]

Practical Application #5:
Declare that You Are Beloved of the Father

While it is true that every day, God is reaching out in certain ways to speak TO you, as a loving Father He is also speaking words OVER you. Words that help you understand that you are loved and beloved!

---

72 Loren Cunningham, Ibid., (Founder of YWAM), p. 172.

"This is My beloved Son" said the eternal, loving Father to His Son. And His Son in turn reveals the Father's love to all who receive Him.

Jesus launched His own ministry in the perfect timing of the Father and with the Father's personal love and voice. He called Him *"My BELOVED Son."*

You are God's BELOVED Son or daughter, prince or princess of the King. Know it. Act like it. Trust it. And live it.

In your prayer life, expect the Father to listen and respond and speak wonderful, truthful words OVER you.

Expect an answer, and allow God to speak to you in any way He chooses.

Sarah Young, in her devotional book with 365 daily revelatory readings from the Lord, shares it this way,

> *"I am a God who gives and gives and gives. I search for people who are able to receive in full measure. To increase your intimacy with Me, the two traits you need the most are receptivity and attentiveness. Receptivity is opening up your innermost being to be filled with My abundant riches. Attentiveness is directing your gaze to Me; searching for Me in all your moments."*[73]

In my experience I have found I needed a new ability in my relationship with the Holy Spirit within to work together with Him in hearing the voice.

Every morning I prepare myself in both prayer and reading of the word, expecting the Lord to guide me, however He chooses to do so, and if indeed He chooses to do so on any particular day. Some days there seems to be no contact from God, and other days there seems to be multiple different contacts and thrilling moments of His voice personally speaking and confirming my path.

Try praying this every day, perhaps every morning:

---

73 Sarah Young, an excerpt from March 28, *Jesus Calling: Enjoying Peace in His Presence* (Thomas Nelson Publishers).

"Father, I set my heart to seek your face today. I declare the truth, I am a beloved (insert the word, SON or DAUGHTER) of God. I receive your love today through hearing your voice. Speak to me above the noise of this world. Speak to me through Jesus or the Holy Spirit. Speak, Father, for your servant is listening."

Practical Application #6: for Holy Spirit Inception:
What do you LOVE to do?

Simple question, right? Take an hour and sit down and write down a list of stuff. On one side, make it negative. Ask yourself and answer honestly, "What DON'T I like to do? What AREN'T I good at?" The other column is, "What DO I like to Do? What AM I good at? What comes naturally to me?"

Now pray over that list. What is the direction of the Spirit for your life? Sometimes you find out by a discipline like this.

As I mentioned in the Holy Spirit Inception chapter, I got my start in the world of media production as a young intern at an organization called The In-Fisherman. It was run by two very gifted brothers, Al and Ron Lindner. They both came to faith and were "relieved" (to put it in their own words) that God was indeed calling them into media and that they could both make their living fishing.

What has followed is a career spanning more than four decades of inventing lures, producing television and radio broadcasts, writing books and publishing magazines, and other fishing endeavors. Both Al and Ron are considered to be two of the top fisherman in the world today.

And when it comes to "Holy Spirit Inception: the Desires of Your Heart," there is no greater example than the two of them, whom God called to fish for a living. "When I received Jesus as Lord of my life" writes Al, "I was relieved that He did not ask me to go into some other endeavor."[74]

---

74 Al & Ron Lindner, *Reflections at First Light: A Fisherman's Devotional* (Eugene, Oregon: Harvest House Publishers, 2015).

What is amazing, too, about the story of the Lindner boys, is how they utilized their influence in the world of fishing to be a very strong witness of Christ. This included putting a sign over their company's headquarters that plainly reads, "Jesus is Lord," and placing a special Christian symbol of the fish in all of their broadcasts. (The ancient fish symbol is what the 1st century Christians used to identify themselves to each other in the midst of the pagan world.)

They also ran a successful camp called "Camp Fish" for ten years, to which they invited evangelists to preach the gospel. Many people of all ages have committed their hearts to Christ through the naturally supernatural witness of the Lindner brothers.

So, what is the desire of your heart? Follow it by faith!

Practical Application #7:
Praise and Worship in the "Thin Places"

You might remember the amazing story of Paul Munson in Chapter 20. He was called "out of the limelight" and "into the lamplight" for a whole lifetime of intimacy with Jesus.

He decided to engage the Lord in relationship in four areas every day.

1) Confession of his sins before the Father in Jesus' name

2) Meditation of the Word of God

3) Prayer and Intercession

4) Worshiping and Praising the Lord in song

I have not spoken very often of the power of ministry to the Lord in worship in these chapters. The teachings of this book flow from understanding the Lord's love in his multi-faceted voice. How is the best way to GROW in deeper love and relationship with the God who IS LOVE? A daily devotion with sincere worship from your heart is a great place to start.

By placing yourself in an atmosphere of praise and worship, you actually posture yourself to be in a better position to hear from God. The Psalmist encourages us,

> *"Enter into His gates with thanksgiving, and His courts with praise!"* (Psalm 100:4). And, *"Worship the Lord in the splendor of His holiness"* (Psalm 96:9).

One of my dear friends in Ireland led an ecumenical community of Catholics and Protestants in Dublin for many years. His name is Rónán Johnston, known by his friends as, Rojo. He is a gifted worship leader and musician. Here are a few thoughts he shares about the power of worship to build intimacy in his recent book.

"What a better way to learn how to be in this place of intimacy with God than worship? Worship is itself time spent in that most intimate place with God, and the more time we spend there, the more familiar we will become with the sound of His voice. I am not in any way advocating a lack of Scripture reading, but rather a deeper knowing of God.

"We learn the nature of God, what He cherishes, what He desires and plans, how He feels about the world, and how He puts it to rights, all from Scripture. The writers of Scripture never intended our relationship with God to end there. Having described God, they hoped we would then spend time with Him, in the Holy of Holies.

"The greatest saints of the past, those who have really stayed with us, inspired us in our own walk with God, and challenged us to take up the cross daily, these are not necessarily people who were great theologians or powerful ideologues. Rather, they are people who loved God more than others.

"Not great thinkers, but great lovers.

"Enter into the Holy of Holies through songs of worship, within the veil of the temple, and live out your life in joyful surrender to the will of the One who knows us, who chose us, and who Himself loves us."[75]

---

75 Rónán Johnston, *Trust, Surrender, Believe, Receive: an adventure in praise and worship.* (Luton, U.K.: First published in 2014 by What's Your Story).

Well said, Rojo!

Within this practical application, may I send you a challenge to create a "holy space" in your home or natural surroundings? An actual place, like a favorite sitting area, or actual room like a study, where you can dedicate that space to God's glory and return there often to pray, to listen, and to praise and worship Him?

The ancient Celtic Christians of the U.K. named places like this, "thin places." The idea was that so much praise, worship, and intimate listening to God went on in certain places, hour after hour or day after day, that the veil of the temple became "thin" which means: the atmosphere became almost heavenly.

Like Heaven touching earth in a particular place, with the veil in the Holy Spirit's realm thin and the ability for one to hear God's voice heightened.

In my story of Ethan and his friend Micah visiting my study to seek the Lord, earlier in the book in Chapter 7, I relate how they heard a song from Chris Tomlin playing on a CD player as they entered the room. That is because my study is my "thin place" and I keep praise and worship music playing there 24/7!

Try this!

Practical Application #8:
Minister in Social Justice and Love Others

As I shared in the Intro to this Section, God has no spoiled children. He loves us, speaks to us, even corrects us and trains us in righteousness, for a purpose: to send us. Jesus sent each one of you and at the same time brought the fresh revelation to mankind of the Trinity in what is known as "The Great Commission." He sends you forward in deploying you as part of His Last Days army of warriors.

He said, *"All authority has been given to me in heaven and on earth. Go therefore and make disciples of all the nations"* (Matthew 28:19).

So you are sent! And in sending you, you discover now some inward and outward dimensions of the Father and His wonderful diverse ways of reaching out to you. He reaches out to us so you can feel His love and acceptance. He expects us to do the same to others in practical ways.

You've learned now to begin to recognize the Father reaching out to you in so many wonderful ways: creation/nature, media like films and music, "Holy Coincidences" or circumstances that reveal His Providence, and even angels on your shoulder sent to intervene in the affairs of men and women.

I want you to recognize the Father. I want you to know Him like Jesus knew Him. When you experience His voice, His reaching out, and His personal love for you, you won't be able to contain that love! You will need to share it.

> *"For I was hungry, and you gave Me something to eat; I was thirsty, and you gave Me drink. Truly I say to you, to the extent that you did it to one of these brothers of Mine, even the least of them, you did it to Me"* (Matthew 25:35a, 40b).

> *"Jesus therefore said to them again, 'Peace be with you; as the Father has sent Me, I also send you'"* (John 20:21).

> *"Beloved, let us love one another, for love is from God; and everyone who loves is born of God and knows God"* (I John 4:7).

> *"Our Scriptures tell us that if you see your enemy hungry, go buy that person lunch, or if he's thirsty, get him a drink. Your generosity will surprise him with goodness. Don't let evil get the best of you, get the best of evil by doing good"* (Romans 12:20-21, The Message Bible).

I love the idea of what we call "incarnational and intentional living," that is, Jesus didn't play it safe for all eternity. Incarnation happened! And He is now incarnate inside of you!

Jesus heard the Father's voice and set about doing Father's business, which included ministry to all the people He came in contact with. You can, too.

This is true intentional discipleship. You make choices to reach out, and usually those choices take you out of your comfort zone and put you in uncomfortable territory. As you choose to reach out and touch the lepers, reach out and touch the poor, or reach out and touch your neighbors, you will help them discover God's love for them.

A modern-day example of a Good Samaritan kind of leader is Brandon Hatmaker and his wife Jen. They are from Austin, Texas. After years of growing in the love of the Father and experiencing personal revival, they felt the calling, through hearing Father's voice, to stop "doing church" and instead became missional strategists who started to "be the church."

They help nonprofits with areas of human sex trafficking, helping the poor and disenfranchised, and their model of church includes regular times where every person involved has practical outreach opportunities to go and serve in the love of Jesus and meet real needs on a real level.

"We feel bad. We recognize need" shares Brandon Hatmaker. "We talk about it with others. But so often we fall short of doing anything. We often confuse the heart of compassion that requires a response with the feeling of sympathy that remains idle. Most of us hear about need and sympathize. But that's not compassion. It's not justice. It's not mercy. Sympathy remains only sympathy until we do something about it. Then it becomes an act of compassion: an appropriate response to the call of need."[76]

N.T. Wright would agree. He explains as he shares about followers of Jesus becoming agents of justice and sharing the love of the Father.

"The church is called to a mission of implementing Jesus' resurrection and thereby anticipating the final new creation. What might that look like? God intends His wise, creative, loving presence and power to be reflected—imaged, if you like—into His world through His human creatures. He has enlisted us to act as His stewards in the project of creation. And, following the disaster of rebellion and corruption, He has built into the gospel message the fact that through the work of Jesus and the power of the Spirit, He equips humans to help in the work of getting the project back on track."[77]

---

76 Brandon Hatmaker, *Barefoot Church, Serving the Least in a Consumer Culture* (Zondervan Publishing, 2011), p. 34.

77 N.T. Wright, *Surprised by Hope* (HarperOne Publishers, 2008).

Let the love of the Father draw you forward in acts of social justice! Real revival and awakening, starting within you personally, can absolutely change the world around you.

People who advocate social justice without a personal relationship with Jesus are not the same kind of people that I am talking about. Jesus lights you on fire; then you move out and spread that fire in any way He shows you.

Love creates love!

Shawn Bolz, who ministers words of knowledge and revelatory words with perfect strangers, once prayed, "Father, I want people to feel your love so much. Take what little I am and multiply me to the world."

Each time he shares a word with someone, he remarks, "I'm learning the love nature of God. He's making us into what His original intention was for our lives when we were created. The world is waiting for us to restore the awe of God's reality."[78]

I like to put it this way: make your altar call immediate if the Spirit is prompting you to pray for or minister or share the gospel with another; don't wait till Sunday or another time. The most opportune time and moment is usually right in front of you and immediate.

Practical Application #9:
Share the Living Word with At Least 1 Person Today

Are you ready to experience the power of these truths by blessing someone else with a fresh word from the Living Word?

Here is a simple, yet profound, method I have learned from God to bless others.

First of all, you can choose to do this particular application every day of your life. There are many people in your mobile/cell phone list who need to

---

78 I heard Bolz preach this live. Quote from my notes of his talk.

hear a word from God. Today. And you can bring them that word.

How do you receive a fresh word from His Word for another person?

There are two main methods that I like to use.

First, I have a small book full of topics and encouraging scriptures to go along with them. This is an excellent tool to have handy.

Second, if you don't have one of those, you only need a copy of the Word and you can begin by PRAYER.

"The next time you read your Bible," wrote Anne Graham Lotz, daughter of evangelist Billy Graham, "pray first and ask the Spirit of Truth to open your eyes to Jesus."[79]

I like those opening words: pray first!

Step 1: Prayerfully choose a person from your mobile/cell phone text messages.

Step 2: Begin quietly to pray for that person for the next several minutes. As you pray, you are expecting God to share a scripture with you that will be one of three possibilities: either EDIFYING, ENCOURAGING or COMFORTING. Believe for a scripture in one of these three categories!

Seek the very presence of the Lord. Praise Him. Thank Him for the many ways that He is revealing Himself in love for that person.

Step 3: Use your Bible. As you wait upon the Lord, wait actively with your Bible in front of you. Perhaps ask Him for a particular book of the Bible from which He desires to speak to you. Some good choices filled with encouragement are Isaiah chapters 40-66, or the Psalms, or the Gospel of John. These are only suggestions. Every page of Scripture is filled with passages that are meant for edification, exhortation or comfort.

Often as I am doing this spiritual discipline, I will be reading through several passages, and suddenly one of them will seem to leap off the page (or

---

79 An excerpt from a blog post by Anne Graham Lotz, 2015. Her blog is: http://www.annegrahamlotz. org/category/messages-from-gods-word/latest-from-anne/

leap off the smartphone screen or iPad screen!), and into my heart and mind for that person.

In the inner-witness of my spirit, along with the Holy Spirit, I quietly sense Him saying something like, "That scripture applies to them."

Step 4: Send it! As soon as you find a Scripture verse that is either EDI-FYING, ENCOURAGING, or COMFORTING, I would like you to use your smartphone in a text, or any form of messaging via social media, and send it to them. Facebook and Twitter both have direct messaging capabilities.

You don't have to freak them out with the words "GOD SAID!"

You can simply text them with, "I was praying for you today and I felt led to send you these words to bless you," and then add the scripture and send it.

You'll be surprised how often you can change a person's perspective in the midst of their circumstances or trials by sending them fresh manna from Heaven! Be sure you add a prayer, too. Pray that encouraging word over their life and context to bless them.

The Psalmist wrote, *"Oh that My people would listen to Me, that Israel would walk in My ways! I would quickly subdue their enemies, and turn My hand against their adversaries. I would feed you with the finest of wheat (the established Word of God); and with honey (the living Word of God) from the rock I would satisfy you"* (Psalm 81:14, 16).

Practical Application #10:
Utilize the Revelatory Gifts to Minister God's Love to Other People

It is my prayer for each of you that you would learn to hear from God in many of the ways I have taught in this book. And as you learn, you would learn this phrase to share with others, in a quite naturally supernatural way:

"I know God is real, because He talked to me this morning."

Learning that phrase, and having a personal testimony of ongoing contact with God, can revolutionize your witnessing life in sharing the Good News with others.

People are longing for relationship! All around you are those who are estranged from God. They are outcasts. They are outsiders. Yet *"God STILL so loves (AGAPE) the world"* and is desiring to reach out in relationship to them.

When you share a fresh testimony of how God spoke to you recently, you can be a more effective witness in sharing His love.

Ready to try another level beyond just sharing a testimony? Many people everywhere are activating their faith in bold new ways in witnessing by hearing the voice of the Holy Spirit and sharing His encouraging words with others. Have you ever tried asking God for a word for the person sitting next to you? Try it, it's dangerous!

When you step out of your comfort zone into the danger zone, anything can happen. Be bold, be humble, and try it.

The chapters on the Revelatory gifts: prophecy, word of wisdom, word of knowledge, and discerning of spirits, were very internally focused for a reason. I wanted you to get familiar with these awesome gifts and see how you can utilize them for yourself.

However, it's just as powerful to begin to activate those gifts for others. They are there, alongside the gift of prophecy and the other gifts, for you to be an extension of the voice of the Spirit for other people. You can also begin to think this way and actively pray for visions and dreams for others.

The POWER of the Spirit is like dynamite and the gifts of the Spirit that Paul lists in I Corinthians 12 are all DYNAMITE!

They are all active! They were all in use in the Book of Acts.

Hence, we call that book the "Acts of the Apostles" and not the "Doctrine of the Apostles." Nothing wrong with strong doctrine, as we learned in Section 1 about the LOGOS, or established truth of the Word. But for that proper balance in your life, you will want to activate especially the gifts of prophecy and the words of wisdom, knowledge, and discerning of spirits.

As I mentioned, Shawn Bolz has learned to do this in some remarkable ways, but he is quite honest that these ways are simple faith ventures, even for him, and not "works" or "gifting" that is causing the kind of accuracy that he is flowing in when giving words to others.

I heard him speak at a conference recently and he shared, "Many times when I didn't feel qualified, or like I didn't have the relational or emotional capacity, let alone the skill set, to speak to different people (it felt way out of my comfort zone), God's personality and his passion possessed me in a way that made it easy. I am not limited to my resources; I am limited to His, even when reaching outside my comfortable space."[80]

Shawn shared the story about being in a coffee shop and the Father directed his attention to one of the women behind the counter. As he looked at her, he began to see in his mind a picture of a worship leader he knew, Joann McFatter, leading worship at a piano.

He began to pray over this word and wondered what God was showing him.

He told his friend who was sipping coffee with him.

"Shawn? Maybe God wants you to know that her name is Joanne. Have you thought of that?"

So he went right up to the counter and said,

"Ma'am? Sorry, I am just letting you know that I felt God wanted me to pray for you and to encourage you. By chance is your name Joanne?"

Suddenly the whole face of the woman changed in amazement.

"Yes!" she said excitedly. He then shared a bit of his testimony and prayed over her a prayer with some other accurate words, and shared the love of God with her (no, she was not wearing a name tag either)!

---

80 Shawn Bolz, *Translating God: Hearing God For Yourself & the World Around You.* www.bolzministries.com

A great story.

So simple. The truth is, God knows your name! And He knows the name of every single person on earth. And the sound of one's own name is one of the sweetest sounds on earth. When He calls you by your name, you feel His love. So Shawn many times gets people's names as a sign of God's personal love for them.

Shawn has many more stories and encouragements in his book, *Translating God*. Maybe God will start to speak to you like that to share His love with others. Be ready and be bold![81]

And practice makes perfect. Try out the gifts of the Spirit for others, and allow the love of God to flow through you in any way that He chooses.

The gifts are full of spontaneity, vitality, and uniqueness, and work equally well inside you whether you are more "reasoning" or "intuitive."

The Holy Spirit is like the lightning rod from God, bringing the reality of the real relationship we have and helping direct us, propel us forward, speak life, and live changed lives for ourselves and others.

I find a great way to step out in faith is to simply ask people if they have any needs you can pray for. If they agree, when you go to pray, start seeking the voice of the Spirit within. Start looking for visions or word pictures, or perhaps a word of knowledge. Pray it out over them, and remain sensitive to the Holy Spirit. I find that when I step out in faith, the Lord always meets me in that place.

Often He will give me more pictures or words, after I have shared or prayed the first one and it is well received by the person.

Put the voice of God's love in motion and He will love people, through you, and His voice will be heard.

---

81 For more info: Shawn Bolz, *Translating God: Hearing God For Yourself & the World Around You.* www. bolzministries.com

And Finally, LORD, We Went...

"Deep in the stone chambers beneath the Church of the Holy Sepulcher in Jerusalem is an inscription bearing silent witness to the early church.

Etched upon the walls are the words, "LORD, we went..."

Next to the inscription is a picture of a fishing boat rowing away from Palestine toward other lands of the Roman Empire.

"Etched in the wall opposite the inscription, "LORD, we went..." is the symbol of the mighty tenth and twelfth Roman legions from whose ranks came the soldiers who crucified Christ.

The early Christians knew and understood the reality of Jesus' message of forgiveness. They put aside their prejudices against the Roman overlords and took the Good News of Jesus' love and forgiveness to lands and peoples whom they had suffered under."[82]

As you keep advancing into these days of uncertainty, you might be in the midst of fiery trials. You might be going through some challenging paths on your journey. You might not have all the answers. And yet, He is calling you to deeper intimacy.

The early disciples did not play it safe by keeping their "religion a private experience." They spoke boldly and openly with the word of their testimony.

May your prayer and testimony of the LOVE and the VOICE at the end of your own journey be, "Lord, I went..."

---

82 An excerpt from a devotional written by Robert Schuller.

CONCLUSION

You Can Recognize
God's Multi-Faceted Voice Today

Gonce revealed a unique, divine connection between His LOVE and His VOICE. He says, *"I have loved you with an everlasting love; therefore I have drawn you with lovingkindness. Call to Me, and I will answer you, and I will tell you great and mighty things, which you do not know"* (Jeremiah 31:3, 33:3).

So in essence God is saying "I have loved you" and "I will tell you." Thus, Love Speaks. Every day. Every week. In every season of your life, be they *mundane* or *extraordinary.*

At all times, His voice will fill you with the personal revelation that the "I AM" is speaking *directly to you,* and He really is *ever-present in your circumstances.*

Common people in history like Martin Luther, St. Francis, John Wesley, Dietrich Bonhoeffer, Corrie Ten Boom, and so many others have reached out in faith in both everyday times and times of great shakings. They heard the voice of God. You can, too. You can hear from Him today.

Why not revisit certain chapters of this book and read them over and over again until you form a new discipline with the Holy Spirit's help of listening to God in that area? Then you and He will be ready to try to listen and recognize His voice in that way, especially if it was new to you. Ask God's help to understand Him better.

Return to this book every week and pray over the ways that seem attractive to you.

Each week, remember the mystery of the Trinity reaching out to you.

1) The Father speaks primarily externally, through His Providence, circumstances, nature and creation, and other ways. These signs of His love are quite literally everywhere. And each sign then bears witness within your spirit, through the Holy Spirit's confirmation.

> *"For God (the Father) so loved (agape) the world that He gave His one and only son"* (John 3:16).

2) The Son, Jesus Christ speaks primarily through both His Word (the Bible) and through His Body (other believers). We are all part of the one Body of Christ no matter what our church background. His Word (the Bible) is the foundation of all revelation and the trusted source of confirmation for everything we hear from God.

> *"The Son of God (Jesus) who loved (agape) me, and gave Himself for me"* (Galatians 2:20).

3) The Holy Spirit speaks primarily internally, from within your human spirit, as He now inhabits your heart with the divine Kingdom of God. His voice flows out of your mind and can be discerned by your spirit. And He confirms all direction at least two or three times through both internal and external means.

> *"I urge you by the love (agape) of the (Holy) Spirit"* (Romans 15:30).

Take a prayerful inventory with the Holy Spirit at the end of each day, or at the end of each week. Ask yourself, and then consider,

"How many contacts did I have with God today or this week?"

The more you pray and learn and recognize God's ways, the more He will be speaking.

And then you will look back at your journey and realize, "God was speaking to me. God was leading me. His love for me is real."

"Call to Me, and I will answer you, and I will tell you great and mighty things, which you do not know" (Jeremiah 33:3).

A Prayer of Consecration to God (pray this as often as you like):

"Dear Heavenly Father, I ask you to forgive me for all my sins in the name of Jesus Christ, and I surrender my life to you today.

"I ask you to speak to me in any way you choose. I set my heart to seek your face today Father, and I set all of my desire towards you.

"Lord Jesus, make yourself known to me today through your Word and through others.

"Come, Holy Spirit, speak within, and confirm your personal guidance today.

"I love you, Father, and I declare I will hear your voice of love and respond to you. I consecrate my whole heart and my whole life to you, and I receive your love today. In Jesus' name, Amen."

NOTES:

_____

_____

_____

_____

Appendix

Counterfeit Voices

The summer before I prayed in surrender to Jesus Christ and gave him my heart and life in personal relationship, I attended the University of Southern California (USC) Film School in Los Angeles. This school is prestigious and is known as one of the top film schools in America. I felt at the time that making movies was to be my career path.

I made friends with an actor who invited me one night to a party. It was hosted by an actress who had been a star in the hit television series "Hogan's Heroes," which aired from the late 1960s to the early 1970s. I used to be a fan of that show and knew who the actress was, so I was excited to meet her.

What I didn't know was that this "good Lutheran boy" was about to meet a woman of unusual powers from the dark side.

Have you ever heard of tarot cards? Ouija boards? Fortune tellers? Palm readers? Television personalities who seek the dead on behalf of the people in the audience? Of course you have. Everybody has.

And many people think that they are legit, or at least, intriguing.

I sure did. Nobody had ever warned me of their powers of deception.

So into the party that night walked this woman who was a New Age fortune teller. She was working the room, going from person to person, reading their palms and telling them details of their life.

That seemed intriguing to me.

How could she know those things? She grabbed my shoulder and muttered something or other. But then she stopped, looked past me, and said, "You are going to have a car accident. I see a red car, and your right rear tire, on the driver's side, is going to explode."

I wandered away that night, wondering if this premonition would really take place. I did not know what to do about it, so I prayed.

In my humble prayer to God, I said, "Lord, I know you are real. Please stop this from hurting me or anyone else." I honestly did not know if God had heard my prayer or not.

I moved back home to Minnesota late that summer and was preparing for returning to college for my senior year.

One hot day, I was driving out in the middle of nowhere, and suddenly I saw my hub cap go rolling off of my right rear tire, on the driver's side, and roll directly in front of me!

I instinctively began to slow down, and as I did so, the tire exploded. I simply pulled over on the deserted road and got out. The tire was shot, but nobody was hurt. Nobody was even around.

God had intervened and stopped Satan's plan of harm!

I will be honest with you, when the tire blew out it shook me to my core. This "voice" had accurately discerned this future event, though not the outcome.

I did not know it at the time, but this was a counterfeit voice vying for my attention through that fortune-teller at the party. (After I came to faith, I then recognized that my agreement with that demonic spirit who spoke that word, helped bring it to pass.) This fortune-teller was flowing in a counterfeit to the gift of the Word of Knowledge.

So let's talk about this.

The reason I wrote this appendix is to awaken you to the reality that the authentic voice of the Lord is not the only voice that is trying to speak to you.

There are counterfeits.

They seem real, and yet will only lead you into bondage.

Sorcery, Witchcraft, Black Magic, & Fortune-Tellers

Let me explain this first from Scripture. I am going to quote here from a friend's blog. Paul Anderson (no family relation to me, except through Jesus!) writes, "Satan has a dossier on you. He knows your history and remembers it better than you do. He does not know your future but has some ideas because of what he has observed.

"Satan is not omniscient, omnipresent, nor omnipotent.

"He can't read minds. Only God exists in the eternal present, the Great I Am. The reason over three hundred prophesies about Jesus all came true is that for God, there is neither past nor future.

"People are intrigued by the seeming accuracy of fortune-tellers and buy in as a legitimate way to come to truth.

> Satan is not omniscient, omnipresent, nor omnipotent. He can't read minds.

"Truth is moral. It requires not only accurate information but a reliable source.

"Fortune telling is meant to intrigue us, so that we open a door to enemy infiltration. Fortune-tellers are influenced by demons (note: demons are fallen angels who are aligned in this "present darkness" with Satan, not with God).

"Sorcery, witchcraft, black magic, and fortune telling have a sinister pull on our flesh. Sorcery is called *a work of the flesh (Galatians 5:20)*, because the person outside of Christ is naturally drawn to the work of demons and Satan.

"The devil gives people the appearance that he is safe, fun and enchanting, and people choose him rather than God.

"The Bible calls it spiritual prostitution, finding pleasure in the underworld rather than in a good God.

"Israel was warned not to dabble with mediums. Many psychics do not even know that they are being used by the devil. They think they are simply "gifted," and they are. They honor demons, who give them a level of information and influence, which they enjoy."[83]

Here is God's word on this issue, and His word is true. *"If a person turns to mediums, I will set My face against that person"* (Leviticus 20:6).

> *"There shall not be found among you anyone who...practices divination or tells fortunes...for whoever does these things is an abomination to the Lord"* (Deuteronomy 18:10-13).

So Satan's counterfeit voices contain real information, but it is only partial information, and by design he is attempting to steal, kill, and destroy people and lure them away from Jesus.

You will find that the nine gifts of the Holy Spirit all have counterfeits from Satan's forces of spiritual darkness.

Those counterfeits are what are operating in palm readings, tarot cards, etc.

The real voice of God was the first voice that Adam and Eve ever heard.

---

83 An excerpt from, *"Dare To Dream"* a blog by Paul Anderson. More info can be found here: www.pastorpaulanderson.com

It wasn't long, however, until they succumbed in sin to the counterfeit. Satan is a fallen angel and has been slithering around with his counterfeit voice since the days of Eden.

You might even say that the first sin that was ever committed, the first act of rebellion against God, was in coming into agreement with a voice that was not God's authentic voice.

That's right. The serpent was crafty, and he twisted the truth of what God had spoken (the real voice) and substituted it with his counterfeit voice and infiltrated their minds.

Their minds thus darkened, they chose to sin and disobey God's word. They ate of the Tree of the Knowledge of Good and Evil, and that knowledge deceived them.

Adam and Eve's sinful actions, caused by them not rebuking the counterfeit voice, changed everything. They themselves changed.

Their hopes of eternal life and ongoing communication with God, through the promise of the invitation to eat of the Tree of Life, disappeared.

Their sin brought curses. Their sin brought death as a physical reality.

Their sin brought a barrier in the Spirit to direct contact with God.

As a result, all of humankind, including you and me, have been affected. Their sinful stain affects every man and woman still being born into this world.

Hence the prophet, thousands of years later and in an atmosphere with loads of satanic counterfeits, could cry out, *"And when they say to you, 'Consult the mediums,' should not a people consult their God?"* (Isaiah 8:19).

When You Possess the Real, the Counterfeit Will Be Close Behind

The counterfeit immediately surfaced when the true reality of the Holy Spirit's power was being displayed through the Apostle Paul in the Book of Acts. Sometimes you can have power encounters where the Holy Spirit in you will be in opposition to people who are working with the demonic world. Paul and Barnabas were asked to share the gospel with a leader and this magician was trying to stop them.

Here is what Scripture says happened.

> "But Elymas the magician was opposing them, seeking to turn the proconsul away from the faith. But Paul, filled with the Holy Spirit, fixed his gaze upon him, and said, 'You are full of all deceit and fraud, you son of the devil, you enemy of all righteousness, will you not cease to make crooked the straight ways of the Lord?'"

Then Paul pronounced blindness on this man, and the power of God made him blind, and the proconsul became a Christian when he saw the true power of God unleashed (*see the whole story in Acts 13:6-12*).

Talk about the original *power evangelism!*

On another occasion we see a certain slave-girl with a spirit of divination who was a fortune teller, *"bringing her masters much profit by fortune-telling. Following after Paul she kept crying out, 'These men are bond-servants of the Most High God, who are proclaiming to you the way of salvation.' And she continued doing this for many days. But Paul was greatly annoyed, and turned and said to the spirit, 'I command you in the name of Jesus Christ to come out of her!' And it came out at that very moment. But when her masters saw that their hope of profit was gone, they seized Paul and Silas"* (Acts 16:16-19).

I love this story. This particular power encounter brought real persecution to Paul and Silas, but it provides an authentic moment in history of the reality of these demonic spirits and how the power and authority of God, in the name of Jesus Christ, is always stronger.

Of course, I hope you are reading this appendix with an open heart and are ready to face the counterfeits with the reality, love, and compassion of the living God!

In C.S. Lewis' marvelous book, "The Screwtape Letters," we find a chief demon, Screwtape, writing to a lesser demon, Wormwood, about a man who became a Christian, with instructions on how to try to corrupt his faith. In his Preface, Lewis writes,

"There are two equal and opposite errors into which our race can fall about the devils. One is to disbelieve in their existence. The other is to believe, and to feel an excessive and unhealthy interest in them. They themselves are equally pleased by both errors."[84]

Pantheism is the Counterfeit of Encountering the Father in Nature

Pantheism can be defined as the belief that the Universe (or nature as the totality of everything) is identical with divinity, or that everything composes an all-encompassing, immanent god.

Pantheists thus do not believe in a distinct personal god.

This whole misunderstanding of mother-nature as divine in itself, which comes through pantheism, is the counterfeit.

The truth, on the other hand, is that God is your Father, and He is the Creator, and He is blessed forever. He deserves your personal worship, and all of His creation shouts praise and glory to Him, every day, everywhere.

Through sin and the curses upon the earth, mankind still denies the existence of God, but God still loves His creation and His people, and is continually reaching His arms of love THROUGH creation and nature to speak and communicate.

I have just quoted a few lines directly from my chapter on the reality of the Father reaching out through all of His creation. Why not have a fresh read of that chapter, and begin today to exercise your faith that He is reaching out to you through His creation?

Satan's Counterfeit Trinity found in the Book of Revelation

The Book of Revelation is filled with symbolic imagery.

As you study Revelation, you find an interesting feature. Satan himself

---

84 C.S. Lewis, *The Screwtape Letters* (Quotes from Preface and Chapter 2, The Centenary Press, 1945).

has established a counterfeit to the Trinity, and his counterfeits all have counterfeit voices that lead millions of people astray every single day.

In Revelation, here is Satan's counterfeit to the Trinity:

The Red Dragon (a counterfeit to the Father, found in chapter 12). Satan aspires to be God and control everything for himself. The Red Dragon is the Satanic counterfeit to the Creator-God we know as "Father."

The Beast (a counterfeit to the Son, Jesus, found in chapter 13). This Beast has "blasphemous names" vs. Christ's worthy names, and he has "great power" while Christ has "divine power and authority." The Beast has a "mark" (yes, the now-famous, "Mark of the Beast"), which is a counterfeit of the seal of the name of Christ upon the foreheads of believers (see Revelation 14:1).

The False Prophet (a counterfeit to the Holy Spirit, found in chapter 13). The False Prophet is even said to work "miraculous signs" and be a "witness" and propagate its false religions. (So real demonic powers are at work within the world's other religions every day).[85]

Remember that every single world religion outside of Christianity is symbolized by the False Prophet.

Remember that the reality of the power of God was poured out upon the Day of Pentecost and empowers normal people to be supernatural witnesses until the day of the Second Coming of Christ.

This includes Islam, Judaism, Buddhism, Hinduism, and even cults like the Jehovah's Witnesses and Mormonism.

And remember the Pharisees? They were the "religious" enemies of Christ.

R. Loren Sandford writes about Jesus confronting the religious spirit of His day. *"Why do you not understand what I am saying? It is because you cannot hear My word. You are of your father, the devil"* (John 8:43-44).

---

85 A summary of some teaching from Vern S. Poythress, *The Returning King: A Guide to the Book of Revelation* (Phillipsburg, New Jersey: P & R Publishing Company, 2000), pp. 17-18.

"The Pharisees had become a people of the Word, but they failed to apprehend God's heart embedded in His Word. Believing that they valued Scripture, they actually listened to demons."[86]

Satan's Counterfeit to the True Church, the Bride

And, yet one more interesting counterfeit. Revelation chapters 17 and 18 picture this Harlot named Babylon. She is a counterfeit for the true bride of Christ.

"Babylon the Harlot is a counterfeit for the church, the bride of Christ. The corruptions of Babylon contrast with the purity of the bride of the Lamb (19:7-9). Babylon sums up in herself the worship of the godless world.

"By contrast, the bride (the Church) represents true worshipers of the true God. Just as Satan masquerading as the Dragon, the Beast, and the False Prophet form a counterfeit Trinity, Babylon is a counterfeit church, seducing the world to give its allegiance to the counterfeit Trinity."[87]

A New Heart Brings a New Voice

The religious and the godless cannot properly hear from God. The Apostle Paul wrote of this in his letter to the Romans. In chapter 1 he addresses the Greeks, which represent the godless, in chapter 2 he address the Jews, which represent the religious. To both groups, godless and religious, he says, *"There is none righteous, not even one. There is none who understand. There is none who seeks after God. All have turned aside, together they have become useless; there is none who does good, not even one"* (Romans 3:10-12).

What is Paul saying? The whole world, every person, whether they are acting "religious" or whether they are "godless," is born in this world in spiritual darkness, and separated by sinful choices from the Father.

There is no real relationship, so no voice to be heard speaking for thousands of years. The only voice of God was heard through the Law and the Prophets, until Jesus.

---

86 R. Loren Sandford, *Visions of the Coming Days* (Chosen Books, a Division of Baker Publishing, 2012), p. 24.
87 Poythress, Ibid., p. 159.

319

God the Father's voice thundered approval of His One and Only Son, being sent as a sacrificial lamb to be slain on behalf of all people of all time. Jesus hinted in John 10 that the Shepherd would *"lay down His life for His sheep"* (John 10:11).

Why was a sacrificial life necessary to return us to right relationship with our Father?

God the Father yearned for relationship, but it was never to be had without a change of heart from within. So Ezekiel, like Jeremiah, prophesied, *"I will give you a new heart and put a new Spirit within you"* (Ezekiel 36:26).

Sin is the breaking of God's moral law, and the punishment for the breaking of that law is physical death.

Death is what mankind is due, unless someone could enter the scene who never sinned. Then they could stand in judgment in place of others, and receive that sentence on behalf of others.

Enter Jesus. He is the answer for this conundrum.

He fulfilled the law of righteousness and never sinned. He is called the "spotless Lamb of God." He was both the Good Shepherd and the spotless Lamb at the same time!

God offered Himself, in the Person of Jesus, in an amazing act of *agape* love, as a sacrifice for all sin. The cross was costly for God. God personally accepted the consequences for man's sin there, and shed His own blood as payment in full.

So to put it simply, the Good Shepherd laid down His life for His sheep (bearing their sins upon His back, upon the Cross).

He died upon the cross as an act of eternal *agape* love. For three days He is laid in the tomb.

Easter sunrise arrives. Jesus received new life: the eternal, pulsating, powerful, communicating life of the Spirit, at the moment of the resurrection. He came back from the dead. He ascended to Heaven and poured out the gift of the Holy Spirit to all who seek to follow Him.

"I will give you a

NEW
HEART

and put a new Spirit

within you."

(Ezekiel 36:26)

And His voice immediately is activated within multitudes of new hearts, as they receive Him personally.

What a Shepherd!

Now His voice will lead the sheep for all eternity.

> *"A hostile world! I call to God, I cry to God to help me. From his palace he hears my call; my cry brings me right into his presence—a private audience!"* (Psalm 18:6, The Message Translation).

His goal has always been to have a dialogue with us! When you cry out, you actually have a private audience with the High King of Heaven, Jesus Christ, and the Father.

Spend Time with the "Original"

In John's gospel He shared with His disciples, *"And the sheep HEAR HIS VOICE, and He calls His own sheep by name, and leads them out. When He puts forth all His own, HE GOES BEFORE THEM, and the sheep follow Him because they KNOW HIS VOICE"* (John 10:3-4).

Sounds so simple! Don't follow another voice. Jesus promises that He has already gone before you, and He is continually calling out to you. Praise Him! Worship Him!

As you spend time with Jesus in praise and worship, you will recognize the real voice of the Good Shepherd, and recognize more clearly the voice of the stranger.

Irish worship leader, Rónán Johnston, writes "You can tell the true from the false just as you can tell the cadence or accent of someone who grew up close to you, or you can tell in one mouthful whether the meal you're eating was cooked by your mother, or you can know by the smell of the air whether you're nearing home.

"You thus know Jesus in a deeply intimate way, and you know the sound of His voice as your Shepherd, as opposed to the myriad of other voices at work in this world. This familiarity can be built into you as you participate in good, Holy Spirit-inspired praise and worship."[88]

Grow in your intimacy with God through a life of devotional prayer, praise and worship. Spend time praising and worshiping the authentic "Original" voice: the Father, Son and Spirit. Thus, you will be able to better discern the counterfeits.

Closing Prayers

You might remember my encounter with the counterfeit in Hollywood.

After I became a Christian I prayed and renounced my agreement, and any other previous agreements I had made, with demonic voices.

You can do the same, right now, if you have ever listened to the counterfeit voices. Have you ever had your fortune told? Had your palm read? Or played with tarot cards or Ouija boards? These are all sinful and an abomination in the eyes of God.

Have you ever participated in New Age religion, or Eastern meditation (through any means)? These are the counterfeits to the real Spirit-led spirituality taught in this book.

Prayer this prayer of repentance, and you can be free. Break any agreements with your enemy now,

> *"Father, I come to you in the powerful name of Jesus. I confess my sin in the past of participating with the Satanic counterfeits in these areas. Please forgive me, in Jesus' name. I ask for cleansing by the blood of Jesus, my Good Shepherd, who laid down His life for me. I renounce any agreements I have had with demonic powers in the name of Jesus Christ. Holy Spirit, I yield to you now and ask for your authentic power to witness the truth and reality of Jesus the rest of my life. Thank you Father, in Jesus' name, Amen."*

---

88 Rónán Johnston, *Trust, Surrender, Believe, Receive: an adventure in praise and worship.* (Luton, U.K.: First published in 2014 by What's Your Story).

And pray this to activate your spirit and open your heart to hear the voice of the Good Shepherd daily:

> *"Father, I give my whole life to you in the precious name of Jesus Christ. Jesus is my Good Shepherd, and I am one of the sheep of His pasture, and I recognize His voice. Speak to me today in Your Word and by Your Holy Spirit. In Jesus' name, and through your love for me, Papa-God. Amen."*

About the Author

was raised as a, "good Lutheran boy." I even preached my first message from a Lutheran pulpit at the age of 17. It finally dawned on me one day, a few years later, that instead of just following Luther's teachings I needed more: I needed to follow Christ Himself!

So at the age of 20, one night during my senior year of college, I repented of my sins and gave my heart and my life to Jesus Christ.

I remember the very morning after I made that commitment in prayer. I was walking to class and suddenly it seemed my entire world was alive in new ways! Everything seemed brighter, more colorful, more vibrant and ALIVE. The Father Himself seemed to be shouting His love to me in all of His creation.

His Word became alive in me, too. I voraciously devoured the Gospel of John and soon after, the entire Bible. He has blessed me time and time again as I have followed Him, journeying into both the world of itinerant ministry and media.

My vision in equipping evangelism is to inspire passionate discipleship, and also help people of all backgrounds hear the voice of God more clearly and help equip people to share their faith in Jesus Christ. I travel extensively, bringing an inspirational preaching and teaching style to churches, seminars and conferences.

My vision in media includes being a producer of great documentary films. I even attended U.S.C. Film School for a summer in Los Angeles, California. I love to study history, and I love to bring history to life for people. I love relating stories of common believers of all times who had extraordinary faith and did great things for God.

In personality I could be described as an "outgoing introvert." That means that I love to network and meet new people and learn all about them. It also means I love to retreat to private places to pray often in seclusion. I get recharged by being alone (even though I enjoy being with people).

In my spare time I love to go fishing, play golf, watch movies, pray, sing and worship God, and do accents and imitations.

If you are ever wanting to "test" me, just shout out, "BRAVEHEART" or, "DO SHAKESPEARE." I might just do a loud Scottish accent with the famous Braveheart speech, or even Shakespeare in an English accent.

In case you are wondering, my favorite Bible verse is John 10:10. I just love it. It is Jesus sharing this, *"The thief comes only to steal, and kill, and destroy; I came that they might have LIFE, and might have it abundantly"* (John 10:10).

I love this verse because the "thief" in context appears to be the "religious crowd" standing there. Religion, without relationship with Jesus, steals, kills and destroys. I experienced "religion" growing up, and once I found the LIFE that Jesus speaks of, it set me free. He came to set us all free and enjoy relationship!

I invite you to subscribe to my Listener Updates e-Letter so we can keep the conversation going. My blog contains sometimes *challenging* but *always inspirational* teachings, with both Scripture and practical application.

I post new devotional blogs and email them often enough, but not too often to overload your email.

Subscribe to the Listener Update e-Letter and receive my special free e-Book, "Love Speaks: Hearing the Voice of Our Father," as a free gift delivered right to your inbox.

Visit our website to subscribe at:
http://www.LoveSpeaks.Today

Enjoy instant access to all of our Love Speaks discipleship tools, including the Book, e-Book, Kindle Edition, Audio Book (read by the Author), the Love Speaks Masterclass (online training course for individuals & small group study), the Love Speaks Documentary Film Series "Video-On-Demand" Service (including Broadcast Versions and Special Director's Cuts), as well as subscribe to our latest "Listener Updates e-Letter."

I'm looking forward to hearing from you!

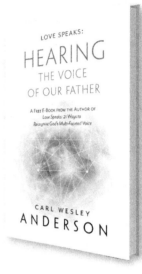

LOVE SPEAKS:

HEARING
THE VOICE
OF OUR FATHER

A Free E-Book from the Author of
Love Speaks: 21 Ways to
Recognize God's Multi-Faceted Voice

CARL WESLEY
ANDERSON

Resources for Further Study:

Love Speaks Masterclass

Do you wish this wasn't the end? Are you hungry to learn more about this subject? You are not alone. Consider enrolling in the Love Speaks Masterclass (perfect for either a small group or individual study).

Join Rev. Carl in many hours of anointed teaching on the themes in this book. Your purchase allows lifetime access to all the online teaching sessions, so you can choose the ones you really like and watch them again and again, anytime, worldwide.

Delve deeper into the themes taught here, and develop new faith in expecting God to speak personally to you in His love, every week, no matter what circumstance you find yourself in.

The Masterclass includes:

— Full teaching on all 21 ways to recognize God's multi-faceted voice

— Challenging exercises to dramatically increase your contact with God on a weekly basis

— Additional inspirational stories not included in this book on several key ways of God speaking

— A Bonus Workbook & Study Guide with "dig deeper" questions, scripture verses for meditation, and a built-in prayer journal

— 5 Bonus Training Sessions of Practical Application, including themes of Fasting, Living the Revelatory Lifestyle, and How to Give a Word from the Word, and more!

Simply visit www.LoveSpeaks.Today for more info.

LOVE SPEAKS™

MASTERCLASS

Resources for Further Study:

Love Speaks Documentary Film Series

The Love Speaks Documentary Film Series is a unique historical, educational, inspirational, and impartational journey for a modern generation. Based on this book, each episode focuses on a "Way" that the Father, Son, and Holy Spirit speak and shares stories of how God has faithfully spoken to every generation—plus **BONUS STORIES** from Salvation-History! If you are yearning to grow in your relationship with the LORD and recognize His voice more clearly, you will be blessed.

Season 1
- Episode 1, Way #1: The Established Word. "To the Ends of the Earth"
- Episode 2, Way #2: The Living Word. "It's Alive!"
- Episode 3, Way #3: The Inner Witness. "Follow the Witness"
- Episode 4, Way #4, The Inner Voice. "The Still, Small Voice"
- Episode 5, Way #5: The Inner Desires. "The River of God's Will"
- Episode 6, Way #6: Nature & Creation. "The Ocean of God's Love"
- Episode 7, Way #7: Providence. "Two Hearts, Strangely Warmed"

Season 2
- Episode 8, Way #8: The Preaching of His Word, "The Fire & the Hammer"
- Episode 9, Way #9: Other Believers, "Christ in Mouth of Friend or Stranger"
- Episode 10, Way #10: Visions, "Visions of the Nations"
- Episode 11, Way #11: Dreams, "I Dreamed a Dream"
- Episode 12, Way #12: Symbolic Speech, "Christ the Warrior King"
- Episode 13, Way #13: Divine Appointments, "Holy Coincidence, Batman!"
- Episode 14, Way #14: All Forms of Media, "God Goes to the Movies"

Season 3
- Episode 15, Way #5: The Gift of Prophecy, "Every Oak was Once an Acorn"
- Episode 16, Way #16: The Word of Wisdom, "Blueprints from Heaven"
- Episode 17, Way #17: Words of Knowledge, "The Revelatory Lifestyle"
- Episode 18, Way #18: Discerning of Spirits, "Spiritual Sight to Reign in Life"
- Episode 19, Way #19: Angels, "Flames of Fire"
- Episode 20, Way #20: Jesus Himself Speaking, "He Moves Among the Candlesticks"
- Episode 21, Way #21: The Audible Voice of the Father, "Some Said It Thundered"

CONTACT CARL

To get the latest Love Speaks resources and updates, visit:
www.LoveSpeaks.Today

Carl travels extensively around the world with his dynamic teaching style and brings the themes of this book to life. He can deliver an engaging 40 minute single message, a half-day, or a full training day for your church, conference, or ministry engagement. He loves to allow time also for live Q & A for people to ask him questions and respond to the material.

If you are interested in finding out more, please visit his Speaking Page here: **http://BornToBlaze.com/invite-carl/**

You can also connect with Carl here:

BLOG: http://BornToBlaze.com/blog/

FACEBOOK: https://www.facebook.com/carlwesleyandersonjunior/

TWITTER: https://twitter.com/BornToBlaze

INSTAGRAM: https://www.instagram.com/born2blaze/

Publisher's Note:

Be a sower of the Word of God and this unique message! Put a copy of this book into the hands of others who need to read it. Many people who need this message may not be looking for it.

Consider extending this ministry by sowing 1 book, 3 books, 5 books or MORE TODAY and become an instrument of changing lives, and increasing hunger for hearing God's voice and sharing God's love around the world!

To purchase multiple copies of Love Speaks to sow to others, please visit us: www.LoveSpeaks.Today

Rev. Carl Wesley Anderson, Founder, Born to Blaze Ministries, Since 1992

A Prayer of Repentance from Sin

Turning to the Lord, and Receiving His Salvation, Eternal Life, and the Voice of the Spirit Communicating within Your Redeemed Human spirit!

To begin an adventure of hearing God's Voice both internally and externally, with the Person of the Holy Spirit coming to reside within you, I have a few questions:

"Will you accept God's love for you?

Can you admit to God you have failed and are a sinner?

Will you believe that Jesus died for you?

Do these things and one step remains: a true Christian accepts Jesus as God and King forever.

Open yourself to Jesus Christ and receive Him into your life as your absolute King and Savior.

If you want to, here is a prayer to pray right now:

*'Father God, I really want to know You.

I want to be truly part of Your family.

Just as I am, I give myself to You.

I am not perfect.

I have done lots of things wrong.

I am a sinner.

Jesus Christ, I believe and trust in You.

I believe You died for me.

I give You all my sin and guilt and failure.

Thank You for forgiving me.

Thank You for making me clean.

I give myself and all I have to You, without holding anything back.

Come in now as my King and Savior forever.

Take charge of my life.

Fill me with Your Spirit.

Make me what I should be.

Thank you, Jesus Christ, Amen.'

You have just put your hand into the hand of God and He will hold you!

As Jesus has promised,

"I give them eternal life, and they shall never perish; no-one can snatch them out of My hand" (John 10:28).

From now on, you belong to Jesus Christ. You have become a Christian."

*(Prayer Adapted from a writing by Eric Delve).

Now you can return to all the Lessons and know that every single, "WAY" is available to you.

Begin recognizing God's multi-faceted voice today!

Please feel free to email any Testimonies of praying this prayer to me: **carl@BornToBlaze.com**

To Subscribe to Carl's unique eLetter (if you haven't done so yet), please visit the following link for receiving his free "Listener Updates."

https://www.lovespeaks.today/listener-updates.html

For additional resources, please visit, **http://www.LoveSpeaks.Today**

 *Keep listening!*

LOVE SPEAKS™

BY CARL WESLEY ANDERSON

QUICK REFERENCE CARD:

21 WAYS TO RECOGNIZE GOD'S MULTI-FACETED VOICE

Very Common Ways	Common Ways	Uncommon Ways
1 The Established Word of Jesus *(John 1:1)*.	**8** The Preaching of the Word of Jesus *(2 Thess. 2:13)*.	**15** The Revelatory Gifts: The Gift of Prophecy *(I Cor. 14:1)*.
2 The Living Word of Jesus *(Romans 10:17)*.	**9** Other Believers Speaking Confirmation *(Matthew 18:16)*.	**16** The Revelatory Gifts: The Word of Wisdom *(I Cor. 12:4-11)*.
3 The Inner Witness of the Holy Spirit *(Acts 9:31)*.	**10** Visions: Conscious Pictures from the Holy Spirit *(Acts 2:17-21)*.	**17** The Revelatory Gifts: The Word of Knowledge *(I Cor. 12:4-11)*.
4 The Inner Voice of the Holy Spirit *(Acts 8:29)*.	**11** Dreams: Sub-conscious Pictures from the Holy Spirit *(Acts 2:17-21)*.	**18** The Revelatory Gifts: The Discerning of Spirits *(I Cor. 12:4-11)*.
5 Holy Spirit Inception: The Desires of your Heart *(Psalm 37:4)*.	**12** Symbolic Speech: Metaphors from the Holy Spirit *(Numbers 12:8)*.	**19** Angels (by Dreams or in Reality) *(Acts 12:7-10)*.
6 Father Speaks Through All of Creation & Nature *(Romans 1:19)*.	**13** Divine Appointments from the Father, "Holy Coincidences" *(Acts 8:27)*.	**20** Jesus Himself Speaks (by Dreams or in Reality) *(John 20:19)*.
7 Providential Outward Signs & Circumstances *(Romans 8:28)*.	**14** Father Speaks Through All Forms of Media & Culture *(Nehemiah 9:6)*.	**21** The Audible Voice of the Father *(Matthew 17:5)*.

What if you could recognize God's voice everywhere?

You can!

In the midst of the uncertainty in this impersonal world, you can discern the personal voice of the Father, flowing through His Son, Jesus Christ, and the Holy Spirit.

All 3 Persons are One God, yet they all have their own unique ways that they communicate with you every week.

The more ways you recognize, the more faith you can apply to be in continual contact with God, feel & know His love for you, and share His love with others.

Keep listening!

Carl Wesley Anderson
Email:

carl@BornToBlaze.com

Subscribe to our monthly eLetter & YouTube Channel for free resources:

www.LoveSpeaks.Today

www.youtube.com/
Search: Carl Wesley Anderson

"I pray that the God of our Lord Jesus Christ, the Father of glory, may give to you a spirit of wisdom and of revelation in the knowledge of Him"
(Ephesians 1:17).

LOVE SPEAKS

Notes: _____

Notes: _____

Printed in Great Britain
by Amazon

44960350R00188